# A PRACTICAL
# THEOLOGY OF
# SPIRITUALITY

Books by Lawrence O. Richards

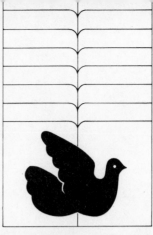

# A PRACTICAL THEOLOGY OF SPIRITUALITY

*Lawrence O. Richards*

Academie
Books
Grand Rapids, Michigan
Zondervan Publishing House

A PRACTICAL THEOLOGY OF SPIRITUALITY

ACADEMIE BOOKS
is an imprint of
Zondervan Publishing House
1415 Lake Drive S.E.
Grand Rapids, Michigan 49506

**Library of Congress Cataloging in Publication Data**

Richards, Larry 1931–
   A practical theology of spirituality.

   Includes index.
   1. Spirituality.     II. Title.

BV4501.2.R5125   1987        248        87–4989

ISBN   0–310–39140–7

*Printed in the United States of America*

87  88  89  90  91  92  93  94  95 / AH / 10  9  8  7  6  5  4  3  2  1

# Contents

# Preface

True Christians have a common desire to be spiritual men and women whose intimate relationship with Jesus Christ actually affects their everyday life. Yet the meaning of spirituality, not to mention its faithful practice, is often elusive. This book is designed to clarify the nature of Christian spirituality and, in a systematic way, to teach and encourage its expression in practical living.

In part 1, I briefly review traditional views of spirituality and look at theological constructs. I suggest an incarnational model to guide our thinking and our search for a rich personal life. In part 2, I examine aspects of the spiritual life and ways that individuals develop spiritually. These chapters are designed (1) to aid in the reader's own personal spiritual growth and (2) to help equip church leaders to guide congregational spiritual growth.

The chapters in part 2 are paired in seven sections. The first chapter in each section examines a deeply personal, inner aspect of the spiritual life. The second chapter of the section then discusses a corresponding outward expression, seen either in the shared life of the Christian community or in expressions of Christian commitment in the world. The inner experience of prayer, for example, has its corollary in worship; morality, a personal commitment to holiness, has its corollary in a commitment to public justice. In the chapters of part 2, I (1) provide a biblical overview, outlining a Christian understanding of each area, (2) explore how the quality is exemplified in Jesus' life and teaching, (3) suggest exercises for personal spiritual development, (4) outline ways in which Christian leaders might stimulate development of this aspect of spirituality in a local fellowship, and (5), in the "Probe" sections, provide action ideas, thought provokers, and suggestions for further reading.

While I hope this book will be profitable for the individual reader, it is intended primarily for classroom use. If I were still teaching regularly in a college or seminary or in a local congregation, I suspect that I would cover part 1 quickly, in a week or so of lectures. Then I would take at least a week on each section or even each chapter in part 2. I would use this text simply as a springboard for discussion, focusing with my students on wider reading in the areas it suggests, on exercises designed to help class members grow spiritually, and on the calling of spiritual leaders—persons called by God not simply to administer ecclesiastical institutions or even simply to preach but to help God's people grow.

I am aware, as I approach this subject, that my own spiritual development is incomplete. I write, therefore, not as an expert, but as a fellow adventurer. My prayer is simply that what is said here will help the reader progress toward a deeper experience of that true spirituality which is our heritage in Jesus Christ.

## Part One

# SPIRITUALITY DEFINED

# 1

# CHRISTIAN
# SPIRITUALITY

I believe that most Christians find the idea of living a vital spiritual life very attractive. But most of us are unsure what that means.

There is good reason for uncertainty. *Spirituality* is a term broadly applied across a range of religions. In some Eastern faiths the spiritual person denies every normal human desire and, by rigid asceticism, seeks to lose his or her personal identity. In some Catholic traditions spirituality is linked with a monastic commitment to meditation and worship, highlighted by momentary numinous experiences of unity with God. In some Protestant traditions the spiritual person is assumed to be a dour traditionalist who seldom smiles and has only a critical look for those who are less holy.

In spite of the stereotypes, most of us yearn for a "vital spiritual life," even though we may be uncertain of its meaning. Perhaps John Westerhoff III and John Eusden are right when they suggest that "at the center of all human life is the quest for the integration of the material and the nonmaterial, the body and the soul, the secular and the sacred." Spirituality "has to do with being an integrated person in the fullest sense."[1]

Their voices are two of many today that are exploring spirituality afresh. It may be helpful to listen to others as we begin our own exploration, at least in order to identify important questions, if not to begin shaping our own answers.

---

[1] John H. Westerhoff III and John E. Eusden, *The Spiritual Life* (New York: Seabury, 1982), p. 2.

*11*

# THE QUEST FOR SPIRITUALITY

What are contemporary writers saying about spirituality? Here are a few modern voices, many echoing views that have long been held in the church, with others staking out newer ground.

Westerhoff and Eusden write from the conviction that "we Christians who have been socialized in Western culture need more than anything else to learn from non-Christians socialized in Eastern culture." Their basic reason is stated later:

> For too long we have thought of the Christian life as essentially either involvement in political, economic, social concerns that wear us out and result in depression, or as activity which keeps the church intact and doctrinally pure. Our primary orientation cannot be to an institution or some great cause or even other people, but first and forever to God.[2]

Westerhoff and Eusden see in Eastern religions not necessarily truth but a spiritual orientation that insists that devotion to God, rather than devotion to good works or religious duty, is central to the meaning of human life.

Devotion to God is central in the Catholic mystic tradition as well. But while this strain of spirituality is not ignored, many contemporary Catholic writers call for a shift of emphasis. A "spiritual catechism" prepared by Thomas Keating says that "the criterion of true Christian spirituality, affirmed by the Gospel over and over again, is the practice of concrete love of neighbor which leads us to make the sacrifice of our own desires, convenience, and comfort, in order to meet the needs of others."[3] Benedict J. Groeschel, in a 1981 work on the psychology of spiritual development, says:

> Perhaps the best description of the spiritual life is *the sum total of responses which one makes to what is perceived as the inner call of God.* However, the spiritual life is not locked up inside a person. It is a growing, coherent set of responses integrated into the complex behavior patterns of human life. To think of the spiritual life as something apart from the rest of one's individual life is to flirt with ancient and persistent errors. When the individual has decided to respond to the call of God experienced within, and strives

---

[2]Ibid., pp. 3, 96.
[3]Thomas Keating, *The Heart of the World* (New York: Crossroad, 1981), p. 13.

to make this call the center of activity and choice, he or she may be called a spiritual person.[4]

Scanning the literature on spirituality, we find many other suggestions of how to view the "spiritual life." Iris V. Cully, a protestant Christian educator, says:

> To live the spiritual life is to be related to God, with this relationship as the basis for all human relationships. To see the image of the Creator in each created being is to have a perspective from which to live among other human beings. The spiritual life, particularly through the forms of prayer, cannot be lived in a possessive sense of closeness to God. The intercessory nature of prayer is a mark of authentic spirituality.

Essentially, Cully believes, "living in the presence of God helps people develop attitudes that are attuned more closely to the purposes of God for the world; living for the fulfillment of the Rule of God proclaimed in Scripture."[5]

The theme of integrating "spirituality" and "real life" is stated powerfully by Edward Carter. He affirms that Christ came

> for a double purpose, or rather for a single purpose with two facets. He was radically to release us from the dominion of sin and to elevate us to a new level of existence. This life which Christ has given us, traditionally termed the supernatural life, is not a type of superstructure erected atop man's normal life. The Christian is not one-half natural and one-half supernatural. He is one graced person. In his entirety he has been raised up, caught up, into a deeper form of life in Christ Jesus. Nothing which is authentically human has been excluded from this new existence. Whatever is really human in the life of the Christian is meant to be both an expression and a growth of the Christ-life.[6]

## THE SOURCE OF SPIRITUALITY

Francis Schaeffer sounds a more traditional Protestant note. He too calls for living a supernatural life now but is

---

[4] Benedict J. Groeschel, *Spiritual Passages* (New York: Crossroad, 1983), p. 4.

[5] Iris V. Cully, *Education for Spiritual Growth* (San Francisco: Harper & Row, 1984), pp. 15, 17.

[6] Edward Carter, *Spirituality for Modern Man* (Notre Dame, Ind.: Fides, 1971), p. 15.

*Spirituality = the mode of seeking after God.*

concerned that our approach to spirituality not take lightly facts the Bible affirms about the condition of humankind. He reminds us that "it is impossible even to begin living the Christian life, or to know anything of true spirituality, before one is a Christian. And the only way to become a Christian is . . . by accepting Christ as Savior."[7]

Schaeffer, in line with historic orthodoxy, takes sin seriously. He realizes that, apart from Jesus Christ, human beings are cut off from God, alienated and hostile to the Father. Thus while true spirituality "does not mean *just* that we have been born again, it must begin there."[8]

Schaeffer offers further descriptions of Christian spirituality. First, Christian spirituality cannot be reduced to getting rid of the don'ts in order to live a looser life. It is a call for a deeper, more committed life. Second, Christian spirituality is not just outward but inward. It involves an orientation of love toward God and toward people. Finally, Christian spirituality is dynamic and positive. There is a positive inward experience of reality, followed necessarily by positive outward results. Spirituality is

> not just that we are dead to certain things, but we are to love God, we are to be alive to Him, we are to be in communion with Him, *in this present moment of history.* And we are to love men, and be alive to men as men, and be in communication on a true personal level with men, *in this present moment in history.*

To Schaeffer "anything less than this is trifling with God."[9] Christian spirituality is a divine calling to experience freedom from the bonds of sin, a calling to experience reality in our Christian life.

Schaeffer is not alone in insisting that we root our understanding of spirituality in personal relationship with Jesus. Groeschel, quoted earlier, also insists that our spirituality be distinctively Christian.

> The center of Christian spirituality is the Incarnate Word of God. He is the center, not as a point of gravity, but as a single source of light in an utterly dark and lifeless universe. Just as He is the source of light and life in the material creation ("Through Him all things came to be,"

---

[7] Francis Schaeffer, *True Spirituality* (London: Hodder & Stoughton, 1972), p. 15.
[8] Ibid., p. 28.
[9] Ibid.

Jn. 1:3), so he is the source of salvation and spiritual life. "To all who did accept Him, He gave power to become children of God" (Jn. 1:12). These words from the great Christological hymn at the beginning of St. John's Gospel give the key to the entire doctrine of spirituality in Christianity.[10]

## SPIRITUAL DEVELOPMENT

The voices calling for a reexamination of spirituality may not agree entirely on the definition of spirituality. Even those writing in the Christian tradition may not agree on the necessity of a new birth or even the centrality of Jesus. But all do agree that the spiritual life must be nurtured. Whatever its exact meaning, spirituality does not come automatically with conversion.

Catholic tradition often conceives of a spiritual journey marked off by the stages of the "three ways." Groeschel notes that

> at some time in childhood or adolescence, or occasionally much later, the reality of grace begins to break through to the conscious mind of the individual in a religious experience. This event, known psychologically as an *awakening*, marks the beginning of conscious spiritual life.[11]

Growth takes place as the believer travels the three ways.

Along the "way of purgation," the believer renounces serious and deliberate sin and becomes increasingly aware of his or her depravity. Gradually forsaking self-reliance, the person learns to rely "on a greater life of union with Christ, with increased prayer, reflection, more listening and less manipulation of and speculation about God."[12] Out of the crucible, gradually and painfully and not without moments of despair, a deeper hope and faith mature.

Along the second way, the "way of illumination," there is relative freedom from a sense of guilt and from anxiety. Love for God grows more intense, as does love for others. "Consequently good works become the hallmark of the illuminative

[10]Groeschel, *Spiritual Passages,* p. 17.
[11]Ibid., p. 72.
[12]Ibid., p. 78.

way." Prayer becomes a joy, and the believer "lives on Scripture and is fed on the writings of the saints."[13] This way too has its "dark night" experiences, yet the desire to remain loyal to God persists, and final surrender of oneself to the Lord marks release.

The "unitive way" is the last and highest stage in Catholic spirituality. "Words fail and thoughts evaporate as one attempts to describe the experience of union with God which comes to the very few who arrive at this way of infused contemplation."[14]

Cully takes a different approach. She argues that "the spiritual life must be cultivated. Cultivation is a process of nurture and education. Spirituality is never a product. It is a process evidenced in a lifestyle." In her book she tries to "help people learn about and nurture spiritual growth in their own lives" and also become teachers who can help others mature.[15]

Cully sees spiritual growth as a combination of nature and nurture. God has granted different gifts and personalities to different individuals, so spirituality may not take the same form in everyone. But spirituality involves growth. "The life with God is cultivated, as is any other relationship. God is the initiator, but the human response is essential."[16] Without in any way discounting the work of the Holy Spirit, human beings must accept responsibility for cultivating their own spiritual life and for helping others along the road of spiritual growth.

Traditionally, theologians agree with such an emphasis on human responsibility. While there may be no place in justification for human works, in sanctification "our cooperation by moral exertion and personal discipline is most necessary."[17] In fact, Wesleyan James Earl Massey is quite comfortable in speaking of the "demands" of the Christian life, insisting that Christians "cooperate with the urgencies of the Spirit of God, and remain committed in a disciplined obedience to the biblical terms for growth in godliness."[18] In his book Massey particularly commends four disciplines: meditation-prayer, fasting, dialogue, and worship.

---

[13] Ibid., p. 83.

[14] Ibid., p. 86.

[15] Cully, *Education for Spiritual Growth,* preface.

[16] Ibid., p. 38.

[17] Kenneth Prior, *The Way of Holiness* (Downers Grove, Ill.: InterVarsity Press, 1982), p. 67.

[18] James Earl Massey, *Spiritual Disciplines* (Grand Rapids: Zondervan, Francis Asbury Press, 1985), p. ix.

## ASSUMPTIONS AND QUESTIONS

Just this brief review of modern ideas about Christian spirituality helps us sense the complexity of our subject and raises a number of questions. Perhaps the most important one is, What are our assumptions as we approach this issue?

My own assumptions about the nature of spirituality are rooted in conservative Christian convictions. I state them, for they are bound to affect everything written here.

- I accept and trust the Scriptures and their revelation of truth as communicated to human beings by God.

- I acknowledge the Scriptures' verdict that human beings are by nature locked in sin, both dead to spiritual realities and hostile to the Father.

- I affirm Jesus Christ as the Son of God, who came in the flesh to bridge the uncrossable gap between material and spiritual reality and, through the Cross, to bring all who trust him into a personal relationship with God.

- I agree with Jesus when he said, "No one comes to the Father except through me" (John 14:6), and take this statement to mean that only in Christ may God be found and true spirituality experienced.

- I assert the utter necessity of divine enablement at every stage of one's spiritual journey and rejoice that the Holy Spirit enables Jesus' people to take each new step in grace. While this book necessarily explores what human beings may do to cultivate their spiritual lives, I am convinced that we can do nothing without the constant supportive action of the Holy Spirit. Nothing written here should be taken to suggest that human beings can achieve anything spiritually apart from the Spirit's grace and activity. Assumptions different from these five may lead to different conclusions about implementing spirituality. It will be important, therefore, for readers to identify and clarify their own basic beliefs.

While the convictions listed above guide my exploration, they do not in themselves answer questions raised by contemporary Christian voices. I outline here some of these questions, without trying now to suggest answers.

First, there are questions about the nature of spirituality. Is spirituality essentially an inner experience, a soul-to-soul communion with God? Or is spirituality different from personal devotion, a sort of "living in the presence of God" while going about our daily duties? If spirituality has both an inner and outer aspect, how are these two related? Is the spiritual person more otherworldly or more "this worldly"? If the latter, how can we distinguish spirituality from a barren activism? Can one be spiritual in one's prayer life and at the same time be unspiritual in relationships with other persons? And if personal relationships are unspiritual, can one's prayer life be real, or must it be merely hypocritical self-deceit?

Second, there are implicit questions about the relationship between *spirituality* and other terms Scripture uses in discussing the Christian life. For instance, how does our concept of spirituality relate to holiness? Or to maturity, sanctification, perfection, growth, or Christ's lordship? Can the concept of spirituality integrate and reflect the meaning of these other, more biblical, terms, or is it merely an aspect of a reality that requires the additional terms to describe?

Third, there are the persistent questions of method: How do we grow spiritually? What disciplines are important? How can we cultivate our relationship with Jesus and experience its effect in our lives? How can we help others grow spiritually? Are there theological concepts we need to understand that can guide us? Or is spiritual growth more a matter of practices that lead to spiritual progress?

Perhaps because of such questions, most Protestant Christians, while drawn to the idea of spirituality, are more than a little hesitant. Although Bible colleges and seminaries teach "spiritual life" courses and churches may have "spiritual emphasis" weeks, too many of the questions raised here remain unanswered for most Christians to feel comfortable with the idea of pursuing "spirituality." In our exploration of spiritual development we may not reach definitive answers. But I do hope we will come up with (1) a fresh way to affirm the fact that Christians are called in Christ to lead unique lives and (2) practical ways to grow toward becoming the persons God calls us to be.

**PROBE**

case histories
discussion questions
thought provokers
resources

1. Quaker leader George Fox wrote the following in his diary. Read and think about this entry, and then write a paragraph about how reading it makes you *feel*.

   Longed with intense desire after God, my whole soul seemed impatient to be conformed to him, and to become "holy, as he is holy." In the afternoon, prayed with a dear friend privately, and had the presence of God with us; our souls united together to reach after a blessed immortality, to be unclosed of the body of sin and death, to enter the blessed world, where no unclean things enter. O, with what intense desire did our souls long for that blessed day, that we might be freed from sin, and for ever live to and in our God! Blessed be God for every such divine gale of his Spirit, to speed me on in my way to the new Jerusalem.

2. In this chapter the author shared his personal theological convictions that must necessarily shape his exploration of Christian spirituality and Christian spiritual development. Make a list of your own theological convictions, including particularly any you believe are likely to affect your approach to this subject.

   When the list is complete, try to spell out just *how* each conviction is likely to color your perceptions and your viewpoint.

3. There are many books on Christian spirituality and related issues. Here is a representative list of recent books, with a brief description of the orientation of each. Why not scan two—one that seems close to your own viewpoint and one that seems different? As you scan, jot down answers you believe the author might give to the questions raised at the end of this first chapter.

   Iris V. Cully, *Education for Spiritual Growth* (San Francisco: Harper & Row, 1984). Cully emphasizes the *process* of spiritual growth and the means to nurture a relationship with God that infuses all of life.

   Benedict J. Groeschel, *Spiritual Passages* (New York: Crossroad, 1983). This well-written book is a psychology of spiritual development that reflects and explores a long Catholic tradition.

   Francis Schaeffer, *True Spirituality* (London: Hodder & Stoughton, 1972). This famous Protestant apologist explores spirituality as freedom in this present life from the bonds of sin, with the attitudes and life style that this freedom implies.

   John H. Westerhoff III and John D. Eusden, *The Spiritual Life* (New York: Seabury, 1982). The authors explore the contributions of Eastern religions and Eastern Orthodox Christianity to the approach to spirituality taken by Western Christians.

David Winter, *Closer Than a Brother* (Wheaton, III.: Harold Shaw, 1971). This brief interpretation of Brother Lawrence's *Practicing the Presence of God* provides a view of the practical strain in some Roman Catholic spirituality that is enriching as well as informative.

4. Before you read on, write out your own brief answers to the questions the author raises at the end of this chapter. The process of revising your answers as you work through the text, or after you finish it, can serve as one measure of how much you have learned and grown.

# 2

# BIBLICAL IMAGES

The meaning of the term *spirituality* is uncertain partially because Scripture uses so many images and concepts to teach us about our Christian experience. Among the most salient images and concepts are several that have implications for our understanding of Christian spirituality, including fruitfulness, growth, maturity, sanctification, holiness, and love.

While none of these biblical images is the same as spirituality, each contributes to our understanding of the Christian's spiritual life. It is likely, however, that much of our confusion about spirituality comes from past attempts to make one or another of these concepts the single key to victorious Christian living, rather than exploring each for different and yet complementary insights into Christian spirituality. Holiness, for example, is a vital aspect of Christian spirituality, but holiness is not an equivalent to spirituality and is not an integrative image capable of putting Christian spirituality in adequate perspective.

We do need to pay careful attention to various biblical images associated with Christian spirituality. But we also need to look beyond them for a more powerful biblical image capable of giving us a distinctive perspective: an image capable of integrating the other images and providing direction as we seek to respond personally to the call of God to live in and by his Spirit in this present world. Before describing that integrative image, I review some of the biblical images linked with spirituality and note the kinds of contributions that such a study can make to our understanding of spiritual life and growth.

## IMAGES

*Fruitfulness.* In the Old Testament, *fruit* is the product of plants or the offspring of animals or of human beings. Fruit also represents the consequences of human choices and acts. Isaiah 5 is the primary example of this use. God personally planted his people Israel as a farmer plants a vine. God placed his people in good ground and tended them carefully. Although he looked for justice and righteousness, the fruit Israel produced was bloodshed and cries of distress.[1]

The New Testament uses *fruit* in the same three senses, especially in the Gospels, where it often refers to words and actions that grow out of and reveal a person's character (see Matt. 7 and Luke 6). The defining passage, however, is John 15:1–16. Here Jesus is pictured as the root and trunk of the vine, to which believers, as branches, are linked. Only a continuing, intimate relationship with Jesus enables the believer to be fruitful; Jesus warns, "Apart from me you can do nothing" (v. 5). Jesus makes it clear that intimacy is maintained by obedience, saying, "If you obey my commands, you will remain in my love" (v. 10).

The Book of Galatians uses *fruit* in essentially the same sense as in the Old Testament. The fruit which grows from the sinful nature of human beings is "sexual immorality, impurity and debauchery; idolatry and witchcraft; hatred, discord, jealousy, fits of rage, selfish ambition, dissensions, factions and envy; drunkenness, orgies, and the like" (Gal. 5:19–21). In contrast, the Holy Spirit produces a fruit in the believer which is a quality both of our inner life and of our relationship with others. The Holy Spirit's fruit in human lives is "love, joy, peace, patience, kindness, goodness, faithfulness, gentleness and self-control" (vv. 22–23).

Fruitfulness is not spirituality. But the life of the spiritual person, lived in intimate relationship with Jesus and marked by an obedience to him, will be rich in that love, joy, peace, and patience which God's inner work provides.

*Growth.* Of three Greek word groups linked with the word *growth* in the New Testament, the most fascinating is *auxanō/auxō,* "grow." Used twenty-two times, the word group suggests natural processes which God has structured into his universe. The words are used of plant and human development

---

[1] Summaries of biblical terms and their use are drawn primarily from Lawrence O. Richards, *Expository Dictionary of Bible Words* (Grand Rapids: Zondervan, 1985).

and of numerical growth of the church. In the Epistles we discover that individual believers grow in faith (2 Cor. 10:15), in knowledge of God (Col. 1:10), and in grace (2 Peter 3:18). There is also corporate growth for the body of Christ as it matures (Eph. 2:21; 4:15–16). All such spiritual growth is superintended by God (1 Cor. 3:6–7; Eph. 2:21; 4:15).

Christian growth, however, is not automatic, nor are believers passive in the process. Christians are to feed on God's Word (1 Peter 2:2; Heb. 5:11–14) and to be rooted deeply in relationships with others in the community of faith (Eph. 3:1–19; 4:13–16).

Growth is not spirituality. Yet the spiritual life draws us into the process of growth. God is deeply involved in this process; indeed, all growth comes from him, for God "makes things grow" (1 Cor. 3:7). At the same time, there is clear human responsibility. We are to feed on the Word and involve ourselves in loving relationships with our fellow believers.

*Maturity.* The Greek terms translated "mature" or "maturity" are *teleios* and *teleiotēs*. The essential notion is that of an end, or goal. The mature person has approached the goal of God's process of growth. What are mature Christians like? They grasp and apply spiritual truth (1 Cor. 2:6), establish right priorities in their life (Phil. 3:15), and stand, confident and firm, in the will of God (Col. 4:12).

Scripture also suggests how maturity is achieved. We reach maturity as we bond with other believers, living together as Christ's church (Eph 4:12–13); as we persevere in our trials (James 1:4); and as we exercise our faculties by using God's Word to guide our choices (Heb. 5:14).

Maturity is not spirituality. Yet the spiritual person is on the way toward maturity. God, by his supernatural power and grace, makes us grow. Yet we are clearly responsible to make the choices which involve us in the processes God has established to stimulate our progress toward maturity.

*Sanctification.* "Sanctify" and "sanctification" are translations of the related Greek words *hagiazō*, and *hagiasmos*. These same words also mean "make holy" and "holiness," which suggests that the concepts of sanctification and holiness overlap and at times are identical. When we look at passages in which *sanctify* appears, we are confronted by what theologians call "positional truth." Hebrews 10:29 concludes that Jesus' blood *has sanctified* the believer. The context argues that Old

Testament sacrifices could not take away sins but that Christ's sacrifice of himself on Calvary has in fact taken away all our sins. "We have been made holy through the sacrifice of the body of Jesus Christ once for all," since "by one sacrifice he has made perfect forever those who are being made holy" (vv. 10, 14). Thus our standing, or position, with God is that of those who have been made holy and who thus *are* sanctified.

At the same time, it is clear that we fall short of actual holiness. Our *state* does not necessarily match our *standing*. Thus the New Testament emphasizes a process of sanctification by which believers increasingly experience that holiness in which we stand. Jesus prayed that his followers might be sanctified by God's Word (John 17:17, 19). The Holy Spirit is also spoken of as the agent of sanctification (Rom. 15:16; see also 1 Cor. 1:2; 6:11). Paul shares his deep desire that God might sanctify his converts "through and through," adding, "May your whole spirit, soul and body be kept blameless at the coming of our Lord Jesus Christ" (1 Thess. 5:23).

Sanctification is thus both a reality and a possibility. It is something we have and are to strain toward. It is something Christ has won for us, as well as something the Holy Spirit is doing in us.

Sanctification is not spirituality. Yet it is clear that our spirituality is rooted in Christ's sanctifying work on the cross and depends on the continuing work of the Holy Spirit in our personalities.

*Holiness.* This vital concept is developed in both Old and New Testaments. The Hebrew term means "to be consecrated" or "to be dedicated." Thus the holy was set apart—particularly in the faith of Israel, the objects, places, and persons associated with Israel's ritual were set apart *from* all common use and contact *to* the realm of the sacred. As Old Testament faith was both cultic and moral, holiness had both ritual and moral aspects. Morally Israel was called to be holy "because I, the LORD your God, am holy" (Lev. 19:2). In context, the morally holy Israeli was to reject idolatry, theft, lying, fraud, and revenge and to follow the rule of loving one's neighbor as oneself.

The New Testament concept is primarily expressed by *hagios,* which has a strong moral overtone, rather than *hieros,* which was linked in Greek culture with religious ritual. This choice of words implies a very significant difference in the two

Testaments' approach to holiness. The Old Testament stressed strict separation between the sacred and the holy. Even a touch of the common could make a holy object unclean. The New Testament emphasizes a dynamic inner holiness which remains unaffected by external contact with the unclean.

The difference in approach is reflected in a familiar incident reported in the Gospels. The Pharisees were upset and angry at Jesus, whom they accused of keeping company with tax collectors and "sinners." Jesus explained that the sick of society, not the well, need the physician. The Pharisees, whose concept of holiness demanded strict separation from sinners, could not grasp or accept his meaning. Their kind of holiness would be polluted by a sinner's touch! But Jesus' holiness overcomes evil and even brings healing to the sinner, for Jesus' holiness is inner and a dynamic quality of his life.

Paul applies this theme in his letter to the Corinthians. "I have written you in my letter not to associate with sexually immoral people—not at all meaning the people of this world who are immoral, or the greedy and swindlers, or idolaters. In that case you would have to leave this world" (1 Cor. 5:9–10). To Paul too, holiness is a dynamic concept, an inner quality which cannot be ruined by externals and which is threatened only by an inner erosion of the individual's or church's commitment to Jesus.

Holiness remains essential to our calling: God still commands us, "Be holy, because I am holy" (1 Peter 1:16). As a chosen people, belonging to God, we are, "as aliens and strangers in the world, to abstain from sinful desires, which war against [our] soul" (2:11). As a holy people, we are told, "Live such good lives among the pagans that, though they accuse you of doing wrong, they may see your good deeds and glorify God on the day he visits us" (v. 12).

Paul gives us a similar picture. Holiness is not a matter of ritualistic or ascetic practices (Col. 2:20–23). Rather, the holy life calls for inner separation from the passions that arise from our sinful nature (3:5–11). What marks believers as God's chosen people, "holy and dearly loved" (v. 12), is their commitment to compassion, kindness, humility, gentleness, and patience. Such traits, along with a quick readiness to forgive and a deepening love for others, express true holiness (vv. 12–14).

We cannot, of course, understand holiness without noting

that most uses of *holy* in the New Testament link this adjective with the word *spirit*—the Holy Spirit, who is the source of our holiness. He powers the inner dynamic that transforms us into good and loving persons. Yet even this fact is an argument for human responsibility, for Paul cries out emotionally, "Don't you know that you yourselves are God's temple and that God's Spirit lives in you?" (1 Cor. 3:16). While the Spirit is the source of the holy and our holiness depends on our relationship with Jesus and his Spirit, we are responsible to make moral choices based on our knowledge of his presence. We are responsible to reject every act which might stain the living temple of our God.

Holiness is not spirituality. Yet spiritual persons will live a holy life. They will exhibit an inner moral dynamic which expresses itself in true goodness, and enables them to walk unstained in our tarnished world, while reaching out to others with Christ's healing touch.

*Love.* Love must be included on our list of images vitally linked with Christian spirituality. On the one hand, the Old Testament and Jesus stress the high priority of loving God and neighbor (Deut. 6:5; Matt. 22:34–40). The love theme is also tightly woven through every New Testament Epistle. On the other hand, we particularly must consider love because, in 1 Corinthians, Paul specifically links love and spirituality.

Corinth was a problem church. The structure of Paul's first letter to the Corinthians is determined by his consideration of this congregation's problems. Each shift from one problem to another is marked in the Greek by a phrase rendered in the New International Version as "now about" and in other versions by "now concerning." First Corinthians 12 begins a new topic with "Now about spiritual gifts."

This rendering leads to some confusion, for a separate word corresponding to "gifts" is not present in the original language. Other versions reflect this omission by suggesting that Paul is now going to write "about spiritual things" or even "about special abilities." I believe, however, that these renderings have obscured rather than illuminated Paul's argument. Paul is actually dealing with the issue of spirituality and with the Corinthians' confusion of more spectacular gifts with spirituality itself. It is probably best if we translate 12:1 as, "Now about spirituality, brothers, I do not want you to be ignorant."

We may quickly trace Paul's argument. In Paul's day, epilepsy was called the "divine disease," and those who had it were thought to have a particularly close relationship with their deity. Ecstatic utterances, furthermore, were considered to be a mark of spirituality. It is therefore not surprising that the Corinthians apparently associated an exercise of the gift of tongues with a special divine touch and thus considered tongues an evidence of true spirituality.

In 12:1–3, Paul expresses his concern that these recent converts from paganism might be led into error by someone whose "qualifications" were simply the ability to produce ecstatic speech. In verses 4–11, Paul explains that there are many spiritual gifts, or enablements. The Holy Spirit *in* each believer gives a divine enablement *to* each believer. Thus no gift is evidence of a special closeness to God or a deeper spirituality. In verses 12–31, Paul likens the church to a body, and each believer to a functioning member of its body. For health and wholeness, every member is necessary, whatever function that member may have. The gift and placing of an individual in the body is not a matter for pride or envy, nor is it evidence of spirituality.

Now Paul makes his pivotal point and shows his readers "the most excellent way." Spirituality is not evidenced by tongues, by prophecy, by mountain-moving faith, or even by self-sacrifice (13:1–3). The key is love. Love, not gifts or position, is a true measure of Christian spirituality. Paul goes on to explain love:

> Love is patient, love is kind. It does not envy, it does not boast, it is not proud. It is not rude, it is not self-seeking, it is not easily angered, it keeps no record of wrongs. Love does not delight in evil but rejoices with the truth. It always protects, always trusts, always hopes, always perseveres (vv. 4–7).

Those looking for evidence of true spirituality are to look, in themselves and in others, for the overflow of such a love.

Then Paul returns to the problems that have been caused by the Corinthians' misunderstanding of spirituality. He affirms the gift of tongues as a valid expression of the Spirit's work but insists that the Corinthians place it in perspective as a relatively minor gift (14:1–25). He lays down some guidelines that will restore order to their church gatherings, which had deteriorated to shouting matches, as first one and then another interrupted with some ecstatic utterance (vv. 26–39).

If love has such primacy, what does the New Testament

suggest about the impact of love on the individual and the Christian community? Briefly, love creates community (John 13:34), prompts obedience (14:21, 23), provides motivation (2 Cor. 5:14), transforms character (Col. 3:12–17), provides purpose (1 Peter 4:8–10), stabilizes relationships (Phil. 2:2), and compels concern (1 John 3:16–18). Even this brief survey makes it clear that love—for God and from God—is the wellspring which vitalizes and characterizes the truly Christian life.

As with the other images, we have two strands in the biblical teaching on love. Love is something that "comes from God" (1 John 4:7). Our love is, at heart, only a response to his initiating love (v. 19). Yet throughout the New Testament Christians are exorted, "Now that you have purified yourselves by obeying the truth so that you have sincere love for your brothers, love one another deeply" (1 Peter 1:22). We are, in fact, as dearly loved children, to imitate God and "live a life of love, just as Christ loved us and gave himself up for us as a fragrant offering and sacrifice to God" (Eph. 5:2).

Love is not spirituality. But true Christian spirituality could not conceivably exist apart from a deep and overflowing love.

## DIVINE AND HUMAN RESPONSIBILITY

So far in this chapter I have suggested that many biblical images and concepts are closely linked with spirituality but that none of them should be identified with it. Fruitfulness, growth, maturity, sanctification, holiness, and love all enrich our understanding of the Christian life and of truly spiritual persons. But none of these images alone can integrate Christian spirituality so that we can grasp its fullest meaning and best be guided on our own spiritual journey. Yet it has been helpful to summarize these biblical images and to note their contribution to our growing understanding of spirituality. Particularly we have noted a number of consistencies summarized in Table 1.

First, each image emphasizes an aspect of the Christian life which the spiritual man or woman will demonstrate. Such a person will be characterized by a righteous character and acts, by involvement in a process of growth which moves toward maturity, and by a dynamic goodness which expresses New Testament holiness and love.

Second, the source of each quality or characteristic is God. Only in God, by virtue of an intimate relationship with Jesus and the work of the Holy Spirit, can any of us hope to live a vital spiritual life.

**Table 1. Divine and Human Roles in Spiritual Growth**

| Image | Essence or Emphasis | Divine Source | Human Responsibility |
|-------|---------------------|---------------|----------------------|
| Fruit | Righteous character and acts | Relationship with Jesus and the Holy Spirit | Obedience |
| Growth | Process, development | God | Word, community of believers |
| Maturity | Goal, fulfillment | | Apply Word, persevere in trial, bond with believing community |
| Sanctification | Process | Holy Spirit | |
| Holiness | Dynamic inner goodness | Holy Spirit | Live good, loving lives. |
| Love | Core quality | God | Live a life of love |

Third, while God is the source and initiator of each positive quality in the believer, there is at the same time clear human responsibility. Spirituality engages every human capacity and calls for an active commitment to God's ways. In this sense we are each responsible for our own spiritual development.

A tension between God's role and the individual's role is reflected in all our theologies. Some emphasize God as sovereign, while others emphasize human beings as responsible moral agents. To the extent that either truth is taught *at the expense of* the other, our theologies will incorporate error. Only by affirming both that God is totally the source of our spiritual life and that human beings are totally responsible for their spiritual progress can we hope to approximate the biblical position.

Unfortunately, these two affirmations seem contradictory

to us. Theologians have thus tended to reconcile the twin themes either by explaining responsibility in the light of God's sovereignty or by explaining sovereignty in the light of human freedom. Such attempts at reconciliation have regrettably not been particularly helpful.

We need to affirm a paradox. We must hold firmly to the total sovereignty of God in our lives and experience. And at the same time we must cling just as firmly to the conviction that we are fully responsible for our own spiritual progress. In line with this conviction, I discuss briefly the role of the Holy Spirit in Christian experience, acknowledging that spiritual growth and vitality are wholly his work. Then, in part 2 of this book, I examine in detail how we believers can fulfill our responsibility and commit ourselves to spiritual growth.

## THE HOLY SPIRIT IN CHRISTIAN EXPERIENCE

The rabbis of Jesus' day believed that the Spirit, silent since the time of Malachi, would be given again only in the last days. When Jesus claimed to speak and act by the Spirit, it was a bold announcement of his own messiahship. It was also something of a mystery: Why did this one who claimed to be God enfleshed draw supernatural power from the Holy Spirit?

The Spirit is constantly associated with Jesus' life on earth. The Holy Spirit was the agent of Mary's conception (Matt. 1:18, 20; Luke 1:35, 41). The Holy Spirit came upon Jesus at his baptism to empower him for ministry (Matt. 3:16). The Spirit led Jesus into the wilderness to face Satan's temptations (Luke 4:1). Jesus performed his miracles "by the Spirit of God" (Matt. 12:28), for he was given "the Spirit without limit" (John 3:34). And Jesus' resurrection was a stunning display of the Spirit's dynamic, vivifying power (Rom. 1:3–4).

While we cannot penetrate the mystery of the Holy Spirit's relationship with Jesus, we do sense his power, and we realize that, during Jesus' time on earth, Christ modeled a reliance on the Spirit that we too must display. As we walk with Jesus through the Gospels, we hear him promise his disciples that the Spirit will be given to them too (John 7:37–39), to be in them (14:15–17) as a source of spiritual power.

The New Testament letters identify several works of the Holy Spirit in the lives of believers, including:

• Baptism, which unites all believers with the living body of Christ (1 Cor. 12:13)

• Filling, which expresses the vitalization available to us as we live and act in harmony with the Spirit (Eph. 5:18)

• Gifts, which represent the Spirit's enablement of individuals for ministries that enrich the lives of others in Christ's church (Rom. 12:6–8; 1 Cor. 12:8–11, 28–30; 1 Peter 4:10)

• Indwelling, which expresses the Spirit's presence within our redeemed personalities (Rom. 5:5; 8:9, 11; 1 Cor. 6:19–20 )

• Sealing, which indicates the Spirit's permanent presence in our lives and which affirms divine ownership and commitment (2 Cor. 1:22; Eph. 1:13; 4:30)

Some results of the Holy Spirit's work are the following:

• Leading in choices and decisions (Acts 11:12; 16:6–7; 20:22–23; 21:10–11)

• Inner transformation of character to become Christlike (2 Cor. 3:17–18; Gal. 5:22–23)

• Power to overcome sin and to live a truly righteous life (Rom. 8:2–11; Gal. 5:5–6)

• Enlightenment as to the divine perspective and spiritual values (1 Cor. 2:12–14)

As Galatians 5 affirms, the Spirit produces change in us, supernaturally producing also the love, joy, peace, patience, kindness, goodness, faithfulness, gentleness, and self-control that can come only from God. The Spirit accomplishes all this work in and for us by carrying out the good will of Christ and of the Father for each believer. These works are all of God— works done for us in grace and love. Yet, though it is all of God, it is our responsibility to "live by the Spirit" and to "keep in step with the Spirit" (Gal. 5:16, 25).

Many biblical concepts and images are related to spirituality. However, none of the images we have looked at sums up in itself what Christian spirituality is and how we make personal spiritual progress. Yet, examining the images, we note that they have much in common. Each suggests an inner and an outer transformation; each affirms a work of God; each demands human responsibility and response.

Spiritual men and women will live their lives illumined by each of these images. They will recognize that every gift comes solely from God. But they will also accept responsibility for their own spiritual progress and will commit themselves to disciplined lives.

## PROBE

**case histories**
**discussion questions**
**thought provokers**
**resources**

1. Are there other biblical images of spirituality that parallel the ones explored by the author? If you believe there are, choose one and write a report on the concept like the brief studies in this chapter.

2. In some theological traditions, "holiness" is taken as an orienting theme. Any good theological library will contain a number of books on holiness. If this has *not* been a focal theme in your own theological tradition, why not survey three books on holiness from a seminary or college library? How would the writers of these books answer the questions about spirituality the author raises toward the end of chapter 1? What do you personally gain that enriches your own understanding of your life with God?

3. For some reason, love has not been given quite the same treatment in theological traditions as has holiness. Using a theological library, study the meaning and role of "perfect love" in the Wesleyan tradition. How does Charles Colson, writing firmly in a Calvinist tradition, deal with this theme in *Loving God* (Grand Rapids: Zondervan, 1984)?

4. Here are quotations from two writers on spirituality. How would you evaluate their comments in these brief excerpts, in view of the images explored in this chapter?

   a. In *The Communion of the Christian with God* (Philadelphia: Fortress Press, 1971), Wilhelm Herrmann discusses some of Luther's ideas on mysticism:

   The mysticism of all ages is intensely attractive, because in mysticism the universal aim of all genuine religion is clearly grasped. In religion man seeks not simply God's gifts but God Himself. What God can give without giving himself does not comfort the soul; the soul never rests until it has pierced through all that is not God; a soul is free when it has risen above all that is not God. Every devout man knows the justice of these propositions (p. 29).

The essence of mysticism lies herein: that its religious life exhausts itself in that long series of experiences just described. When the influence of God upon the soul is sought and found solely in an inward experience of the individual, that is in an excitement of the emotions taken, with no further questions, as evidence that the soul is possessed by God; without, at the same time, anything external to the soul being consciously and clearly perceived and firmly grasped, or the positive contents of any soul-dominating idea giving rise to thoughts that elevate the spiritual life, then that is the piety of mysticism.

He who seeks in this wise that for the sake of which he is ready to abandon all beside, has stepped beyond the pale of truly Christian piety. For he leaves Christ and Christ's Kingdom altogether behind him when he enters that sphere of experience which seems to him to be the highest. It is possible that an earnest and intimate attachment to Christ and a powerful impulse towards love of our fellow men may co-exist with this. But although this is abundantly seen, even in the great mystics of the Roman Catholic Church, yet is it not the less clear that whenever the religious feeling in them soars to its highest flights, then they are torn loose from Christ and float away into a sphere where they meet the non-Christian mystics of all ages (pp. 22–23).

b. Alfons Auer, a Catholic writer, analyzes lay spirituality in *Open to the World* (Baltimore: Helicon, 1966). Auer argues that spirituality must be worked out in the everyday world, finding and expressing Christ in "all earthly realities":

This task requires that he combat the obdurate and obstinate nature of things created, a struggle in which he must overcome first and foremost his own proneness to selfishness, lest this tendency induce him to impose his own will instead of God's upon things.

Spirituality is spiritual training for, the spiritual carrying out of, and spiritual insight into secular activities through meditation. Only regular and intense meditation can prevent a person from becoming so engrossed in the things of this world that he loses sight of their meaning in terms of creation and salvation. Requisite for one's development are tranquility, recollection and concentration on the inner self, so that a person may keep himself open to the mystery and may search for and find it in his day-to-day life, and so that he may moreover hold on to it and confront the realities of each day with it and make it visible and fruitful in his life. It is only in this way that daily life and service to the world can be brought to perfection by virtue of creation and salvation. And this spiritual accomplishment of one's existence as a man and as a Christian is the essence of spirituality (p. 337).

# 3

## THEOLOGIES AND SPIRITUALITY

One way to think biblically about spirituality is to study biblical images of Christian life and experience, as we did in chapter 2. But there are other ways to explore Christian spirituality. For instance, we might study the verbs that the Bible associates with the believer's spiritual life. This approach is fascinating because verbs portray action or process, and they should allow us to see the spiritual person in action in his or her relationship with God and with the world.

When we look at the verbs Scripture uses, we are flooded with a range of impressions. Spiritual persons follow Christ, abide in him, and walk as he walked. They also walk in the light, as God is in the light, and, as many have pointed out from Romans 6, they know, reckon, yield, and obey. They seek, submit, and stand. They deny themselves and take up their cross daily. They live by the Spirit, live according to the Spirit, and are controlled (filled) by the Spirit.

None of these verbal expressions dominates; none in itself can lead us to *the* theology of spirituality. Instead, each adds its insights to the interaction which takes place between God and believers as we work out our relationship with him.

These verbal phrases are fascinating and present a varied impression of our response to God. Other verbs, however, emphasize divine action. For example, the Spirit seals, baptizes, and fills. The blood of Christ cleanses and redeems. In Christ we have been given fullness and were spiritually circumcised by the "putting off of the sinful nature" (Col. 2:11). The

Spirit gives life to our mortal bodies, lifting us, as he lifted Jesus, beyond the limitations imposed by our spiritual death.

From this brief survey of the verbs of Scripture it is clear that the spiritual life involves us in interaction with God, who has unveiled his work for us in the written and living Word and who has outlined the response he seeks as he comes to us in Christ. But Christians have not been satisfied with complex images. We have been willing to say that spirituality is expressed in the composite of knowing, yielding, counting as true, submitting, following, walking, abiding, obeying, seeking, standing, denying, etc. In our theologies we have struggled to define abstractly just what we do, just what happens in us, and just how it "works." In defining spirituality, the various theological traditions have developed different descriptions of the believer's interaction with God. Too often, however, such theologies have fastened on one or two of the verbs as the unique key to understanding spirituality or as the single element that will lead to becoming spiritual and living a spiritual life.

## THEOLOGICAL FRAMEWORKS

In his audio tapes on learning to pray, Jim Howser defines two traditional frameworks for Christian thinking about spirituality. He calls one a scriptural, or "self-in-God," model; the other he calls an American, or "self-outside-God," model. Howser compares the two frameworks in the following list:

| Scriptural Model | American Model |
|---|---|
| God initiates and the person responds. | The person initiates and God rewards. |
| Grace is a transformation of the total person into the likeness of Christ by the freely given gift of the Holy Spirit. | Grace is a treasury of merit stored up in heaven and earned by good deeds. |
| The focus is on love of God and others now. | The focus is on reward for self now or in heaven after death. |
| The emphasis is on internal and continual awareness performed of the Spirit's movements. | The emphasis is on sporadically external deeds. |

Howser elaborates on the two models as follows:

To gain the most from this analysis it is important to be very concrete. The practical question is: Do I adequately acknowledge the Spirit's role in the good actions I perform every day, or do I attribute them only to my own initiative and hard work? The scriptural model insists that if the action was good, the Spirit was present from the beginning to the end. Since I am a teacher of theology it is most important for me to acknowledge God's role in this area. Do I see the desire in me to teach well for the love of God and others as coming from the Spirit? Do I recognize that the strength and insight to carry out the good desire well are also infused by the Spirit? At the end of the day, do I adequately acknowledge God's role in my successes and give Him appropriate thanks? In addition to my teaching, I must do the same review for my counseling, my committee work at the university, my writing, my prayer, my helping others in any way throughout the day. I have allowed grace to be present and operative in myself to the extent that I have tried to do my daily service for the love of God and others. To this extent the Spirit of life in Christ Jesus our Lord has been dominant over the pressures on me not to serve with love. To the extent that I have not served with love, I humbly admit my faults and ask for a greater increase of grace to transform these areas. My reward for living in the Spirit is habitual peace and joy.

It cannot be stressed enough that the self-outside-God approach to spirituality is a distortion of the New Testament. It attributes to the self what in truth flows from the Spirit. In it God is not permitted to be God; grace is not grace. The saddest fact of all is that the conscientious person living under the Western model will never truly appreciate the presence and power of God in daily life. Erroneously attributing to the self what clearly is of God, the person will never understand the all-pervasiveness of God's love and activity.[1]

I include this extended quotation in order to point out that each theology of the Christian life summarized below assumes the scriptural rather than the Western framework. Each sees God as initiator, and grace as all-pervasive. Each is concerned with inner attitudes from which good actions flow as the Spirit of God moves. Yet each has a different conception of how the scriptural model actually works.

[1]"Learning to Pray" audio tapes (Dade City, Fla.: St. Leo's College, n.d.).

*Reformed: the lifelong process.* Reformers in both Calvinistic and Lutheran traditions have held a common view of Christian faith and life. In their view the Christian life is a lifelong process of growth toward a Christian perfection that will be achieved only in eternity. According to Calvin, one must adopt the basic attitude of piety, or *pietas,* in order to experience this growth. Calvin's Catechism of 1537 says, "True piety consists rather in a sincere feeling which loves God as Father as much as it fears and reverences Him as Lord, embraces His righteousness, and dreads offending Him worse than death." Out of reverence and love for God, the Christian learns dependence upon God and hopes for an increasing experience now of the righteousness which is guaranteed in the afterlife.

Luther maintains the same emphases as Calvin, as reflected in this excerpt from a sermon given one Pentecost Sunday.

> Here we should be intelligent and know that in one sense all is not accomplished when the Holy Spirit is received. The possessor of the Spirit is not at once entirely perfect, pure in all respects, no more sensible to the Law and of sin. We do not preach the doctrine that the Spirit's office is one of complete accomplishment, but rather that it is progressive; he operates continuously and increasingly. Hence, there is not to be found an individual perfect in righteousness and happiness, devoid of sin and sorrow, ever serving all men with pleasure.
>
> The Scriptures make plain the Holy Spirit's office—to liberate from sin and terror. But the work is not then complete. The Christian must, in some measure, still feel sin in his heart and experience the terrors of death; he is affected by whatever disturbs other sinners. While unbelievers are so deep in their sins as to be indifferent, believers are keenly conscious of theirs; but Christians are supported by the Holy Spirit, who consoles and strengthens till his work is fully accomplished. It is terminated when they no longer feel their sins.
>
> There will ever be in us mingled purity and imperfection; we must be conscious both of the Holy Spirit's presence and of our own sins—our imperfections. We are like the sick man in the hands of the physician who is to restore him to health. Let no one think: "Here is a man who possesses the Holy Spirit; consequently he must be perfectly strong, having no imperfections and performing only worthy works." No, think not so; for so long as we live in the flesh

here on earth, we cannot attain such a degree of perfection as to be wholly free from weakness and faults.[2]

The Reformed concept of an increasing and continuous spiritual growth, which nevertheless fails to lift believers beyond a mingled purity and imperfection, can be diagramed as in figure 1. Each dot along the ascending line represents reliance on the Spirit, while the upward slant of the line suggests progress toward a maturity exhibited in increasing reliance on the Spirit and progress toward perfection.

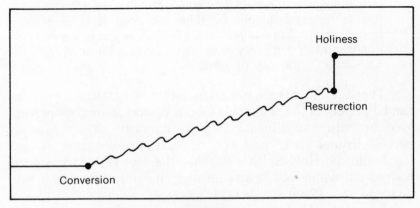

**FIGURE 1**

The Reformed View of Spiritual Growth

*Wesleyan: the pursuit of holiness now.* Those in the Wesleyan tradition, which include many "old" and "new" Pentecostals, reject the Reformed vision of the Christian life as inadequate. They argue that Jesus came to deliver believers from the power of sin and that the Christian life must therefore contain the possibility of holiness now, not just the certainty of perfection in eternity.

To understand the Wesleyan and similar systems, we need to understand three key terms and concepts. First, *entire sanctification* involves a specific and definite act of God, subsequent to salvation, by which a believer is given, or baptized with, the Holy Spirit. While this event is instantaneous and cleanses the believer from sin (see discussion below), entire sanctification does not end the need for continuing growth.

---

[2]Quoted in Hugh T. Kerr, ed., *A Compend of Luther's Theology* (Philadelphia: Westminster, 1943), pp. 71–72.

Instead it represents a special empowerment for continuing
one's faithful service and for more rapid spiritual progress. In
this sanctifying work God acts to stamp his moral image deep on
the heart, and all the processes of grace follow that act. Both
instantaneous and progressive grace are thus essential to the
perfection for which Wesleyans yearn.

A second key term is *perfect love,* which is a favorite
Wesleyan way of speaking of entire sanctification. In his "Plain
Account of Christian Perfection," Wesley maintained:

> (1) That Christian perfection is that love of God and our
> neighbour, which implies deliverance from all sin. (2) That
> this is received merely by faith. (3) That it is given
> instantaneously, in one moment. (4) That we are to expect
> it, not at death, but every moment; that now is the accepted
> time, now is the day of salvation.[3]

These comments are not intended to imply that the believer
can be perfect in the sense that God is perfect. Nor does perfect
love or entire sanctification imply maturity as a Christian
person. Instead each speaks of "a heart cleansed from sin and
filled with the Holy Spirit" so that "the love of God has been
poured out within our hearts through the Holy Spirit who was
given to us" (Rom. 5:5 NASB).

Third, the Wesleyan system maintains a distinctive view of
*sin.* In a letter to a Mrs. Bennis, Wesley wrote that "Nothing is
sin, strictly speaking, but a voluntary transgression of a known
law of God. Therefore, every voluntary breach of the law of
love is sin; and nothing else, if we speak properly."[4]

This definition of sin rules out much that the Calvinist
includes. It dismisses—though not lightly—our sins of falling
short of God's character, calling them "infirmities." According
to Wesley,

> The highest perfection which man can attain, while the
> soul dwells in the body, does not exclude ignorance, and
> error and a thousand infirmities. Now, from wrong judg-
> ments, wrong words and actions will often necessarily flow:
> And, in some cases, wrong affections also may spring from

[3]John Wesley, "A Plain Account of Christian Perfection as Believed and Taught by
the Reverend Mr. John Wesley, From the Year 1725, to the Year 1777," in *The Works
of John Wesley,* 14 vols. (London: Wesleyan Conference Office, 1872; reprint, Grand
Rapids: Zondervan, 1958), 11:393.

[4]Charles W. Carter, ed., *A Contemporary Wesleyan Theology,* vol. 1 (Grand
Rapids: Zondervan, Francis Asbury, 1983), 1:270–71.

the same source. I may judge wrong of you; I may think more or less highly of you than I ought to think; and this mistake in my judgment may not only occasion something wrong in my behavior, but it may have a still deeper effect; it may occasion something wrong in my affection. From a wrong apprehension, I may love and esteem you either more or less than I ought. Nor can I be freed from a liableness to such a mistake, while I remain in a corruptible body. A thousand infirmities, in consequence of this, will attend my spirit, till it returns to God who gave it. And, in numberless instances, it comes short of doing the will of God. . . . Therefore every man living needs the blood of atonement, or he could not stand before God.[5]

Perfection, then, is a matter of the heart and restores to human beings a pure desire to love God and others. One who has experienced entire sanctification is cleansed from domination by the old sin nature and will choose that which is good and right, *as far as he or she knows it.* However, entire sanctification does not release human beings from fallibility, which is linked to the natural limitations of Adam's race, living in a tangled world. Thus even the "perfect" may think, feel, and do wrong. Even the sanctified need to pray daily, "Forgive us our trespasses." Yet, because such failures do not involve a "voluntary transgression of a known law of God," they are, in the Wesleyan view, not rightly called "sins."

We can represent the Wesleyan understanding of the Christian life as in figure 2, which shows a second work of grace experienced subsequent to salvation. This baptism, or coming, of the Holy Spirit—which takes place when the believer reaches the point of total commitment—purifies the believer of sin (as willful disobedience), removes the dominion of the sin nature, and gives the individual a perfect love for God and for others. From this point onward, the believer will live a holy life, for he or she will not sin, that is, will not voluntarily transgress a known law of God.

The line following the second-blessing experience, however, still moves upward. Even the perfected must continue to grow and mature, deepening their knowledge of God and of love's way. Yet, while in the body, the sanctified believer is still subject to human imperfections and ignorance, so that only the resurrection can provide ultimate perfection; in eternity,

---

[5] Ibid., p. 539.

infirmities will be sloughed off, and believers will experience a full transformation into the image of Christ.

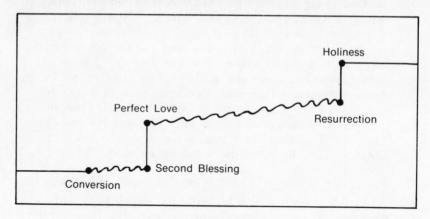

**FIGURE 2**

The Wesleyan View of Spiritual Growth

*Dispensational: the struggle of two natures.* Another approach to Christian spirituality is commonly adopted by those who take a dispensational approach to interpreting the Bible. This view focuses on biblical terms which indicate that believers have an *old nature,* or *sin nature*—the *flesh.* These terms stand in contrast with the *new nature,* or the *new self,* which at conversion was "created to be like God in true righteousness and holiness" (Eph. 4:24). Romans 7 is thought to describe an ongoing conflict within the believer between these two natures. As long as believers struggle in their own strength to keep God's law, the old nature dominates and they fall short. The solution is to rely wholly on the Holy Spirit, who, energizing the new nature, enables Christians to live a holy life, in which "the righteous requirements of the law" are "fully met" (Rom. 8:4). The key is to be "controlled not by the sinful nature but by the Spirit" (v. 9).

How does one give control to the Holy Spirit? Typically a pattern is drawn from Romans 6. The believer *knows* from Scripture that we died with Christ "so that the body of sin might be done away with" (v. 6). In fact, believers are told, "*Count yourselves* dead to sin" (v. 11). Paul next commands, "*Offer yourselves* to God" (v. 13) and *obey* him.

In this system, "spiritual" persons are yielded to the Holy Spirit and live in their new nature. The choice to yield to the promptings of the old nature, or flesh, shifts the individual immediately to an unspiritual, or "carnal" (fleshly, soulish), state. Growth takes place as the Christian learns to live more and more in the yielded state. A mature Christian has grown, over time, by living more and more in a spiritual way rather than a fleshly way.

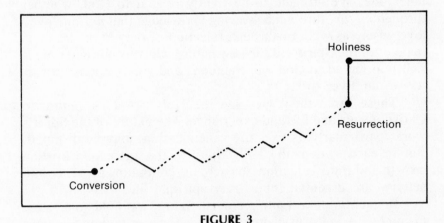

**FIGURE 3**

The Dispensational View of Spiritual Growth

Figure 3 represents a diagram of this concept of spirituality and the Christian life. Believers are given a new nature at conversion, and—by yielding to either their new or their old nature—they experience shifts back and forth between spirituality (- - -) and unspirituality (——). But the trend is upward, toward maturity and toward a greater and greater proportion of life lived in a spiritual state as believers grasp what Christ has accomplished and learn to rely on the Spirit's enablement as they step out in faith to obey the Lord.

## SOME CONCLUSIONS

Each of these attempts to describe the dynamics of Christian life and spirituality operates in what was called earlier a biblical rather than a Western framework. There are many obvious differences between them, yet there are also a number of similarities. For example, each system sees the spiritual life as a struggle against the limitations of our humanity. The Calvinist's portrait of the Christian as simultaneously saint and sinner, the Wesleyan's view of even the sanctified as subject to multiplied infirmities, and the Dispensationalist's vision of conflict between two natures all teach that Christians must commit themselves to disciplined effort and, when failures come, must continually return to and rely on the cleansing blood of Christ.

Each system also sees the real battle in spirituality as an inner one. We struggle to be rightly related to God, whether through *pietas,* through a growing knowledge that permits us to love wisely as well, or through rejection of the old nature in us in favor of the Spirit and the new nature. Only as our inner life is rightly oriented to God will righteous and good actions characterize our lives.

These three theologies see the Holy Spirit as central to Christian spiritual life and experience. The nature of the Spirit's work, particularly as to entire sanctification, may be disputed. But in each system the Holy Spirit is the agent of Christian growth and transformation; in each, his continuing presence and activity are essential for a truly spiritual life.

In each system, faith is crucial. What God holds out to us, in and by his Spirit, is claimed by a response of faith in response to his promise. Faith, as trust in God and his Word, is an individual's appropriate response to every revelation of God.

Finally, in each system, faith finds expression in obedience to the revealed Word and the promptings of the Spirit. Enabled by the Spirit, the Christian lives a righteous and holy life, expressing in his or her daily activities the priorities and the practices enjoined in the Word of God.

Each system, then, despite very real differences, does display a common underlying view of Christian life and spirituality. In each system it is recognized that, despite the limitations under which we, as Adam's children, labor now, our calling is to an obedient and holy life. Morever, each affirms that holiness of life flows from within, is worked by the Holy Spirit, is claimed by faith, and is expressed in righteous and loving acts. In each there is a level of perfection that can be experienced only in the resurrection.

Some theologies are undoubtedly better approximations of spiritual reality than are others. Yet in our quest for an understanding of spirituality and personal spiritual vitality, we may be better off to set aside the theologies and to retain the convictions they have in common.

I do not suggest that these theologies that analyze spirituality are unimportant, for we should study the Christian life at the traditional theological level. Rather, Reformed, Wesleyan, and Dispensational theologies deal with spirituality in ways which are not particularly helpful in our personal quest for practical spirituality or for helping others grow spiritually.

By way of illustration, consider the different ways in which a chemist and an atomic physicist analyze and deal with substances. The chemist deals with substances on the molecular level; the physicist, on the atomic level. Each one's approach can discover truth about the substance. Yet each one deals with the material on such a different level that the truths found and stated by one scientist make no practical contribution to the other. Similarly, it is entirely possible that we will find more practical help in dealing with spirituality on a level different from that of the traditional theologians.

Or consider a newborn baby boy. He takes his first breath and utters his first loud cry. In the course of time he grows, learning to crawl, toddle, and run, maturing in the way healthy children mature. Much later the young man, now in college, studies human development. Now he knows "what really happened" in his birth and growth. But knowing this information was not necessary for his growth, any more than he needed to master obstetrics in order to be born.

These analogies are inadequate, of course. But perhaps they clarify my point that there is often more than one valid way of approaching an issue. In fact, some ways of dealing with issues at theoretical levels are not particularly helpful to us when our concern is practical.

I am suggesting simply that there are better ways to explore spirituality and spiritual growth than to determine which theological formulation best approximates "what really happens" within the believer who grows. We do need to hold firmly to the underlying realities which our theologies affirm in common. And we do need to accept the biblical verbs and images, viewing none in isolation as the key but using each to gain additional insight into a reality more complex than a single set of terms or theological formulations can adequately portray. We need to be concerned, not with "what really happens" within, but with how we work out our relationship with the Spirit in practice so that we may grow spiritually.

**PROBE**

case histories
discussion questions
thought provokers
resources

1. At the beginning of the chapter the author listed a number of verbs used in conjunction with the New Testament's teaching on Christian spiritual life. Is this a complete listing? What verbs do you believe should be added?

   Select the five verbs which seem to you to make the greatest contribution to an understanding of spirituality. Explore their use in the New Testament. Then sum up, in one paragraph for each, the insights you gained into the spiritual life from each word and its use in context.

2. The following three books approach the Christian life from the viewpoint of holiness. Each, however, reflects a different theological position. Compare the three books and their conclusions. In particular, ask yourself as you read, What practical steps toward holiness does this author suggest I take? When you have finished reading, are you satisfied that you understand spirituality? Do you understand how to become a more spiritual person in a significantly Christian sense?

   Donald S. Metz, *Studies in Biblical Holiness* (Kansas City, Mo.: Beacon Hill, 1971).

   Kenneth Prior, *The Way of Holiness: A Study in Christian Growth* (Downers Grove, Ill.: InterVarsity, 1982).

   J. C. Ryle, *Holiness: Its Nature, Hindrances, Difficulties, and Roots* (Westwood, N.J.: Revell, n.d.).

3. In this chapter the author sketches three Protestant theologies of Christian life and spirituality and suggests that perhaps the traditional theological exploration of "what happens" is not the most helpful in one's search for a practical theology of spirituality and spiritual development. The following excerpt from a letter in *Closer than a Brother,* a work by David Winter cited in chapter 1, is also concerned with the spiritual life but approaches it from a different standpoint than the theologians do. Both approaches deal with truth, and neither invalidates the other. But is one approach more helpful?

   So even this accident, you see, can have a good result, because it can compel you both to turn your minds to serious and important matters. Michael, certainly, will have plenty of time in the hospital to do some real thinking — do urge him, won't you, to see how what has happened to him underlines his need of God? He may feel it proves God has deserted him. But that kind of thinking makes God little more than a good-luck mascot. In fact, an accident like this should drive a spiritual man to renew his total trust in God, who goes with him everywhere, and keeps him in joy and pain, in pleasure and sorrow, in life and in death.

Turn it all to prayer and faith. That's my advice in a nut-shell. Think of God as often as you can, and especially in times of danger. Just a little lifting up of the heart is enough—a little remembrance of God, a brief act of inward worship—even out on patrol, or on guard with a rifle in your hands: God hears and understands. He is near, and you will know it.

Don't think this in any way lessens your ability or efficiency as a soldier. Far from it. The man whose courage is built only on his own resources can never match the man who is drawing on the courage of Christ.

So here is my advice to you both. Think of God as often as you can. Cultivate the habit, by degrees, of turning consciously to him at every opportunity, no matter how briefly. Make these small, holy acts of worship and prayer. No one need see or know (none of those barrack-room bedside dramatics—prayer is not for public performance), and what I am suggesting is not very difficult. All it requires is the will to do it. And it seems to me absolutely necessary for men in your position, whose lives and whose spiritual standing are under constant attack, to know where to turn for help at any moment.

God bless you both. You know I am praying for you, and I trust you pray for all your former colleagues and brothers in Christ here, and for me (pp. 82–83).

4. Donald Metz has developed two lists of "practices which assist the Christian in living a holy life" (*Studies in Biblical Holiness*, p. 272). Which of the following practices do you think *only* Wesleyans would affirm? Which of the practices might be just as easily suggested by one in the Reformed or Dispensational camps?

## LIST 1

1. Hold on to faith, and do not depend on feeling.

2. Testify to the grace received.

3. Beware of spiritual pride.

4. "Beware," said John Wesley, "of that daughter of pride, enthusiasm [fanaticism]."

5. Welcome all new light.

6. Abstain from doubtful things.

7. Do not wonder at temptations, nor be discouraged by them.

8. Watch.

9. Work.

10. Let love keep guard over your speech and control your life.

11. Guard your thoughts.

12. Associate with holiness people.

13. Read holiness literature.

14. Beware of schism—separation of yourself from your brethren.

15. Live moment by moment.

## LIST 2

1. You must maintain a continuous, entire consecration—a complete self-abandonment to God.

2. To retain full salvation, you must continue to believe.

3. To retain the witness of the Spirit and continue in the light of purity, you must confess it.

4. You must live constantly in the spirit of self-denial.

5. You must live in the spirit of watchfulness.

6. You must be faithful to the teachings and drawings of the Holy Spirit.

7. You must read the Holy Scriptures daily.

8. To retain the blessing of perfect love, you must constantly aim at growing in grace.

9. You must live constantly under a sense of the presence of God.

10. You must lead a life of prayer.

11. You must labor faithfully for the salvation of sinners.

12. To retain it, you must oppose sin of every name and kind, without any compromise.

# 4

## LIVING IN UNION
## WITH GOD

We may be comfortable with the affirmation that true spirituality must be Christian spirituality, rooted in personal relationship with God through Jesus Christ. But this position does not in itself tell us what spirituality is or give us direction in our quest for a theology of spiritual development.

The various New Testament images associated with spirituality, as suggestive as they are, do not provide definitive help. The active verbs used in Scripture to describe the believer's ongoing experience with God provide kaleidoscopic impressions rather than definition. Protestant theologians have generally approached spirituality by arguing Reformed, Wesleyan, or Dispensational versions of "what happens" in the Holy Spirit's work within the spiritual person. But the theologians' concern with defining their tradition's distinctives has not been particularly helpful in defining spirituality nor in directing us toward a practical spirituality.

It seems that we need a different approach and a common image which will help us define Christian spirituality in simpler terms. The spiritual writers have tended to sense that both can be found not in theological formulations but in the person of Jesus himself: Jesus Christ took on a body and nature like our own and stepped into our world. In our space and time, he lived a truly spiritual life.

A number of passages in Scripture—particularly in John's gospel—emphasize the truth that Jesus lived in complete and total harmony with God the Father. In Jesus' daily life, spirituality and normal human experiences were perfectly unified. The following are a few of Jesus' claims about himself:

> I tell you the truth, the Son can do nothing by himself; he can do only what he sees his Father doing, because whatever the Father does the Son also does. For the Father loves the Son and shows him all he does (John 5:19–20).

> I have come down from heaven not to do my will but to do the will of him who sent me (6:38).

> I do nothing on my own but speak just what the Father has taught me. The one who sent me is with me; he has not left me alone, for I always do what pleases him (8:28–29).

> When a man believes in me, he does not believe in me only, but in the one who sent me. When he looks at me, he sees the one who sent me (12:44–45).

> Don't you know me, Philip, even after I have been among you such a long time? Anyone who has seen me has seen the Father. How can you say, "Show us the Father?" Don't you believe that I am in the Father, and that the Father is in me? The words I say to you are not just my own. Rather, it is the Father, living in me, who is doing his work. Believe me when I say that I am in the Father and the Father is in me (14:9–11).

 These statements help us understand that *Christian spirituality is living a human life in this world in union with God.* While this definition is apparently simple, its implications are far reaching. In fact, when correctly understood, Christian spirituality as modeled by Jesus challenges many common notions of the "spiritual" life.

## LIVING IN THIS WORLD

Early in the first century, distorted notions of spirituality infected the church. One of the most persistent distortions cast spirituality as asceticism and called for self-denial and strict religious observances and duties. This misunderstanding grew out of and expressed a dualistic view of reality. The religious dualist recognizes two opposing realms—the material and spiritual. The material, or physical, realm is assumed to be evil. The spiritual, the realm of God, is good.

In the strict dualism of the later Gnostics, the two realms

were in such drastic conflict that it was assumed God could bear no contact with the material world. Creation was the work of a lesser deity or angel. Jesus himself was a lesser being or perhaps a "shadow." Theological dualism simply could not conceive of a real union of the spiritual God with the material creation.

Paul deals with seeds of this heresy in Colossians. There he insists that Jesus Christ is the "image," or exact representation [*eikōn*] of the invisible God. Jesus is not a shadow but a solid and visible expression of God in our world. Not only is Jesus God, it is "by Christ's physical body through death" that human beings are presented to the Father "holy in his sight, without blemish and free from accusation" (Col. 1:15–22).

In this statement dualism is decisively rejected. There is no essential conflict between the spiritual and the material realms. In fact, the material world is the locus in which God chose to accomplish his redemptive work. One who is fully God became a true human being, and in his physical body the God-man died for us. The pivotal point in Paul's argument is that the spiritual and the material are not at odds. In fact, for God's work to be accomplished, the spiritual and the material must be united.

With this point established, Paul moves on to demonstrate that asceticism is no friend of spirituality. Spirituality cannot be described as a self-denying disconnection from the world of everyday experience. Rather, the spiritual life involves connection with others in the world of everyday experience. Here is Paul's critique of ascetic spirituality and the reason for its ineffectiveness:

> Do not let anyone judge you by what you eat or drink, or with regard to a religious festival, a New Moon celebration or a Sabbath day. These are a shadow of the things that were to come; the reality, however, is found in Christ. Do not let anyone who delights in false humility and the worship of angels disqualify you for the prize. Such a person goes into great detail about what he has seen, and his unspiritual mind puffs him up with idle notions. He has lost connection with the Head, from whom the whole body, supported and held together by its ligaments and sinews, grows as God causes it to grow.
>
> Since you died with Christ to the basic principles of this world, why, as though you still belonged to it, do you submit to its rules: "Do not handle! Do not taste! Do not touch!"? These are all destined to perish with use, because they are based on human commands and teachings. Such

regulations indeed have an appearance of wisdom, with their self-imposed worship, their false humility and their harsh treatment of the body, but they lack any value in restraining sensual indulgence (Col. 2:16–23).

The ascetic way of disconnection from everyday experience and its allegiance to the immaterial may appear spiritual to some. In fact, however, it has nothing to do with Christian spirituality. Paul goes on to describe the life style of the truly spiritual person. Such an individual has turned from the old way of sin and has chosen to live in this world as God's new person (Col. 3:5–11). Paul portrays the behavior of the spiritual person as follows:

> As God's chosen people, holy and dearly loved, clothe yourselves with compassion, kindness, humility, gentleness and patience. Bear with each other and forgive whatever grievances you may have against one another. Forgive as the Lord forgave you. And over all these virtues put on love, which binds them all together in perfect unity.
>
> Let the peace of Christ rule in your hearts, since as members of one body you were called to peace. And be thankful. Let the word of Christ dwell in you richly as you teach and admonish one another with all wisdom, and as you sing psalms, hymns and spiritual songs with gratitude in your hearts to God. And whatever you do, whether in word or deed, do it all in the name of the Lord Jesus, giving thanks to God the Father through him" (vv. 12–17).

Paul's argument in Colossians decisively rejects dualism in our thinking about Christian spirituality. The spiritual realm lies beyond this world of space and time, but it is not a "good" realm that stands in opposition to an "evil" material creation. The call to spirituality is not a call for withdrawal from involvement in the everyday experiences of this life.

Instead, the incarnation of Jesus and his death on the cross teach us that true spirituality is expressed *within* the present material universe. The spiritual person does not withdraw, to seek God in a life that is disconnected from ordinary human experience. The opposite is the case! A person finds true spirituality in becoming involved in ordinary human experiences and relationships.

Earlier we noted that Jesus, in his incarnation, claimed to live his human life in such intimate union with the Father that his actions and words perfectly expressed the Father himself. In this way Jesus lived a life of true and perfect spirituality. But what kind of life did Jesus lead? Was it the disconnected life of ascetic withdrawal? Not at all. Jesus' life was the active adventure of a totally involved human being. Jesus did need his times alone with the Father, because intimate prayer was an expression of his spiritual life. But Jesus' spirituality was also expressed in constant, tiring interaction with others. This ultimately spiritual man drained himself to heal the sick, gave himself to teach the crowds, drove himself to train the disciples, and endured the repeated challenges of his antagonists.

In his life Jesus demonstrated compassion, kindness, humility, gentleness, and patience. He bore with others and forgave freely. Jesus loved totally. In his incarnation Jesus lived God's life in this world—*and we are to understand our spirituality by the example that Jesus provides.* The spiritual life is thus first of all a life of active involvement in the ordinary experiences shared by human beings who live in the real world.

## UNION WITH GOD

Earlier I suggested that a simple definition of spirituality as seen in Jesus is *living a human life in this world in union with God*. This definition is drawn first of all from Jesus' words about himself and his relationship with God. In John's Gospel such statements consistently stress the harmony that existed between Jesus and the Father in everything that Jesus did.

The striking feature of John's description is that union with God makes it possible for Christians to live Jesus' kind of spiritual life. We see this view expressed most clearly in what has been called Jesus' High Priestly Prayer.

> I pray also for those who will believe in me through their message, *that all of them may be one,* Father, *just as you are in me and I am in you.* May they also *be in us* so that the world may believe that you have sent me. I have given them the glory that you gave me, *that they may be one as we are one: I in them and you in me.* May they be *brought to complete unity* to let the world know that you sent me and have loved them even as you have loved me (John 17:20–23; italics mine).

Commentators have typically understood this passage as speaking about interpersonal unity within the church. In fact the prayer focuses on the sanctification of individual believers in the world. The prayer assumes that our spiritual experience depends on a supernatural union with God which is similar to the union of Jesus and the Father.

Note the emphasis on sanctification in Jesus' prayer of intercession for us.

> They are not of the world any more than I am of the world. My prayer is not that you take them out of the world but that you protect them from the evil one. They are not of the world, even as I am not of it. Sanctify them by the truth; your word is truth. As you sent me into the world, I have sent them into the world. For them I sanctify myself, that they too may be truly sanctified (John 17:14–19).

Jesus sees the believer as *in* but not *of* the world. Yet, like Jesus, we are set apart to God. We have been sent into the world in order that we might live the kind of life that Jesus himself lived here.

But how is this life possible? Jesus was able to live as he did because he was in fact one with the Father. In his prayer to God he said, "You are in me and I am in you" (John 17:21). Christ's complete union with God was the secret of his spirituality. Now we see that Christ seeks experience of a similar union for you and me! Jesus prays, asking "that they may be one as we are one: I in them and you in me" (vv. 22–23). The heart of Christian spirituality is to experience union with God as we live our human life in the world.

The mystic strain in Christianity has always yearned to experience union with God. Protestants have tended to see this union not so much as some ineffable experience but as a theological reality. Martin Luther understood union with Jesus as something that exists, as he says in his *Commentary on Galatians* at 2:20.

> [Christ] is my form, my furniture and perfection, adorning and beautifying my faith, as the colour, the clear light, or the whiteness do garnish and beautify the wall. Thus are we constrained grossly to set forth this matter. For we cannot spiritually conceive that Christ is so nearly joined and united unto us, as the colour or whiteness are unto the wall. Christ therefore, saith he, thus joined and united unto me and abiding in me, liveth this life in me which I now live;

yea Christ himself is this life which now I live. Wherefore
Christ and I in this behalf are both one.[1]

Other passages in Scripture affirm the existence of a real
union between Jesus and believers. In Romans 6, for example,
the promise of the Christian's freedom from sin's mastery is
based on our having been united to Jesus. We are buried with
him and raised with him (vv. 3–5). Because of our real union
with Jesus, the old nature is "rendered powerless" (v. 6), its
domination of our personalities is ended, and Jesus' resurrection power is available to us today.

Paul then urges Christians to consider themselves dead to
sin and to resist sin's promptings. We are to yield ourselves to
God, surrendering every part of our body to him to be an
instrument of his righteousness (Rom. 6:11–14). In other words,
we are to proceed from the fact of union to the experience of
union, by living a righteous life in this world.

As we look at such passages we note two things. First, a
real union between the believer and Jesus does exist which
makes it possible for the Christian to live a spiritual life. But
second, union with Christ produces no automatic change in our
experience. Although we are one with God through Christ,
Jesus must still pray that we might *be* one, "just as you [the
Father] are in me [Jesus] and I am in you" (John 17:21). Christ's
prayer assumes union but implies that we must go on to a full
experience of the union that exists.

Paul has the same understanding of spirituality. In Philip-
pians he says, "If you have any encouragement from being
united with Christ [a condition which exists], . . . make my joy
complete by being like-minded, having the same love, being one
in spirit and purpose" (2:1–2). Paul thus asks his readers to
express that union in the ordinary experiences of human life.
Paul continues, "Do nothing out of selfish ambition or vain
conceit, but in humility consider others better than yourselves"
(v. 3). As we humble ourselves to live an obedient life, our
"attitude should be the same as that of Christ Jesus" (v. 5). In
this way, we are told, "Work out your salvation with fear and
trembling, for it is God who works in you to will and to act
according to his good purpose" (vv. 12–13).

In summary, the example of Jesus and the teaching of the
Epistles agree that spirituality involves living a human life in

---

[1]Martin Luther, *Commentary on Saint Paul's Epistle to the Galatians*, trans.
Erasmus Middleton (Grand Rapids: Eerdmans, 1930), pp. 144–45.

this world in union with God. Furthermore, the spiritual life is possible because a real union in fact exists between the believer and Jesus. Finally, the existence of that union does not guarantee the experience of that union. The spiritual life is one of working out in experience our union with Jesus.

## CHRISTLIKENESS

Jesus is the key to Christian spirituality in several senses. Jesus is our leader: his example shows us that spirituality is expressed in living a human life in this world. Jesus is our source: only union with Jesus provides the power for the spiritual life. And Jesus is our model: the New Testament consistently directs us to become like him.

The Christian's union with Jesus brings with it the possibility of a Christlike life. This truth moved Wesley deeply and became one of his favorite ways of explaining what he meant by holiness.

> In the year of 1792, I began not only to read, but to study, the Bible, as the one, the only standard of truth, and the only model of pure religion. Hence I saw, in a clearer and clearer light, the indispensable necessity of having "the mind which was in Christ," and in "walking as Christ also walked;" even of having, not some part only, but all of the mind which was in him, and of walking as He walked, not only in many or most respects, but in all things. And this was the light, wherein at this time I generally considered religion, as an uniform following of Christ, and entire inward and outward conformity to our master.[2]

Others have been captured by the same image. Thomas à Kempis wrote of the *Imitation of Christ*. Sheldon captivated a generation with a call to live *In His Steps*. The insight of each is based on a distinctive line of biblical teaching. The Christian is destined for perfect conformity to the likeness of God's Son: "We know that when he [Jesus] appears, we shall be like him, for we shall see him as he is" (1 John 3:2; see also Rom. 8:19). Yet, ultimate transformation is not the Christian's only hope. Paul emphasizes the fact that God's Spirit is writing Jesus on our hearts even now. We "are being transformed into his likeness with ever-increasing glory, which comes from the Lord, who is the Spirit" (2 Cor. 3:18).

---

[2]*The Works of John Wesley*, 14 vols. (Grand Rapids: Zondervan, 1958), 11:367.

Union with Jesus means that, as God's "dearly loved children," we are to imitate God and to "live a life of love, just as Christ loved us" (Eph. 5:1–2). This life is possible only because Christ "dwells in [our] hearts through faith" and is present to help us "to the measure of all the fullness of God" (3:17, 19). Because of our union with Jesus we are to put off the old self, which is corrupted by deceitful desires. We have been taught, "Be made new in the attitude of your minds; and . . . put on the new self, created to be like God in true righteousness and holiness" (4:22–24).

In fact, the call to a Christlike life is so critical that John insists, "Whoever claims to live in him [God] must walk as Jesus did" (1 John 2:6). This call to imitate Jesus is not an invitation to humanistic self-effort. It is rooted in the reality of Jesus' work for us and his union with us. But given that reality, Christianity clearly calls us to live our human life in the world just as Jesus lived his. As Jesus obeyed the Father, we are to obey. As Jesus was fully involved with others, we are to be involved. As Jesus actually enfleshed God in this world, we are to enflesh God in this world. Christian spirituality is nothing more and nothing less than living our human life in this world in union with God.

In this chapter, then, we have come closer to a definition of Christian spirituality. We Christians affirm two realms, the spiritual and the material. But we reject religious dualism and the idea that the spiritual and material are in opposition. We see in Jesus a perfect blending of the two, expressed by living his human life in union with the Father. We see in Jesus' life on earth no disconnection from the ordinary but, in contrast, a total involvement in life's experience. Christian spirituality is essentially incarnational, a person's enfleshing the life of God in the world of humankind.

## PROBE

case histories
discussion questions
thought provokers
resources

1. Which of the following do you think are most important in the spiritual life, as defined in this chapter? Which do you think are most important to one who views the spiritual life in a mystic way? Which elements seemed most important to you before you began this study? Make three lists, in each ranking the following elements from "most important" to "least important."

| | |
|---|---|
| prayer | witnessing |
| Bible reading | completing a task |
| study | talking with a friend |
| resisting a temptation | running for office |
| calling a lonely acquaintance | confessing a sin |
| meditation | exercise |
| going to a wedding | buying a car |

2. The concept of spirituality presented here stresses the incarnation of Christ, seeing spirituality as *living a human life in union with God.* Does this position mean that we can see the Christian life as a continuing incarnation of Jesus? Read the two paragraphs below. Then write a critique, evaluating carefully the areas with which you agree or disagree.

Christian spirituality is incarnational in that Christ really is in us and in that the Spirit's transforming power enables acts of ours to express the beauty of Jesus. As you and I choose to live by the Spirit's promptings, "the righteous requirements of the law" are "fully met in us." As Romans 8 teaches, since "Christ is in you, your body is dead because of sin, yet your spirit is alive because of righteousness. And if the Spirit of him who raised Jesus from the dead is living in you, he who raised Christ from the dead will also give life to your mortal bodies [i.e., you in your mortality] through his Spirit, who lives in you." Bonded thus to Jesus by faith, living in him, our life on earth is an expression of Christ's words, his works, or his life. As the disciples saw the Father in Jesus, so others are to see Jesus in us.

Jesus' continuing incarnation is in his body as well as in believing individuals. Jesus is seen imperfectly in the individual, more perfectly in his body. Mother Teresa's dedication to the poor of India is a beautiful expression of Christ's compassion. Not everyone is called to demonstrate that facet of Christ so perfectly. But each of us does have a gift, a special enablement by which we serve others. In the distribution of these gifts through the body and in their expression in individuals, the many-faceted perfections of Jesus can be seen. George Muller's prayer life was deep and intimate, and the ministry to England's orphans which grew from it was Christlike indeed. An incarnational spirituality calls on each believer to pray. But it does not demand that we each have a prayer life like Muller's. We can look at other spiritual qualities and make the same point. We are all called to worship. But incarnational spirituality does not demand that each of us experience the heights of worship that others may know. Yes, Jesus is expressed in his body as well as in individuals, and more perfectly in the body. No one individual can display the perfections of Christ. Yet, by distributing gifts in the body of Christ, enabling one to display a particular facet of Christ to a heightened degree and another to display yet a different facet, Jesus continues to reveal the fullness of his beauty in our world.

3. Here is a list of critical concepts for an adequate theology of spirituality as presented by the author. Based on these statements, how do you think the author would answer the questions he raised at the end of chapter 1 (p. 18)?

    1. Spirituality in Jesus meant living an involved human life in union with God.

    2. The spirituality of Jesus was rooted in his union with God and was maintained as Jesus chose to do always those things that pleased the Father.

    3. Jesus was energized and empowered to please God by the Holy Spirit.

    4. Spirituality in us means living an involved human life in union with God.

    5. Our spirituality is rooted in our union with Jesus and is experienced as we choose to do always the things that please him.

    6. We are energized and empowered to please God by the Holy Spirit.

    7. As we live in and by the Spirit, growth in Christlikeness takes place.

4. Write out your own conclusions concerning spirituality at this point. How are they similar to and how are they different from the author's?

5. Study John 15:1–17. What does this passage tell you about Christian spirituality? Write an analysis.

# 5

## LIVING A HUMAN LIFE

Christ himself is our key to understanding the nature of Christian spirituality. Jesus is our model of the spiritual person, one who lived his human life in union with God. Our real union with Jesus makes a spiritual life possible. And in Jesus we see the goal of spirituality: Christlikeness.

Too often, writers on spirituality focus on Jesus in a devotional, mystical way. They speak of union with Jesus or God as a direct, numinous experience. Yet, if Jesus' union with the Father is a model for our union with him, we need to focus rather on Jesus' life on earth. When we do, Christ's own words provide a healthy corrective for our mystical yearnings. (All italics are mine.)

> The Son can *do nothing* by himself; he can *do only what he sees his Father doing,* because *whatever the Father does the Son also does*. For the Father loves the Son and *shows him all he does* (John 5:19–20).

> I *do nothing on my own* but speak just what the Father has taught me. The one who sent me is with me; he has not left me alone, for *I always do what pleases him* (8:28–29).

> It is the Father, living in me, who *is doing his work* (14:10).

Note that Jesus' union with the Father was experienced in what he did. The essence of spirituality as we see it in Jesus is not found in some direct "spiritual" experience of his union with the Father but rather is seen in Jesus' living his human life—in doing his human activities—in full and complete submission to God.

If we are to understand spirituality as it is demonstrated in Jesus, we must then look carefully at what it means to live a human life in this world. As Jesus' spirituality is understood by seeing him live his human life in union with God, our own spirituality must also be sought in the way we live our human life in union with him.

We will look at prayer and worship—at communion with God, for these activities were part of Jesus' life in this world. Prayer and worship are vital in every human life, if one is to live as God intends. But prayer and worship are only one aspect of Christian spirituality. If spirituality is experiencing union with God in living and being human here on earth, we need to look beyond prayer and worship to examine all that it means to live a human life.

## GENESIS REVISITED

We cannot understand the human experience apart from reading Genesis. There we find the origin of our species; there we discover vital insights into what it means to live a human life in this world. While the Genesis story is familiar, I would like to highlight a few salient points.

In eternity past, God made a decision: "Let us make man in our image, in our likeness, and let them rule . . . over all the creatures" (Gen. 1:26).

Then, in the echo of a spoken word, space was born, and the heavens were hung with a myriad of shining lights. The next words focused on a tiny speck circling a minor sun in the spiral arm of an unremarkable galaxy. At that word, earth suddenly sparkled with water and clouds and was decorated with plant and animal life.

All was now ready. God himself bent down to mold the dust of earth. Into the shape he had formed God breathed the breath of life. And thus there was the first man, joining in his nature the material universe of which he is part and the image and the likeness of the Spirit who is his Creator.

On this planet God planted a garden, where Adam, the first human being, explored. Adam's capacities for appreciating beauty, for displaying creativity, and for doing significant work were all exercised in the garden. His capacity for intimate relationship with God was also developed, for the Lord often visited in the cool of the evening. With the creation of Eve, humanity's ability to enjoy fellowship and intimacy with others was also extended. Finally, a tree in the garden permitted Adam and Eve to exercise a moral capacity. To be truly like God, human beings too must be able to make a real choice between good and evil.

We have no idea how long the first pair enjoyed their idyll. We do not know how many times they wandered in the garden, glanced at the forbidden tree, and passed by. But one day, incited by the Tempter, Eve ate its fruit and gave some to Adam. Then Adam ate as well, fully aware of his disobedience.

When God came that evening, Adam and Eve fled in fear. When God confronted them, each tried to blame another. Then God pronounced the doom of which they had been warned. Spiritual death shrouded the guilty pair, and through that death, sin gripped the human personality. Also mortality began its work: Adam and Eve now were (and all their eventual children would be) subject to suffering, pain, and death.

But the settling of the cloud of death was not the end. God clothed Adam and Eve in animal skins and taught them sacrifice. Each new generation was taught to do right, and some people, such as Abel and later Noah, chose the way of commitment. Others, such as Cain and Lamech, were unwilling to recognize the lordship of God. These men turned from the way of holiness to do wrong and to cause others harm.

Spinning outward from this beginning, time has woven each thread more tightly into the experience of every individual and into the history of our race. The features we find in Genesis recur in every age and help us identify what it means to live a human life in our present world. The early chapters of Genesis sketch the greatness and the glory of humanity, as well as its fall and the spreading stain of sin. And these chapters suggest the gathering clouds of a judgment to come at the end of history.

It is important here to identify the defining features of human life in this present world. They are present in the Genesis account and can give us an adequate understanding of what human life is. And since spirituality is living a human life in union with God, we must identify these elements if we are to develop a theology of spiritual development.

*Identity.* To be human means to accept the burden of God's image. We see the image of God in everything that makes persons distinct—in our capacity to appreciate beauty, to

perform meaningful work, to be creative, and to enjoy fellowship with others. In mind and emotions and will, we human
beings reflect something of God's being. But perhaps our
identity is most clearly reflected in the symbol of Eden's
forbidden tree: we are responsible beings; we have the freedom
to choose. Nothing can diminish the awesome responsibility of
free choice that we as human beings bear.

To live a human life in the world means to accept the
burden of our identity and to live responsible lives.

*Intimacy*. To be human means to walk with God in the cool
of the evening. Only human beings are created with the capacity
for fellowship with the divine. Only human beings are creatures
of the material universe and yet are infused with God's image
and likeness. Intimate experience with God is therefore vital to
us all. Human beings were created for fellowship with God, and
we are restless until we find our rest in him.

To live a human life in the world means to seek and to find
intimacy with our God.

*Sinfulness*. To be human means to carry the burden of
Adam's legacy. Sin is a reality. We find sin coiled deep within
us; we feel sin striking at us from within others; we are crushed
by the institutionalization of sin in society. We are warped
beings, picking our way through a tangled world, familiar with
the anguish sin causes through our own faults and through the
faults of others. Cain still claims his victims. Yet we must learn
to deal with sin—our own and that of others. We are not to be
defeated by either but, as Jesus did, are to find the way of
victory through union with God.

To live a human life in the world means to learn to live with
sin, yet also to free ourselves of its mastery.

*Mortality*. To be human means to be vulnerable to suffering. We live in weakness. We are vulnerable to pain. Even the
joy of childbirth is marred by suffering, and work has become
struggle. In this world we have little or no control over the
things which cause us suffering. Cancer strikes without our
assent. Loved ones die despite our earnest prayers. Wars or
inflation spoil all that we have set aside. In the last analysis, we
must face our ineffectiveness: we do not control the forces or
the persons that shape our lives.

To live a human life in the world means to surrender to the
God who does control and, in our pain, to find comfort in our
knowledge of God's wisdom and love.

*Lordship*. To be human means to take our place as creatures before the living God. Genesis constantly affirms God's primacy. He is the Creator, the Shaper. God initiates, and human beings respond. While God has showered gifts on humankind, he has also reserved the right to command. God planted the tree in the garden and exercised this right. He continued to speak, calling on Cain to do what Cain knew was right. In every human affair, we creatures are to subject ourselves to God.

To live a human life in the world means to acknowledge the lordship of the living God.

*Holiness*. To be human means to respond to God by pleasing him in all we do. Cain lived in shadows, fleeing from the holy. Unlike his brother Abel, Cain chose his own way, and when rebuked, his anger erupted in open hostility and murder. Holiness here is understood as the opposite of Cain's behavior. To be holy is to do what pleases God. In pleasing God, we do good to every neighbor. As we set ourselves and our lives apart to God, the right we do blesses rather than brings harm.

To live a human life in the world means to be holy in all we say and do.

*Commitment*. To be human means to live with a sense of purpose. At a time when all humankind wallowed in a morass of sin, Noah heard God's voice and chose to obey. For 120 years he and his family labored at the task they had been given. When the floods came Noah received his reward. Each human being is faced with a similar choice. We hear God's clear call; we see his priorities set out before us and must decide what will be of ultimate concern to us.

To live a human life in the world means to commit ourselves to what God says gives purpose and meaning to our existence.

## ASPECTS OF HUMAN LIFE

In his life here on earth, Jesus, while truly God, was also fully human. Jesus shared our identity: he lived as a fully responsible individual, exercising his freedom to choose the Father's will. Jesus shared our need for intimacy with God: he frequently slipped away to meet God alone, in prayer. Jesus lived among sinners, experiencing all it means to be tempted. He was sinned against, even though he himself was without sin. Jesus responded fully to the lordship of the living God, doing only God's will, and then was raised from the dead to become Lord of all. Jesus shared our mortality: he learned obedience in the crucible of suffering. He lived a life of holiness: he pleased God and did good to others. And Jesus made his own full commitment to the priorities established by his Father.

In short, Jesus lived his human life in this world in union with God. In his life, Jesus, the Second Adam, established the true meaning of Christian spirituality for us all. In the sections to follow, we will look at each of these aspects of human life. We will consider Jesus' example of living a human life in union with God as well as his teaching about the way of spirituality.

Besides studying Jesus' example, we will examine carefully the Bible's teaching regarding the basic issues of human life. In doing so, we will note that each issue has both individual and interpersonal aspects. In our identity as beings who bear the image of God, we are responsible for ourselves—but we also owe a duty to others. In our search for intimacy in relationship with God, we experience his touch in private prayer—but we also meet him in the worshiping community. In our struggle with sin we must learn to deal with it in our own lives—but we must also learn to deal with sin as it surfaces in others whose lives touch ours. In fact, every human issue has these paired aspects, as listed in table 2.

**Table 2. Aspects of Human Life**

| Human Issue | Individual Aspect | Corporate Aspect |
|---|---|---|
| Identity | Personal Responsibility | Accountability |
| Intimacy | Prayer of the Heart | Corporate Worship |
| Sinfulness | Confession | Forgiveness |
| Lordship | Choice | Freedom |
| Mortality | Suffering | Compassion |
| Holiness | Personal Morality | Doing Justice |
| Commitment | Discipleship | Servanthood |

The rest of this book is devoted to examining each issue in both of its aspects. I believe that we will thereby be able to grasp the meaning of living a human life, which in turn will unveil the true nature of Christian spirituality.

## SUMMARY

So far in this book I have surveyed approaches that Christians have taken to spirituality. I have considered contemporary and historic voices, surveyed biblical images, and looked at three Protestant theologies of spirituality. I then argued that Christian spirituality must be understood by looking to Jesus, not in his essential nature as God in his present glory, but in his life on earth. In the incarnate Christ we see true spirituality, a perfect blending of the material and immaterial universes. In Christ we see a spirituality which is not retreat or disconnection from the world of people but rather is the living of a human life in perfect union with God.

The spirituality that Jesus Christ models forces us to ask two questions. First, on what basis can *we* live a spiritual life? The answer is found in the Bible's teaching that through faith a real union that makes living the spiritual life possible is established between the believer and Jesus Christ. But we must go on, as Jesus did, and experience the union by in fact living our human life in fellowship with our Lord. The phrases that teach us how to live in union ("do always those things that please him," "doing his work," etc.) focus on an obedient responsiveness to God as he guides us through life.

But our definition of spirituality raises another question. If spirituality is living a human life in union with God, we must ask what it means to live a human life. The answer is found first in the Genesis portrait of our beginnings, in which we learn the distinctives of being human. As we will see, the seven human issues I have identified are so basic that they appear and reappear in the life and teaching of Jesus and throughout Scripture. By examining the personal and interpersonal aspects of these basic issues, we find unexpected direction for living the spiritual life.

## A LOOK AHEAD

So far in this book I have simply defined Christian spirituality and identified the issues with which we must deal if we are to live our human lives in union with God. In the rest of the book I examine further each of these issues, focusing on growth. Every writer on spirituality agrees that spiritual growth and change are outcomes of a disciplined life. I examine the disciplines of the Christian life, considering how the reader can

grow spiritually and how leaders in the local church can guide
congregations into more vital spiritual growth.

My method is simple. In each chapter I discuss biblically
one of these human issues in its personal or interpersonal
aspect. We will see the issue in Jesus as he lived his human life
in union with God. And we will examine how to follow Jesus'
example and apply relevant teachings of the written Word.
Finally, I suggest disciplines through which individuals and
congregations can confront each issue and can take steps
leading to personal spiritual growth.

In taking this approach, I hope to accomplish several
objectives. First, I wish to encourage a fresh view of Christian
spirituality. Study of the various theological explanations of
"what happens" within the believer in his or her relationship
with God does not necessarily produce vital spiritual growth.
The mystics' notion that spirituality involves seeking some
direct, private experience of God is not distinctively Christian
or biblical. I propose a vision of Christian spirituality which
places an appropriate emphasis on the inner life but which is
balanced by a focus on the totality of our human experience as it
is lived in union with God. Christian spirituality suggests not
withdrawal from life or denial of our humanity but an active and
involved human life, such as Jesus Christ lived.

Second, I intend to link all our thinking about spirituality to
Jesus Christ. He is the focus of our faith. He is our model of
Christian spirituality, the one through whom our union with
God is established and maintained. The goal of our spiritual
journey involves growth in Christlikeness.

Third, I hope to define the critical issues of our human
experience, in both their personal and interpersonal aspects, as
these are related to our walk with God. I seek to discern
biblically the meaning of intimacy, sinfulness, commitment, and
each of the others. Such understanding is necessary in order to
grasp the nature of spirituality as Christians are called to
experience it.

Finally, I seek to suggest disciplines which will help
individuals and congregations grow spiritually. I explore ways
in which Christians can respond to God's call and the disciplines
by which we can live out our union with Jesus in this world.

Realistically speaking, I expect to scratch the surface of
what it means to live the spiritual life. Each issue, each aspect,
deserves treatment in a book rather than in a single chapter. But

this volume is a textbook, intended not so much to give answers as to stimulate learning. If studying this book stimulates the reader to search and find more of what it means to live one's human life in union with God, then the book will have served its purpose indeed.

**PROBE**

**case histories**
**discussion questions**
**thought provokers**
**resources**

1. Here are several excerpts from chapter 1 that describe various approaches to Christian spirituality. In view of the author's definition of Christian spirituality as "living a human life in union with God," how do you suppose he would evaluate each? How would *you* evaluate each one?

> "Perhaps the best description of the spiritual life is *the sum total of responses which one makes to what is perceived as the inner call of God.* However, the spiritual life is not locked up inside a person. It is a growing, coherent set of responses integrated into the complex behavior patterns of human life. To think of the spiritual life as something apart from the rest of one's individual life is to flirt with ancient and persistent errors. When the individual has decided to respond to the call of God experienced within, and strives to make this call the center of activity and choice, he or she may be called a spiritual person" (pp. 12–13).

> "To live the spiritual life is to be related to God, with this relationship as the basis for all human relationships. To see the image of the Creator in each created being is to have a perspective from which to live among other human beings. The spiritual life, particularly through the forms of prayer, cannot be lived in a possessive sense of closeness to God. The intercessory nature of prayer is a mark of authentic spirituality" (p. 13).

> Catholic tradition often conceives of a spiritual journey marked off by the stages of the "three ways." Groeschel notes that, "at some time in childhood or adolescence, or occasionally much later, the reality of grace begins to break through to the conscious mind of the individual in a religious experience. This event, known psychologically as an *awakening,* marks the beginning of conscious spiritual life." Growth takes place as the believer travels the three ways.

> Along the "way of purgation," the believer renounces serious and deliberate sin and becomes increasingly aware of his or her depravity. Gradually forsaking self-reliance, the person learns to rely "on a greater life of union with Christ, with increased prayer, reflection, more listening and less manipulation of and

speculation about God." Out of the crucible, gradually and painfully and not without moments of despair, a deeper hope and faith mature.

Along the second way, the "way of illumination," there is relative freedom from a sense of guilt and from anxiety. Love for God grows more intense, as does love for others. "Consequently good works become the hallmark of the illuminative way." Prayer becomes a joy, and the believer "lives on Scripture and is fed on the writings of the saints." This way too has its "dark night" experiences, yet the desire to remain loyal to God persists, and final surrender of oneself to the Lord marks release.

The "unitive way" is the last and highest stage in Catholic spirituality. "Words fail and thoughts evaporate as one attempts to describe the experience of union with God which comes to the very few who arrive at this way of infused contemplation" (pp. 15–16).

2. Chapter 2 notes a number of biblical images which are associated with spirituality. From the following list of images, select at least one to explore directly in the New Testament. How does this image support or bring into question the author's contention that Christian spirituality is living a human life in union with God? Write a five to six page paper on your discoveries.

| | |
|---|---|
| fruitfulness | sanctification |
| growth | holiness |
| maturity | love |

3. Chapter 3 notes a number of active verbs associated with living out our relationship with God. From the following list, select at least one item to explore directly in the New Testament. How does the use of the verb support or bring into question the author's contention that Christian spirituality is living a human life in union with God? Write a five to six page paper on your discoveries.

| | |
|---|---|
| follow | abide in |
| walk | know |
| reckon | yield |
| obey | seek |
| submit | stand |
| deny self | take up cross daily |

4. Reevaluate the three theological formulations considered in chapter 3 of "what happens" inside believers that enables them to live a Christian life. Is any of them more compatible than the others with the concept of spirituality developed in this book? Be ready to support your conclusion.

## Part Two

# SPIRITUALITY DEVELOPED

# Section A: Identity

Genesis emphasizes the creation of human beings in God's image (Heb. *ṣelem*) and likeness (Heb. *dᵉmûṯ*). The key Hebrew words here are linked in contexts where the Old Testament intends to make a significant statement about human nature (see Gen. 1:27; 5:3). Together they teach us that, to understand the nature of human beings, we must look to God, even though in his essential being God is not comparable to anything which exists (Isa. 40:18). *Image-likeness* thus is a technical theological term, identifying human beings as unique in all creation. While God cannot be compared to us, our human life can be understood only by comparing ourselves to him.

The image-likeness affirmed in Genesis 1 and taught throughout Scripture is seen in the capacities which we share with God. In our inner nature each of us reflects an intellectual, moral, and emotional similarity to God. Together these capacities make each of us an individual, responsible self. As God is a personal being, we too are personal beings with our own separate identity. But with separate personal identity comes a dual burden: we have become fully responsible for our own actions, and yet we are also accountable for our influence on others.

To live a human life means to accept fully the reality of personal responsibility and accountability to others. Christian spirituality calls us to live responsibly and accountably in union with God.

# 6

## PERSONAL RESPONSIBILITY

An eighteen-year-old was tried in Tampa, Florida, for killing three coeds. Drunk, he drove the wrong way onto an interstate entrance, striking their VW head-on. He had had several convictions for drunk driving in his home state (Massachusetts).

That same week the papers reported the trial of two brothers. They hammered a man to death who had given them work just a month before. The victim's family asked that one of the two be investigated, because they thought he had drowned his own younger brother some years earlier. The defense lawyer argued that in childhood the two killers had been sexually abused by their father and older brothers.

The question often raised in such cases is one of diminished responsibility. Even if such defendants are guilty, how much is really their fault?

At a Bible study in my home recently, I asked our group, "How much guilt is involved in these two cases? What percentage of responsibility would you assign?" Most suggested something between 90 and 100 percent responsibility. One estimate in the second case was as low as 70 percent. But then I asked another question: "Can you think of a situation in which you felt that other people were at least partly responsible for your actions?" Yes, there were instances. A family argument in which a sister's reaction to a rebuke made another's anger flare up. An order from a military superior that did not seem right but still was followed. Nearly everyone had made choices for which others seemed at least in part to blame.

## THE QUESTION OF BLAME

Seeking to shift responsibility for one's actions was one of the first indications of the Fall. After Adam and Eve ate the forbidden fruit, they were overwhelmed by feelings of guilt and shame. They sewed leaves together in an attempt to cover their nakedness, and then they tried to hide from God. Adam reluctantly answered when God called and explained that fear made him flee. Confronted then with his sin, Adam tried to shift responsibility. "The woman you put here with me—she gave me some fruit from the tree, and I ate it" (Gen. 3:12).

We can understand Adam's twisted reasoning. Perhaps he said or thought, "God, you created the circumstances of my life. You put a woman here with me. You knew how her presence would influence me, and so to some extent you are responsible for how I responded to her. God, the woman actively influenced my choice. She bears at least some of the responsibility, for she gave me the fruit. Yes, I ate it. But both you, as sovereign Lord of circumstance, and she, by her actions, are at least partly responsible for my choice."

*Influences.* Two parallel accounts of David's numbering Israel (2 Sam. 24 and 1 Chron. 21) help us understand the role of influence in human responsibility. The first verse of each account reveals a different source influencing David to act as he did. In one, "The anger of the LORD burned against Israel, and he incited David against them, saying, 'Go and count Israel and Judah'" (2 Sam. 24:1). In the other, "Satan rose us against Israel and incited David to take a census of Israel" (1 Chron. 21:1).

Each passage tells us that Joab and the rest of David's commanders resisted the king. The text does not suggest the reason, but the military recognized that such a census was clearly wrong. But David's command overruled. The census took over nine months, and when it was completed David realized that he had done an evil thing. In some unidentified way God had begun to convict him, and David was suddenly conscience-stricken. Each passage reports David's next act: "Then David said to God, 'I have sinned greatly by doing this. Now, I beg you, take away the guilt of your servant. I have done a very foolish thing'" (1 Chron. 21:8; cf. 2 Sam. 24:10). ("Foolish" here implies not unwise but morally wrong. The "fool" in the Old Testament lacks spiritual insight, and foolish actions reveal this deficiency.) In his confession David appropriately accepted total responsibility for his action. Note that each person identified took and was responsible for certain actions. God is responsible for inciting David, with an implied motive of giving Israel needed discipline. Satan is also responsible for inciting David to order the census of Israel. David too must accept that responsibility and be judged for his action and for his unstated but sinful motive.

Table 3 is a diagram of the dynamics of this interaction.

**Table 3. David's Census of Israel**

| Actor | Action | Motive |
|-------|--------|--------|
| God | incited David | to discipline Israel (for her good) |
| Satan | incited David | to harm Israel ("rose against") |
| David | numbered Israel | unstated, but sinful |

Each of these actors is fully responsible for his own behavior alone. None is responsible for the actions of another. God and Satan incited David, but neither was the cause of David's act. David alone was responsible for his own action. In his confession of sin, David recognized and accepted full responsibility. Inciting by God and Satan provided a context in which David made a personal choice, just as in Genesis, Eve's invitation provided a context in which Adam made a personal choice. But in the last analysis, neither God nor Satan was responsible for David's choice.

To be human means to bear complete responsibility for the choices we make in life. To try to excuse our acts or to claim diminished responsibility because of circumstances or because of the influence of others is to deny what makes us human—the image-likeness of God.

*Determinism.* One popular modern view, with many parallels in ancient philosophy, argues that human choices are not simply influenced but are actually determined. We act as we do because we have to. Behavioral psychologists argue that notions of human freedom and dignity should be discarded; if we only knew enough about the complex factors involved, every individual "choice" would be recognized as a necessary action. Psychiatrists have for decades offered comfort by suggesting that their patients' present difficulties or foolish actions were caused by painful childhood experiences. This modern view, however, has many ancient parallels.

One parallel is seen in the Book of Ezekiel. The Jews in Jerusalem, warned that the judgment threatened by the prophets was about to fall on their generation, simply shrugged it off. They dismissed Ezekiel's warnings with the saying, "The fathers eat sour grapes, and the children's teeth are set on edge" (Ezek. 18:2).

The reasoning is familiar. Do people lack motivation? Probably their mother caused it by tying their shoelaces instead of letting them do it themselves. Do people steal? It must be the fault of society for not giving them the opportunities of the rich. Do people have lung cancer? They should sue the tobacco company. It cannot be their fault for smoking two packs a day.

The argument of the ancient Israelites—there is nothing they can do if some fault of the fathers is about to be visited on them—is decisively rejected by Ezekiel. Inspired by God's Spirit, he announces to these ancient determinists, "The soul who sins is the one who will die" (Ezek. 18:4). *Soul* here does not mean the immaterial self, and the passage is not speaking of eternity. As in most biblical passages, *soul* means the personal self, the self-conscious "I." And the death that Ezekiel speaks of is physical, not spiritual. In the coming holocaust, as Jerusalem and its temple are consumed by flames, individuals who sin will die, and those who do right will survive.

In his argument Ezekiel stresses repeatedly the theme of individual responsibility. A wicked person can change, do good, and survive. A good person can turn to evil and die. The good son of a wicked father and the wicked son of a good father will each be dealt with according to his own and not his parent's ways. The actions of others do not determine a person's present choices. In fact, even one's own past choices do not determine an individual's present or future behavior. Each human being, reflecting the glory and bearing the burden of God's image-likeness, is truly and fully responsible for his or her own acts.

## JESUS' EXAMPLE

Genesis affirms Adam's full responsibility for his actions, which it defines as his being responsible to live by the will of God. God's will for Adam was simple and clear. Adam was free to enjoy and care for the garden given into his care and free to enjoy the woman God had given him to share it with. The sole restriction placed on the first pair was not to eat the fruit of the tree of the knowledge of good and evil. For us, discerning the will of God may be more complicated. But our human calling— to live responsibly by the will of God—remains unchanged.

Jesus is our model for this kind of life. In his humanity, he set the example, saying, "I do nothing on my own but speak just what the Father has taught me" (John 8:28). There was a unique closeness between Jesus and the Father: "He has not left me alone, for I do always what pleases him" (v. 29). Doing the Father's will in no way robbed Jesus of his freedom, which we see most clearly in the choice that led him to the cross. "No one takes it [my life] from me," he said, "but I lay it down of my own accord. I have authority to lay it down and authority to take it up again. This command I received from my Father" (10:18).

The Greek word for *authority* here is *exousia,* a word that has a range of meanings but whose central concept is "freedom of choice." The greater one's *exousia,* the greater the extent of one's unrestricted freedom of action, and vice versa. For instance, an army private has less freedom of action than a sergeant, who has less than a lieutenant, who has less than a colonel, etc. Each higher rank has authority to command the lower ranks and thus to limit their freedom of action.

But in this passage Jesus focuses *exousia* on a single issue. The unique freedom of action that Jesus enjoyed was to lay down his life and then to take it up again. He possessed all the freedom he needed to do what he understood to be the Father's will for him. Ultimately Jesus' authority was the freedom to obey the Father within the context of his own personal circumstances and calling. Jesus had this freedom because he had received it from his Father (John 10:18).

Scripture's view of human responsibility is closely linked with its teaching on authority, or freedom of action. Scripture recognizes that individuals are living in different circumstances. Some are slaves, some are masters. Some are women, with all this means in different societies, while others are men. Some are wealthy, some are poor. Some live in free lands, some live under repressive regimes. Occupations differ, states of health differ, and, within the church, spiritual gifts differ. Such factors create our individual circumstances and limit the choices open to us. A woman in the 1700s could not have chosen to become a doctor. A slave in the Roman Empire could not have chosen to move to another city. A poor person in the modern world cannot choose to fly to another country for a vacation.

Such circumstantial restrictions on freedom of choice always exist but are completely irrelevant to the issue of human freedom and responsibility, which is a *moral* responsibility. Our *exousia* is nothing more or less than the freedom to obey God within the framework of our individual circumstances and calling.

Within my circumstances, then, I hear the voice of God; I sense his call, I see that which is right. In the moment of decision I become aware that, like Jesus, I have authority. I have all the freedom that I need. I can choose to do what I believe to be the will of God, or I can choose not to do it. I, like Adam, am responsible. And if I choose wrong, no matter how much I, like Adam, attempt to shift blame for my choice to others, the fact remains that I, and I alone, chose. No matter what my circumstances are or what the issue that demands decision, I still can choose to do the will of God.

## GROWTH IN RESPONSIBILITY

My spiritual growth and development demand that I learn to see myself as a responsible person and that I accept full responsibility for my actions. Fully aware of my freedom to choose, I must consistently choose, as Jesus did, to do what I believe to be the will of God. I discuss here some practical steps for growing in this area of responsible personhood.

*Dismiss fantasy.* Imagination is a gift of God which we need to affirm. But imagination can also be an enemy. Fantasy can lead us to shift the focus of our freedom to choose from the real world to a realm which simply does not exist.

Suppose I daydream about winning a sweepstakes or inheriting a million dollars. I plan how much I will spend, how much I will save, or how I will help others. I lose myself in my fantasy and, in my imaginary life, feel a sense of joy that I am able to do so much for others and for God. But in my focus on fantasy I tend to ignore a simple fact: I do not have millions. I do have a few thousand dollars, or a few hundred. Life does not consist in what I *might* do if my fantasy came true. Life consists in what I *do* do with my reality.

In focusing on my fantasy I am comforted by a pseudospirituality. But I have lost sight of the fact that I remain responsible for the choices I make in the real world of my present circumstances. To be responsible in terms of my finances, I must understand that my stewardship is of the little I possess, not the millions of which I dream.

*Examine habits.* Each of us understandably lives much of our life by habit. A good deal of life consists of constantly repeated patterns: we get up about the same time each day, take the same route to work, bring the same lunch, we put in the same hours on the job, and we return home at the same time, where we eat the same meals and spend the same evenings. Such patterns of life are not bad, for we all need the sense of stability that they provide.

But patterns may become a problem when they become habit and when the habits wrest from us control of our lives. We may develop the habit of eating dessert and also may be concerned about our weight and the health problems that overweight brings. But we take the piece of cake unthinkingly, by habit. We may have nagging thoughts that we should read more or find more time to pray. But from habit we go out each morning to get the paper to read at breakfast, or we thoughtlessly turn on the TV. We may be aware of being overtired, but still we stay up late each night to watch a favorite program.

If I am to grow as a responsible human being in union with God, I need to become aware of my habits. I need to examine them honestly and evaluate their impact on my life. And I need to take charge of my life, by consciously choosing how I will act and what I will do rather than drifting on, living merely by habit. To live life in accordance with God's will I need to make my choices in full awareness of the meaning of each act, not to surrender my authority to habit.

*Focus on the moment.* Many persons feel bound by their past. At times the bondage is to a series of sins repeated until one is convinced that change is impossible. Each temptation seems so overwhelming; the past demonstrates only one's helplessness and suggests that there is no alternative. The bondage may be to an image of oneself as a failure, nurtured by a parent who constantly held up one's failures and doubted the possibility of one's success. When coming to a new challenge or facing a new decision, such a person fails again, believing that defeat is inevitable.

We forget that the Bible speaks of an image each human being bears and that Jesus proclaimed freedom to choose.

However we may try afterward to excuse the choice we made, we each know that, in that awesome moment when we stand at a crossroad, we have the authority, or freedom, to choose. We can go one way or the other. We have felt the responsibility, known the burden of the image-likeness of God.

All too often we try to deny that knowledge and avoid the moment of choice. We put it off or make a disguised choice by refusing to act. If we are to grow as responsible persons, we need instead to become more aware of such moments. In the moment of choice we *know* that a real choice exists and that the past does not bind us unless we surrender to its power. To live a human life I need to become more aware of such moments and to affirm in them both my freedom and my responsibility. To sense the will of God at such times and to choose it is to live my human life in union with my God.

*Refuse to make excuses.* How we deal with our choices after we have made them is in some ways as important as being aware of our freedom in the moment of decision. All too often, when others challenge us or when we feel a sense of shame over a bad decision, we make excuses. We blame others or circumstances, trying to show why it was not our fault—or at least not *all* our fault.

This pattern is especially dangerous because it shapes our thinking and can even lead us to suppose that others really *were* to blame. It is one thing to explain a decision to others—even a bad decision. But it is something different to try to deny personal responsibility for the decisions that we make.

Instead of making excuses when caught at a fault, we need, like David, to confess our failures, to apologize, and to accept any blame. The course of offering excuses leads surely to self-deceit and to denial of personhood. To live a human life means to accept without empty excuses the responsibility for our acts.

*Determine now to do God's will.* Living a human life means to affirm our human identity as persons made in God's image. It means to acknowledge responsibility for our acts, to affirm that, in the moment of choice, each of us has authority, or freedom, to act. As we become more sensitive to the reality of this freedom, we also become aware as Christians that the touch-stone of our choice must be the will of God.

Each time we come to the moment of choice, we will decide to follow either what we believe to be God's way or what we know is another direction. In that choice and in that moment, we will live or not live in union with God. While no one can make the existential choice before the moment arrives, there is one thing that Christians can and need to do.

We can face the fact that, like Adam and like Christ, we too have a commitment to make. We must decide whether we believe God's will for us is good and whether we will commit ourselves to do it. If we so decide—consciously and intelligently—we will then surrender our lives to God humbly, with the awareness that, in the moment of each future choice, we will need divine grace to help us live out our commitment. To truly live as a human being, then, is to acknowledge God's right to guide us and to choose, as Jesus chose, to please the Lord.

## PROBE

exercises for personal development
case histories
thought provokers

1. For one week, keep a daily diary recording the significant decisions that you are aware of making. At the end of the week, study what you have written. Distinguish between decisions you are pleased with and those you wish you had not made. Do you see any pattern in either kind of decision that helps you understand your decision-making process? (Check such things as the influence or presence of others, your motives, etc.) Were you conscious of the moment of decision at the moment, or after you had made your decision?

   You can continue this process, which is designed to help you make responsible decisions by becoming more aware of the decisions you actually make, for as many weeks as it takes to sensitize you to the *exousia*, or authority and freedom, that you have.

2. Memorize John 8:29: "The one who sent me is with me; he has not left me alone, for I always do what pleases him." Meditate on this verse for at least ten minutes a day for ten days. As you do, open your heart to God and ask him to show you choices you can make that day to please him.

3. List experiences, events, and persons that have had a shaping impact on your life.

   Consider each item listed. Have you used it in any way as an excuse for choices you have made in your life? Have you blamed any of the experiences or persons for your present situation? Be honest in searching out ways you may have attempted to shift responsibility for your acts and decisions.

   Now imagine that each circumstance, event, or person who has had this kind of impact on you is the bar of a cage. Imagine yourself pulling that bar from the cage and giving it to God. When each bar has been pulled out and handed to God, imagine looking around.

Sense your freedom. Feel the new openness that removal of the bars brings.

Ask God to free you from bondage to the past as you make each future choice, aware that, as a person created in his image-likeness, you are free to choose God's will within your circumstances.

4. Write a short study of the Book of James, showing what it means for a believer to live a truly responsible life.

5. Look over the writings of Glasser and/or other proponents of what has been called "reality therapy." What insights do they give you into the dynamics of accepting responsibility for one's actions? What guidelines do they suggest for helping others live as responsible persons in union with God?

6. You are a pastor, counseling a Christian young woman who is very upset. Her former husband, who is not a believer, has asked her to remarry him. He has even promised to start going to church if she will. The young woman has talked with many people and gotten conflicting advice. All of the people who counsel her to remarry and those who tell her not to have explained how the Bible supports their position. Now, confused and upset, she says, "You're the pastor. You tell me what to do."

Write out the interview, showing as you report the dialogue what you think a responsible spiritual leader should do in such a situation.

7. You have been asked to conduct a workshop at a denominational retreat on the theme "Building Responsible Christians in the Church." Which of the following would you develop for this worship? Which would you leave out? Defend your choices—and develop an outline for one section you would include.

*Teaching personal responsibility.* Show how sermons, studies, and classes can explore this area. Suggest passages of Scripture, or biblical incidents that illustrate or teach the theme.

*Modeling personal responsibility.* From 1 Thessalonians 2 and other passages, develop how a leader models personal responsibility. Suggest situations in the church where a pastor needs to act responsibly. Point out factors that make it difficult for a pastor to make and explain responsible decisions.

*Affirming personal responsibility in others.* Present a model of counseling that treats others as responsible adults. Evaluate how to deal with subordinates in ways that encourage them to grow in personal responsibility. Examine how use of the Bible can support or discourage responsible action.

*Structuring the congregation for responsibility.* Discuss how structure discourages personal responsibility. Show how structure can encourage personal and congregational responsibility. Suggest how to help workers develop a sense of personal responsibility for their ministry. (For ideas, see *A Theology of Church Leadership,* by the author, with Clyde Hoeldtke [Grand Rapids: Zondervan, 1980].)

# 7

## ACCOUNTABILITY

The eight-year-old boy in a northeastern state watched the TV in open-mouthed amazement. He could not believe the huddled men and even women he saw crouched outside in the cold. Without telling his parents, the boy gathered up blankets and carried them through the snow toward downtown. The story was picked up in the press, and this child's spontaneous action led to a local movement to care for the homeless.

Margaret had heard the blows, the sharp cries, and the moaning next door just one time too many. She watched through the curtains until he left. Then she slipped across the narrow alley. When the door opened Margaret gathered the bruised woman into her arms and let her sob. Then she said in her most businesslike voice: "Now. Come on. We're going next door and make some phone calls. We're going to find out what we can do."

From early Genesis we learn that humans cannot live isolated lives. People were not intended to live alone. Even the commission to rule was given to Adam and Eve together. Each human being, possessing God's image-likeness, is a responsible person. We each bear full responsibility for our choices, and we are to affirm our freedom to choose even as we exercise that freedom in choosing to obey God. But the very image-likeness which makes us responsible also conveys immense personal worth. Each individual has value to God and is to be valued by others.

Because each person has worth and value, we, as members

of the human family, live in one another's debt. We remain responsible for our own choices. But at the same time we are in some sense accountable to and for others.

## IMAGES OF ACCOUNTABILITY

In Scripture, many threads reflect the theme of accountability. We are accountable not only for the well-being of others but also for the influence that we exert in their lives as the following expressions of accountability indicate.

*In the Old Testament legal system.* God's law established religious, moral, and civil standards. But that law set up no central criminal-justice system for enforcement. Responsibility for administering justice was instead distributed to every member of the community. Each individual was fully responsible for his or her own choices. But the community was accountable both to and for its individual members.

We see accountability for others in the biblical notion that the whole community could be called to account for the sins of individuals, even as the nation experienced defeat at Ai because of the sin of Achan (Josh. 7). We see accountability in Joshua's resolution of that incident: "Then all Israel stoned him [Achan], and . . . the LORD turned from his fierce anger" (vv. 25–26). Leviticus 24:10–23 picks up the same theme. The individual who sins will be held responsible, and the whole community is accountable for doing so.

But accountability is not simply a matter of punishing criminal or sinful acts. Israelites are accountable to their neighbors for volunteering honest testimony in any dispute. A witness is to show no partiality to either poor or rich; all are to be treated with scrupulous fairness (Lev. 19:15).

One fascinating feature of Old Testament law, which we will examine more carefully later, is mechanisms designed to help the unfortunate—no-interest loans, gifts, apprenticeship training, and other ways. The law of Israel made God's Old Testament people fully accountable for the welfare of the needy in the community, while carefully preserving the dignity of the poor (see chapter 17).

An Israelite was even accountable for offering to help an enemy. If an enemy's donkey falls, a neighbor is to help him lift it up (Exod. 23:5). If an enemy is seen doing wrong, the law says, "Do not hate your brother in your heart. Rebuke your neighbor frankly so you will not share in his guilt" (Lev. 19:17).

We are accountable to one another and for one another; we are accountable for helping others in need and for influencing others for good.

*In the Prophets.* While the law suggests that individuals are accountable for the purity of the community and its members, the Prophets affirm a limited responsibility to and for the wicked. The clearest example is found in Ezekiel's image of the watchman. "If the watchman sees the sword coming and does not blow the trumpet to warn the people and the sword comes and takes the life of one of them, that man will be taken away because of his sin, but I will hold the watchman accountable for his blood" (Ezek. 33:6). In this powerful passage Ezekiel makes it clear that the believer-watchman is accountable to the wicked for speaking out "to dissuade him from his ways" (v. 8).

The watchman is *not* responsible for how the wicked respond once they have been warned. And even if the watchman fails to cry out, the wicked one who dies will be taken away "because of his [own] sin." Each of us, however, remains responsible for our own choices and accountable to others, owing each neighbor help, influence, and encouragement to do good.

Hearing the prophet's words, I realize that I owe a duty of love to members of my community and to individuals whose lives touch mine. Living a human life means acknowledging and sensing this accountability. Living a human life in union with God means that I must fulfill my calling as an accountable person. I must be ready to help, quick to warn the wicked, and always eager to do good to others.

*In Jesus' teaching.* Jesus Christ's teaching on accountability is sharp and clear and parallels that of the Old Testament and the Epistles. Christ tells us to confront those who sin against us with a view to restoring them and then outlines a process by which the purity of the community can be protected (Matt. 18:15–17). We are commanded to love others as Jesus has loved us (John 13:34–35) and warned against causing any who believe in Jesus to sin (Matt. 18:6–7). Our responsibility also involves warning the wicked. Like our heavenly Father, who gives rain to the righteous and wicked alike, we are to do good to our enemies (Matt. 5:43–48). We are to share with them Christ's own transforming gospel, for he said, "Go and make disciples of all nations, baptizing them in the name of the Father and of the Son and of the Holy Spirit, and teaching them to obey everything I have commanded you" (Matt. 28:19–20).

*In the Epistles.* The Old Testament believer was a member of a faith community which was at the same time a nation. In contrast, the church exists as colonies of faith scattered through the world, we live in clusters of fellowship, seeded in pagan societies and cultures. No New Testament passage establishes the kind of civil law found in the Old Testament because we simply are no longer a nation but rather are aliens visiting a foreign land. Thus some elements of accountability found in the Old Testament are not repeated in the New.

But there are parallels. Israel's law describes a just, moral community. The church of Jesus is also a holy community, intended to reflect God's love and purity. In view of this calling, Christians are to guard the purity of the church. We are accountable to exercise church discipline when a member of the body chooses a life style of sin (1 Cor. 5:1–13). The goal of such discipline is not to punish but to turn the sinner back to righteousness. But if a person will not turn, that individual is to be expelled from the fellowship. Christians, like Israel, are accountable for the purity of the faith community.

The Epistles state our accountability to others in a powerful, positive way. Paul speaks of a "continuing debt to love one another" (Rom. 13:8) and teaches that the law was always intended to guide God's people into a life of love. Aware of our accountability, believers are told, "Make up your mind not to put any stumbling block or obstacle in your brother's way" (14:13). We are consciously to "make every effort to do what leads to peace and to mutual edification" (v. 19). And both James and John remind us that real love for others will issue in action to meet material as well as spiritual needs (James 2:14–17; 1 John 3:16–20).

The Epistles also contain parallels to Ezekiel's watchman theme. James concludes his book, "If one of you should wander from the truth and someone should bring him back, remember this: Whoever turns a sinner away from the error of his way will save him from death and cover over a multitude of sins" (James 5:19–20). Paul adds, "Brothers, if someone is caught in a sin, you who are spiritual should restore him gently" (Gal. 6:1). It is as much a part of our accountability for others to "correct, rebuke and encourage" (2 Tim. 4:2) as it was for the Old Testament saint to warn the wicked. (See table 4 for a comparison of various biblical teachings on accountability.)

Christian spirituality can never survive an isolated life. We are linked by God's Spirit to Jesus and to each other, and our life is intended to be lived in supportive, caring community. To live a human life is to live in relationship with others. To live in union with God is to commit ourselves to be accountable, always considering "how we may spur one another on toward love and good deeds" as we meet to "encourage one another" (Heb. 10:24–25).

**Table 4. Biblical Accountability**

| Accountable for | OT | Jesus | NT teaching |
|---|---|---|---|
| *Purity of the community* | Punish the guilty; volunteer honest testimony | Go to the one who sins against you to seek reconciliation | Exercise church discipline |
| *Well-being of others* | Care for the needy; help even one's enemy | Cause no one to sin; love as Jesus loved; do good to one's enemy | Care for the needy; put no obstacle in anyone's way; pray for your persecutor |
| *Warning the wicked* | Rebuke neighbor frankly; warn the wicked | Spread gospel to all | Restore a sinning brother; correct and rebuke |

## JESUS' EXAMPLE

While we catch glimpses of the meaning of our accountability in the written Word, the most powerful revelation is seen in Jesus. Hebrews expresses the basis of Jesus' commitment to human beings in this powerful passage:

> Since the children have flesh and blood, he too shared in their humanity so that by his death he might destroy him who holds the power of death—that is, the devil—and free those who all their lives were held in slavery by their fear of death. For surely it is not angels he helps, but Abraham's descendants. For this reason he had to be made like his brothers in every way, in order that he might become a

merciful and faithful high priest in service to God, and that
he might make atonement for the sins of the people (Heb.
2:14–17).

When Jesus entered our world through birth, he assumed a
truly human nature. And in taking on humanity, Jesus also
became accountable to and for others. He became accountable
for our welfare. In his life and death for us, Jesus fulfilled every
obligation of one person to another. Jesus also became accountable for the purity of the human family. At his return Jesus will
fulfill this obligation as completely as he has the rest.

One sequence of events reported in Mark's gospel illustrates Jesus' commitment to accountability. Jesus had been
pressed constantly by crowds who heard of his miracles.
Unable to enter any town openly, Christ stayed outside in
lonely places. Even so, streams of people still gathered to him
from everywhere.

Some days later Jesus slipped quietly into Capernaum. But
again, people heard he was home, and soon the house was filled,
with others pushing close to doors and windows so they could
hear. As tired as Jesus must have been, he preached to them.
Four men hurried to the home with a paralyzed friend. Unable
to get through the crowd, they climbed to the top of the house
and dug through the roof. Jesus responded to their faith and said
to the paralytic, "Your sins are forgiven" (Mark 2:5).

Some teachers of the law looked on grimly, for they
considered his words blasphemy: only God could forgive sins.
Sensing their rejection, Jesus immediately confronted their
unbelief. To demonstrate the truth that the Son of Man had
authority on earth to forgive sins, Jesus told the paralytic to get
up and go home.

Later, as Jesus walked by the lake, crowds gathered again.
Jesus taught them as he walked but stopped at a tax collector's
booth. He called Matthew, the despised collaborator with the
Romans, to follow him and later went to dinner at his home.
There Jesus ate and talked with many other tax collectors and
"sinners," who were rejected by pious society. Jesus' actions
were severely criticized by the Pharisees, who took pride in
their separation from evil and from those who did evil. Jesus'
explanation was simple: "It is not the healthy who need a
doctor, but the sick. I have not come to call the righteous, but
sinners" (Mark 2:17).

In events captured in a few verses of Mark 2, we sense

what it meant for Jesus to share not only our humanity but our accountability to and for others. We see Jesus respond with help to the needy, spend himself to teach and encourage, then both rebuke and act to redeem sinners. All this action was taken at significant cost to himself. Yet, in doing it, Jesus demonstrated his willingness to be accountable for others. Jesus heals. Jesus feeds the hungry. And Jesus' anger flares against the heartlessness and sins of his contemporaries. We need to see that anger in perspective, for it is not hatred but love; it is Jesus, the accountable man, rebuking the wicked for their own good.

In the Gospels we do not see Jesus punishing the guilty, as one who is accountable for the purity of the community, although one day he will. Christ himself said, "The Father judges no one, but has entrusted all judgment to the Son" (John 5:22). By taking on human nature, Jesus accepted the full weight of personal accountability to the community. When Jesus returns and the day of grace comes to its end, then he will judge the lost and fulfill this dark dimension of humankind's responsibility to the human family.

## GROWTH IN ACCOUNTABILITY

Living a human life means living with others. To live my human life in union with God means that, in my society and in my faith community, I must be accountable to and for others. This requirement seems paradoxical. As a human being made in God's image, I am fully responsible for my own actions. Yet, while not responsible for the choices others make, I am to hold myself accountable to them. I am to be involved. I am to participate in church and society, to care for persons in need, and to witness against and to the wicked. How, in these relationships, can I live an accountable life in union with God?

*Stand against evil in society.* When Isaiah's eyes were filled with his vision of the holy God, he cried out in pain. "Woe to me!" Isaiah wailed. "I am ruined! For I am a man of unclean lips, and I live among a people of unclean lips" (Isa. 6:5). Isaiah, despite his own relative purity, shared in the uncleanness that marked his society. While not directly responsible for the sinful choices of others, Isaiah remained accountable for the condition of the society in which he lived. Like Isaiah, you and I need to identify ourselves with our society and to acknowledge our participation in it and our accountability for its moral condition.

Whenever sin is institutionalized in a society, individuals are influenced toward sin. For instance, pornography distorts attitudes and thinking about sex, which is intended by God as a sacramental bond between husband and wife. A man, for example, whose thinking about sex is distorted will remain responsible for his choices, but the choices he makes are more likely to be shaped by his false perceptions and to be wrong. By working to limit or eliminate access to pornographic materials, we help members of our society make better choices and preserve them from tragedy, even as we preserve our society from greater sin.

Many areas in our society reflect distorted thinking and values. Many today seek to rob the unborn of their humanity by calling the fetus a "part of the woman's body." Tobacco growers continue to receive subsidies from the federal government to grow a plant that slowly kills thousands. Drunk drivers who kill and maim and kill again are still given a license to drive. Yet living a human life binds us with others who share our society with us. To live a human life in union with God means we must stand against the evils in our society and stand for what will help rather than harm others.

*Identify with other human beings.* The eight-year-old whose true story introduced this chapter was not sophisticated enough to distance himself from people who were different from him. He could not, as many of us do, comfortably classify others as "them," someone different from "us." In his willingness to identify with others, this child affirmed the basic truth of human identity on which accountability rests. Each human being reflects the image-likeness of God. Each is precious, with an incomparable value and worth. Each is part of "us," for in our common humanity no one, however different, is "them."

Classifying persons into "us" and "them" groupings is one way humanity tries to avoid the accountability which one young boy intuitively recognized and acted on. If we are to grow spiritually, we need to restructure our perception of others. We need to identify with others consciously and feel with them. We need to refuse to isolate ourselves mentally by verbal games and instead to link ourselves mentally with others in their needs. Human life is lived among others with whom we share the human identity. Living in union with God means affirming, in thought and action, our solidarity with others in the one human family.

*Respond to known needs.* An expert in the Scriptures admitted to Jesus that the law might be summed up in its command to love God and love one's neighbor. Christ agreed and challenged him to do so. The man hesitated. Then, hoping to justify himself, he asked, "And who is my neighbor?" (Luke 10:29).

The story that follows is familiar. Jesus told of a man robbed on the road to Jericho. A priest and then a Levite saw his battered body and hurried by. Then a Samaritan, whom the Jews despised as "them," came by. He saw the man, took pity on him, and brought him to a nearby inn. The Samaritan bandaged his wounds and, after caring for him personally, paid the innkeeper to let him stay as he convalesced.

When he finished, Jesus asked, "Which of these three do you think was a neighbor to the man who fell into the hands of robbers?" (Luke 10:36). The answer was obvious: "The one who had mercy" (v. 37).

This story, a favorite of generations, carries a potent message. One's neighbor is anyone in need; one's neighbor is anyone able to help. The antagonism that divided Samaritan and Jew did not block the concern that sprang up in the Samaritan's heart when he saw a fellow human being in need.

New Testament teaching on giving seems to be based on this principle. The basic word for giving is *koinōnia,* meaning "fellowship" or "sharing." The purpose of giving is to meet the basic needs of destitute Christian brothers and sisters, both in the local community (Acts 2:44–45; 4:32–35) and in the world at large (2 Cor. 8–9). And New Testament giving is based not on an established tithe but on heart searching. It is based on sensitivity and caring as Christians become aware of others' needs and, in view of those needs, give with eager willingness (see 2 Cor. 8:10–15).

Living a human life means we will constantly be thrown in contact with those who have needs of every kind. To live a human life in union with God means that we will respond caringly and freely when we become aware of those needs and are able to help.

*Confront lovingly.* All too often, Christians hold back from involvement in others' lives. We are too ready to say, "It's not my business." There may be a thin line between meddling and being accountable. Yet, willingness to confront evil and willingness to confront a brother or sister lovingly and with concern are marks of Christian spirituality.

Scripture does give us guidance in how to confront. Paul tells Timothy, "The Lord's servant must not quarrel; instead, he must be kind to everyone, able to teach, not resentful. Those who oppose him he must gently instruct, in the hope that God will grant them repentance leading them to a knowledge of the truth" (2 Tim. 2:24–25). Anyone who wanders from the truth is to be brought back (James 5:19). One caught in a sin is to be restored gently by those who are spiritual. We are commanded, "Carry each other's burdens, and in this way you will fulfill the law of Christ" (Gal. 6:2).

Living a human life puts us in contact with others who will at times make tragic and wrong choices. Living our human life in union with God means reaching out lovingly to confront and to restore.

*Love fully*. When Jesus gave his disciples his "new commandment," he reiterated a duty which had been established from the beginning. The command to love is a call to involvement in the lives and needs of others. It is a command that is universal and specific at the same time. In its universal sense we are to love and do good to everyone (Rom. 13:8–10; Titus 3:1–2). We are, like Jesus, to brave the criticism of those who cannot understand that the sick need the physician; like Jesus, we are to be with "sinners."

In its specific sense, the command to love is a call to intimacy in Jesus' church. Here too Jesus is our example, for he said, "As I have loved you, so you must love one another" (John 13:34). In the words of Hebrews, we are to "consider how we may spur one another on toward love and good deeds" (Heb. 10:24). We are not to "give up meeting together, as some are in the habit of doing, but let us encourage one another—and all the more as you see the Day approaching" (v. 25).

Living a human life means that we must live among other men and women. Living a human life in union with God means that we reach out to know and to love other people and that we draw especially close to those with whom we share faith in Christ.

**PROBE**

exercises for personal development
case histories
thought provokers

1. Find a partner with whom you will focus for one week on identifying with others. As you read about people in the newspaper or watch

them on television, consciously choose to think of them in terms of "us" rather than "them." Pray for persons as those whose pain you sense.

Record your thoughts and feelings daily in a dairy. Then at the end of the week, share your diary with your partner and compare experiences.

2. The following is a true story. How would you evaluate the action of the pastor and that of the woman in this situation? If you were a pastor and this situation occurred, what do you think you might have said to the woman? What could you have done? What could the woman have done instead of resorting to divorce? How might your congregation have been involved?

Karen wept as she spoke with her pastor. She had not wanted to come, but she said she was desperate now and terribly afraid. Her husband, John, was one of the trustees of the congregation. From what she said, he was also a wife beater. She claimed that at first he hit her only now and then, and he was always sorry afterward; now, with new pressures on his job, he did not stop with just one blow. According to her, he hit her again and again, beating her almost weekly. Karen told her pastor that she was afraid, terrified that someday John would kill or cripple her. And she accused him of beating the children, too. What could she do?

The pastor was disturbed. But he felt there was only one thing she could do: she had to go back to her husband and try to please him. He was the head of the house, after all. Perhaps if she worked harder at being a good wife, the beatings would stop.

Later the pastor spoke to John, who denied ever striking his wife— except maybe once or twice when she needed it. Karen missed church that week and the next. But John was there, so the pastor did not ask any questions.

When Karen finally filed for divorce, she was told she had no right to desert her husband and that, while she could attend the church, she could never sing in the choir or teach Sunday school again.

3. Hold a debate to explore the relationship between responsibility and accountability. Consider this resolution: *Resolved:* Parents should not offer housing or financial help to children past college age.

Give teams preparing the debate time to research the issue. Consider the fact, for example, that today some 55 percent of single adults between the ages of twenty-three and thirty live at home. Why? When does giving help harm another? When does it truly help? Team members could interview parents who have given this kind of help, as well as parents who have not.

4. Select one Old Testament prophet, one gospel, and one New Testament epistle. Prepare a chart such as table 4 above, in which you analyze and compare what each source suggests about accountability. Write a summary of your findings. From this study, how significant would you say the theme of accountability is in Scripture? How important is it in living the spiritual life?

5. The author suggests that New Testament giving is rooted in the concept of accountability, in its aspect as a spontaneous Samaritan-like response to another person's needs.

First, study 2 Corinthians 8–9 to establish principles that should guide Christian giving.

Second, develop a plan for guiding a congregation's giving by the principles you have discovered. For instance, since giving is a response to need, church giving programs should make people aware of needs. An effective stewardship program in the church calls for effective ways of communicating those needs to which believers might respond.

Alternatively, evaluate the existing stewardship program of your local congregation. Does it express or ignore biblical principles found in 2 Corinthians? How might it be modified to fit those principles more closely?

Every church has some approach to giving, both in gathering and expending funds. One of the best avenues for helping Christians develop a sense of accountability is to use the stewardship program as an avenue of education in accountability. Designing an approach to stewardship in the local church that is built on the biblical principles found in 2 Corinthians, which themselves reflect overall scriptural teaching on accountability, is a practical way to nurture the spirituality of a local congregation.

6. You and three others have been led to start a "Samaritan's Club" to help average people demonstrate a Christian accountability to and for others. First, write the constitution and rules of your club. Then outline at least ten projects your club might undertake, describing each project in one or two paragraphs.

# Section B: Intimacy

Genesis 2 breathes intimacy. We sense it in God's personal creative touch. It was not enough to speak man into existence. God had to bend down, knead the clay, and, gently holding the empty form, breathe into it his own life's breath.

We see intimacy in God's gift of the garden. The Lord guided Adam, pointing out the wonders and warning him about one special tree. We sense intimacy as God points out each living creature to the man, watching Adam as he studies each and gives each a name.

The spark in Adam glowed as, warm and close, the man and his Creator kept company in the fresh purity of that young and innocent world.

The thing that surprises us as we read this chapter is the naturalness of it all. Adam turned spontaneously to God. God came to meet and be with him. Even after Eve was shaped from Adam's rib, intimacy with God was a normal, necessary aspect of life. In the cool of the day God walked in the garden, showing himself a friend to the man and the woman he had created.

# 8

## PRAYER OF THE HEART

"My prayers never seem to get beyond the ceiling," Kelly was saying. "I mean, I pray. But I don't seem to get any answers. And I don't *feel* like I'm getting through. It's like I'm trying to talk to God, but he isn't there or something."

Ruth had a similar observation. "I can remember times when I really prayed fervently. Once, before I became a Christian, my brother-in-law had a heart attack. Everywhere I went I was praying for him with all my heart. When I was coming down the stairs one afternoon, I suddenly just knew he'd be all right. It was as if God said right out loud, 'I've answered your prayer.' You know, that was one of the things that convinced me that God exists, and I became a Christian a couple of years afterward. But it's bothered me in a way. How fervently do I have to pray to be really close to God like that? I mean, I've never been able to put my whole heart into prayer except for a few times when I was really hurting."

Kelly and Ruth, like so many others, are uncertain about prayer. In particular, they have not made an important distinction between prayer as request or intercession and prayer as a way simply to be with God.

There are many different Hebrew and Greek words in our Bible that are translated "prayer." In studying them, we discover the wonder of having access to a God who cares about everything we experience. In them we also discover important truths about the nature of our relationship with God. For instance, *pālal* and its derivatives picture calling to God, urging him to see our present need and act to meet it. This kind of prayer expresses dependence and humility; we appeal to him, and we acknowledge that he is the only one who can act.

*Nā'* is a simple expression of entreaty, while *'ātar* suggests that intensity that Ruth associates with her most significant experiences in prayer. The verb *šā'al* ("ask, inquire") is often associated with seeking God's guidance. When used in the context of prayer, *'ānâh* is an urgent cry. *Pāga'* is intercession, while *hānan* is an appeal to God's grace and mercy.

The words of the New Testament show a similar complexity. *Proseuchomai* in Greek culture was used of prayer in general, but in the New Testament it suggests the warmth of genuine conversation. *Aiteō* and *erōtaō* mean "ask; request," while *deomai* emphasizes a request that springs from awareness of deep need. Finally, *entynchanō* pictures intercessory prayer.

The prayer language of both testaments is rich in encouragement. The complex terminology tells us clearly that we can come to God freely with every need, in every situation. But none of the terms recaptures Eden or focuses specifically on the intimacy Adam and Eve knew through simply being with God. Clearly, however, communing with God—simply being with him and aware of his presence—is intended to be our experience. Intimacy with God is available to us, an intimacy that some writers have called "prayer of the heart."

## THE NATURE OF HEART PRAYER

The best way to sense the nature of this kind of prayer is to listen to God's saints who have tuned their hearts to being with the Lord. Here are two beautiful examples from the Psalms.

> O God, you are my God,
>     earnestly I seek you;
> my soul thirsts for you,
>     my body longs for you,
> in a dry and weary land
>     where there is no water.
>
> I have seen you in the sanctuary
>     and beheld your power and your glory.
> Because your love is better than life,
>     my lips will glorify you.
> I will praise you as long as I live,
>     and in your name I will lift up my hands.

My soul will be satisfied as with the richest of
   foods;
   with singing lips my mouth will praise you.

On my bed I remember you;
   I think of you through the watches of the night.
Because you are my help,
   I sing in the shadow of your wings.
My soul clings to you;
   your right hand upholds me.

                                        (Ps. 63:1–8)

How lovely is your dwelling place,
   O Lord Almighty!
My soul yearns, even faints
   for the courts of the Lord;
my heart and my flesh cry out
   for the living God.

Even the sparrow has found a home,
   and the swallow a nest for herself,
   where she may have her young—
a place near your altar,
   O Lord Almighty, my King and my God.
Blessed are those who dwell in your house;
   they are ever praising you.                *Selah*

Blessed are those whose strength is in you,
   who have set their hearts on pilgrimage.
As they pass through the Valley of Baca,
   they make it a place of springs;
   the autumn rains also cover it with pools.
They go from strength to strength
   till each appears before God in Zion.

Hear my prayer, O Lord God Almighty;
   listen to me, O God of Jacob.            *Selah*
Look upon our shield, O God;
   look with favor on your anointed one.

Better is one day in your courts
   than a thousand elsewhere;
I would rather be a doorkeeper in the house of my
   God
   than dwell in the tents of the wicked.
For the Lord God is a sun and shield;
   the Lord bestows favor and honor;
no good thing does he withhold

from those whose walk is blameless.

> O LORD Almighty,
>   blessed is the man who trusts in you.
>                    (Ps. 84:1–12)

We discover the nature of intimacy and the pattern for prayer of the heart not in Hebrew or Greek words but in the shared experience of God's saints. These psalms and other models in Scripture teach us characteristics of such prayer.

*Prayer of the heart implies personal relationship.* The person who is drawn to God knows him in a personal way. Only a person who can cry "O God, you are *my* God" (Ps. 63:1) will eagerly approach God.

The writer of Hebrews focuses on Jesus' priesthood as the source of confidence in our relationship with God. Jesus' sacrifice provides assured access (7:25–27). With Jesus as our high priest, we "approach the throne of grace with confidence" (4:15–16). Assurance of salvation precedes prayer of the heart. The altar of sacrifice assures us that the "LORD Almighty" is at the same time "my King and my God" (Ps. 84:3).

*Prayer of the heart is impelled by a desire to be with God.* There are many valid motives for prayer. When we have needs, we are invited to bring them to God. When we are overwhelmed with despair or fear or are in the grip of jealousy, we are invited to share our emotions with God. But prayer of the heart has a different motivation: a simple desire to be with God.

This element is powerfully expressed in each of the two psalms we have just looked at. In Psalm 63, David says,

> Earnestly I seek you;
> my soul thirsts for you,
>   my body longs for you,
> in a dry and weary land
>   where there is no water.
>                    (Ps. 63:1)

And one of the sons of Korah says,

> My soul yearns, even faints
>   for the courts of the LORD;
> my heart and my flesh cry out
>   for the living God.
>                    (Ps. 84:2)

There are many valid reasons for us to come to God in prayer. But to experience the intimacy with God for which we were created, we need to come simply to be with him, simply because our hearts yearn for his touch.

*Prayer of the heart involves meditation.* Each of these psalms helps us sense the importance of meditation. David recalls his personal experience with God in the sanctuary (Ps. 63:2). At night he remembers all that God has done for him.

> On my bed I remember you;
>> I think of you through the watches of the night.
> Because you are my help,
>> I sing in the shadow of your wings.
> I stay close to you;
>> your right hand upholds me.
>
> (Ps. 63:6–8)

In glancing at these psalms, we see clearly that meditation is a rich and complex experience. Each psalm portrays remembrance of personal experiences with God. Each has images that provide depth and texture to one's vision of God. Like a fledgling, the psalmist sings in the shelter of God's wings (Ps. 63:7). God is pictured as a shield, protecting his worshiper; as a sun, warming and maintaining life (84:11).

Besides images there are also symbols of God's power and glory. The ark of the covenant, for example, contained the tablets of the law and a jar filled with manna. What visions of the thundering mount and of God's daily provision the sanctuary must have stimulated (Ps. 63:2)!

*Prayer of the heart incorporates praise.* Being with God is a quiet—and quieting—experience. There is a deep satisfaction here. David says, "My soul will be satisfied as with the richest of foods" (Ps. 63:5). That satisfaction comes as we respond in praise to the God we have paused to be with. Because prayer of the heart brings us close to God, we sense again the wonder of his love and can say,

> My lips will glorify you.
> I will praise you as long as I live,
>> and in your name I will lift up my hands.
> My soul will be satisfied as with the richest of
>> foods;
>> with singing lips my mouth will praise you.
>
> (Ps. 3–5)

Although no specific Hebrew word designates this prayer of the heart (unless perhaps the word for "praise"), Scripture nevertheless testifies to the importance of times when we seek only to be with God. The Old Testament may not define exactly how we experience prayer of the heart. But it does help us realize that, despite the Fall, those who trust God can have an intimate, private time with the Lord such as Adam enjoyed. And the Old Testament suggests disciplines that believers can follow in seeking the Lord.

## JESUS' LIFE AND TEACHING

Most of the prayers of Jesus that are recorded in the Gospels are public prayers. Yet we know that Jesus often slipped away to be alone with the Father. At such moments Jesus, in his human life, met his own deep need for private, intimate times with God.

After one busy day, Jesus "went up on a mountainside by himself to pray" (Matt. 14:23). Another time, "very early in the morning, while it was still dark, Jesus got up, left the house and went off to a solitary place, where he prayed" (Mark 1:35). Luke says that, as more and more crowds surrounded him, "Jesus often withdrew to lonely places and prayed" (Luke 5:16). He also reports that, as Jesus' enemies began to plot against him, Jesus "went out on a mountainside to pray, and spent the night praying to God" (Luke 6:12). Luke tells us that Jesus went up to the Mount of Transfiguration "to pray" and that, "as he was praying, the appearance of his face changed, and his clothes became as bright as a flash of lightning" (9:28–29). Finally, Luke is the one who tells us that, after Jesus "was praying in a certain place," the disciples asked the Lord to teach them to pray, "just as John taught his disciples" (11:1).

In each of these references the biblical writers chose *proseuchomai,* the general word for prayer which in the New Testament suggests warm and intimate conversation. Strikingly, the same term is used by each writer in describing the scene in Gethsemane (Matt. 26, Mark 14, Luke 22). But it is not found in Jesus' High Priestly Prayer of John 17. There Jesus is described simply as looking up to heaven and "saying." In his prayer Jesus uses *erōtaō,* meaning "request" or "intercede for."

Two conclusions can be validly drawn from what the Gospels tell us of Jesus' prayer life. First, even though Jesus lived in perfect union with the Father in all he said and did, he still needed time for prayer of the heart. Quiet hours of simply being with God were so vital that, when the pressures of his ministry demanded every daytime moment, Jesus often spent the nighttime hours with God. If Jesus needed time to be alone with God, how much more do we need it?

Second, while we do not know just how Jesus approached God in private prayer, there are clues. In fact, it is most instructive when the prayer taught to the disciples is compared with Jesus' prayer of the heart in Gethsemane (recorded in three Gospels). The parallels are outlined in table 5.

**Table 5. Jesus' Prayers and the Prayer of the Heart**

| The Lord's Prayer (Matt. 6:9–13) | Jesus' Prayer in Gethsemane (Matt. 26:39–41) | The Prayer of the Heart |
|---|---|---|
| "Our Father in Heaven | "My Father. . ." | Rest in personal relationship |
| "Hallowed be your name" | [Demonstrated in Jesus' submission to the Father] | Acknowledge God, honoring him as God |
| "Your kingdom come, your will be done on earth, as it is in heaven." | "Not as I will but as you will." | Submit to him, surrendering your self and your will |
| "Give us today our daily bread." | | Acknowledge dependence on God, expressing trust in him |
| "Forgive us our debts as we also have forgiven our debtors." | | Accept God's forgiveness and freely extend it to others |
| "And lead us not into temptation, but deliver us from the evil one." | The three should pray so that they will not fall into temptation | Submit to God's leading, relying always on his protection. |

As seen in these examples, the practice of intimate prayer calls for us to approach God, acknowledging who he is and the nature of our relationship with him. We submit our wills to be fulfilled in his will. We surrender our bodies to him, trusting him totally for daily needs. We surrender our pride, taking our place as creatures who are in constant need of forgiveness and who live with others just as needy. Ultimately we surrender our futures to God, committing ourselves to follow his leading, realizing that any act that does not flow from his will will sweep us into the realm of the Evil One.

## GROWTH IN EXPERIENCING INTIMACY

The teaching of Jesus focuses on our attitude as we approach God to be with him, while the Old Testament illumines what happens in his presence. As we approach God and affirm him as Father, we quiet ourselves before him. We empty ourselves of self-will, worry, and pride, and in so doing we focus completely on the moment we are about to spend in his presence. In that moment we meditate on who God is in his essential person and in his relationship with us. We may use images and symbols, but our goal is to see the Lord. As we discover him afresh, we respond with praise.

This experience is prayer of the heart—Eden in the cool of our evening, communing with God for his sake and for ours. We come to the Lord, not because we want something from him or even because we have something we need to share with him, but simply because we want to be with him and with him alone. Scripture and the experience of God's saints provide suggestions for cultivating prayer of the heart.

*Establish prayer of the heart as a priority.* All agree that prayer of the heart is no casual endeavor. The cares of life rush in to occupy all of our time. Yet if we are to know intimacy with God and find the strength Jesus found for a human life lived in union with God, we must set aside time to *be with* God.

Many suggest periods of time ranging from twenty to forty-five minutes, although ten minutes may at first seem more than enough. All suggest finding a place where we can be quiet, without interruption. There, in our privacy, we must make a focused effort to open our awareness to the reality of God—not to ask for anything or even to share our feelings but just to be with him.

*Develop an effective pattern.* Most suggest beginning with a time of quieting, or self-emptying. The technique of breathing deeply and focusing on that breathing has been an approach taken by Christian mystics as well as others. This method can become more meaningful if it is accompanied by a patterned meditation, such as the following one on the Lord's Prayer.

| Breathing deeply in | Breathing deeply out |
|---|---|
| Father, your will be done. | I surrender my will to you. |
| Father, give this day's bread. | I surrender my anxieties to you. |
| Father, forgive my sins. | I surrender my pride to you. |
| Father, lead me not into temptation. | I surrender my future to you. |

As this meditation is repeated, breathing deeply and slowly, the one praying consciously surrenders to God and, in trust releases personal tensions, fears, and needs in order to be able to concentrate on him. As tensions and needs are released to God, the individual consciously focuses on God in meditation. This activity may take a variety of forms, but one might meditate on God and one's relationship with him as viewed in a psalm, especially a passage that can be easily memorized and has a number of suggestive words, such as the verses below. A person could meditate on these verses for a week, each day concentrating on just one of the italicized words or phrases.

> How great is your *goodness,*
>     which you have stored up for those who *fear* you,
> Which you bestow in the sight of men
>     on those who take *refuge* in you.
> In the *shelter* of *your presence* you hide them
>     from the intrigues of men;
> *in your dwelling* you keep them *safe*
>     from the strife of tongues.
>                         (Ps. 31:19–20).

As one's thoughts of God are shaped and guided by the word about him, one's heart will begin to fill with praise that can be expressed by telling the Lord how great and wonderful he is and how much he is appreciated for himself. This pattern seems to be common in prayer of the heart: first quieting and self-emptying, then meditation, and then spontaneous praise.

It is important not to mistake prayer of the heart, which is intent simply on being with God, for what many have called "quiet time." In general, Protestant quiet time has been viewed as a time for studying the Bible, making requests, expressing needs and problems, etc. Such a time is surely valuable. But it is not the same as prayer of the heart, in which the focus is on intimacy—on simply being with God, sensing his presence, and responding to him with praise.

*Use Scripture as a guide.* The Bible is more than a revelation *from* God. It is a revelation *of* God. We meet God there—in the simple statements, images, and symbols. In a real sense, Scripture is this age's Eden. Scripture is the garden of delight, the field and forest where the Lord meets us in the cool of our evenings.

The many biblical images help us sense who he is and help us warm to his presence: shepherd, gardener, father, husband, mother hen, fortress, eagle's wings, vine. And many symbols speak of what he has done for us: shewbread, altar, sacrifice, bread, door, veil, high priest, prophet, king.

These images and literally hundreds of others are food for our times of being with God, for they nourish prayer of the heart and our awareness of who God is. How important it is that we use God's Word not simply as a source of doctrine but as a love letter that reveals our beloved and draws us deeper and deeper into his presence.

*Practice the presence of God.* We grow in our capacity for prayer of the heart as we grow in all areas of life. At first the disciplines that help us consciously be with God may seem artificial and strange. But as they become more and more a part of our relationship with him, they begin to seem increasingly natural. Then we begin to find ourselves surprised by sudden awareness of his touch—when we're driving on the highway, relaxing for a moment after a day's work, waiting for that next appointment, preparing supper, drying the day's dishes, or lying in bed awaiting sleep.

We can be with God at any and every moment of our day. But typically, such awareness of his presence is an outgrowth of a more disciplined setting of intimacy as a priority in our lives. We cannot doubt that Jesus uniquely lived in the awareness of God's constant presence. Yet Jesus, while living on earth, sensed a need for special, intimate times alone with God that often extended through the night. If we are to live in union with God, we too need to cultivate prayer of the heart.

**PROBE**

**exercises for personal development**
**case histories**
**thought provokers**

1. John Westerhoff III suggests that we take the following questions implicit in the Lord's Prayer as a guide to prayer, posing these questions to God and waiting quietly, listening as well as meditating and offering praise. What do you think of this approach to personal prayer? Does it illustrate prayer of the heart?

   | | |
   |---|---|
   | Our Father in Heaven. | What do you want to make possible for me this day that neither I nor any other human can make possible? |
   | Hallowed be your name. | What do you want to make holy in my life this day? |
   | Your kingdom come. | How can your kingdom come through me this day? |
   | Your will be done on earth as it is in heaven. | What are my Gethsemanes about which I need to say, "Your will be done"? |
   | Give us this day our daily bread. | What nourishment or help do I need most this day? |
   | Forgive us our sins as we forgive those who sin against us. | For what do I need most to be forgiven, and who do I need most to forgive? |
   | Save us from the time of trial, and deliver us from evil. | From what do I need most to be protected this day? |

2. What time and what place might you set aside for meeting God each day this coming month? Commit yourself for at least thirty days simply to be with God, practicing the discipline suggested above in the section "develop an effective pattern." Or use another pattern with which you feel more comfortable.

   At the end of thirty days, explore your experience in writing. How did God touch your life and your awareness of him? What about him has stayed with you? Have you seen any impact of time with God on what the author calls "living your human life in union with God?"

   Talk over your experience with someone else who undertook the same discipline, or see if you can find someone who has practiced prayer of the heart for years. What can they tell you about this private prayer avenue to intimacy?

3. Select any block of ten psalms. Read through them carefully, and write down the images and/or symbols the psalmists use. Then in meditation consider each image and symbol you have recorded. What does each suggest to you about God? Which images seem to draw you to him? Which ones add richness to your vision of the Lord? Which images are most linked in your own heart with praise?

4. Check with your local Catholic or Episcopal diocese office. See whether any prayer retreats are planned and whether you can participate. If you can, take part in such a retreat, first, for your own personal benefit and, second, to see if anything you learn might be applied to training members of your local congregation in prayer of the heart.

   Go with an open mind. After such a retreat write out a careful report, discussing processes used, your personal reactions and values, and suggestions for strengthening what you view as weaknesses.

   If possible, visit with the retreat leader to share your reactions and to ask about reasons for any practices you did not understand.

5. It is suggestive that, when Luke reports a disciple's request that Jesus to teach them to pray, the disciple adds, "as John taught his disciples" (11:1). Apparently, discipling in Jesus' time involved teaching others how to pray. If you were to attempt to teach members of a local congregation today how to pray, how might you go about it? What would be the most appropriate setting: a small group? a Sunday congregational meeting? an adult Sunday school class? a retreat? How would you go about it in each setting?

6. Do you agree or disagree: Christian spirituality absolutely requires the believer to practice prayer of the heart.

   What are implications of your agreement or disagreement for your own life? For Christian congregations?

# 9

# CORPORATE
# WORSHIP

"You Evangelicals don't know anything about worship. You meet in churches with all the aesthetic appeal of a barn. You ignore God and sing not about him but about how 'happy, happy, happy' you feel. Instead of quieting your hearts before the Lord when you come to the sanctuary, your pastors tell you, 'Say a friendly hello to at least three people around you.' And your song leaders are always telling you to sing louder, as if you were in a contest with the church next door. No, you Evangelicals just have a 'church service.' It's like having a party, talking and laughing and making speeches about each other and completely ignoring the one who is supposed to be the guest of honor."

Well, Evangelicals do tend to be weak on worship. For years I have heard remarks such as, "I didn't get anything out of the service today" and "What I like is that people are so friendly" or "Why do we have to sing all four verses of the hymns?" I suppose that it is hard for us to realize that worship, like prayer of the heart, is simply *being with God*.

Our gatherings as the people of God include much that is exciting: a sense of shared faith, a hearing of God's Word, and community prayer and praise. Yet our gatherings should include worship as a major emphasis—a worship which, like prayer of the heart, seeks to draw God's people close to the Lord to enjoy, to affirm, and to praise him. Like prayer of the heart, intimacy with God in shared worship is important to our spiritual growth and walk.

## WORSHIP IN SCRIPTURE

The words translated "worship" in our versions have a common meaning of bowing down, or prostrating oneself, out of respect.[1] In essence they focus on the attitude of believers as they approach the Lord. In any consideration of worship, however, we should focus our attention on praise. A number of different Hebrew words express the praise aspect of worship. They share the following elements: (1) praise is addressed to God or to his "name"; (2) praise is associated with the joy of the believing community in God's person; and (3) praise exalts the Lord, acknowledging and affirming and expressing appreciation for who he is.

The Old Testament firmly establishes the basic nature of praise. Greek terms in the New Testament reflect the Old Testament meaning and add nothing that is new or different. Greek terms do seem to emphasize, however, one or more of the three common elements. Various words imply commending God, publicly confessing allegiance to him, and giving glory to him in prayer or song. Both testaments show us that praise is infused with a sense of wonder and delight. We who see God as he has revealed himself revel in him. Our heart responds in worship and praise, motivated by love and wonder, affirming God for all he is.

The praise terms in Scripture help us sense the exalted and joyous nature of worship. But they do not in themselves teach us how to worship corporately. In the patterns of worship that we find in Scripture, we have clues to enriching corporate worship today.

*Festival and remembrance.* Worship wells up as a response to God's self-revelation. God is the great initiator; our role is to respond to him. The structure of Israel's events of community worship reflects this reality. Three central festivals were established by Old Testament law. For each of them, all the people were to gather, first at the tabernacle and later at the Jerusalem temple.

Passover was the most important of these festivals and the first one established. Held in the month of Nisan (April), the festival commemorated Israel's deliverance from Egypt and,

---

[1] In the Old Testament and in the Gospels, words that are rendered "serve" are generally linked to cultic aspects of worship, though in the later Epistles *latreuō* ("serve") implies a worshipful attitude, expressed in serving the Lord in one's heart and by one's life.

specifically, the sparing of Israel's children when death struck the firstborn throughout that land.

Pentecost was the second annual festival. It was held seven weeks after Passover, on the sixth day of Sivan (June). Pentecost was a harvest festival and also the anniversary of giving the law at Mount Sinai.

The Feast of Tabernacles, or Booths, was the third annual festival. It was held from the fifteenth to the twenty-first day of Tishri (October). Beginning just five days after the Day of Atonement, this celebration marked the end of harvest and represented the years of wilderness travel as Israel waited to enter the Promised Land. During this week of joyous celebration, the people lived outdoors in temporary booths. They shared the meat of the many sacrifices and spent the evenings in song, dancing, and praise.

Each of these festivals focused on remembrance. Not only did the festivals give structure to Israel's religious year, but they also focused the attention of the worshiping people on God's acts in history. This aspect of the festivals is rooted in the important Old Testament concept of *zikkârôn,* meaning "reminder" or "remembrance." It identifies certain events (such as the Passover [Exod. 12:14]) and certain objects (such as the stones Joshua ordered piled beside the Jordan where Israel crossed [Josh. 4:7]) as *memorials.* As such, a *zikkârôn* was more than a monument to the past. It was an aid to the living, a call to identify with the events of sacred history and, by identifying, actually to participate in God's work for his people.

Through the *zikkârôn* festival of Passover, each new generation relived the night that God made his distinction between Israel and Egypt. In that remembrance, the community experienced God's salvation afresh. Through the *zikkârôn* monument by the Jordan, children touched a pile of stones and, in their imaginations, walked through the river that God dried up—for them. The worship ordained in the Old Testament often has this dimension of God's worshiping people coming together to affirm their participation in God's historic acts and, by their praise, to respond to history's revelation of their God.

*Psalms and celebration.* The nature of Israel's worship can be established by identifying the festivals with the Hebrew concept of *zikkârôn.* And the content of that worship can be seen in the Psalms. The Psalms also show pattern and progression, which can guide the structure of our worship services as well as guide us in private prayer.

Most, if not all, of the psalms were intended for use in public worship. Liturgical use is indicated by musical instructions (e.g., "for the director of music") and by other introductory notes. For instance, the "Psalms of Ascent" (Pss. 120–134) are usually viewed as psalms sung by pilgrims on their way to participate in one of the three required festivals. The "Hallel Psalms" (Pss. 113–118) are associated with the Passover, and Psalm 92 is specifically designated "for the Sabbath day."

In exploring the psalms as liturgy, we are struck immediately by the range of topics specifically designated for worship. They are not all praise but instead span a wide range of subjects and of human experiences. The liturgy of Israel drew God's people to himself and involved sharing all that they were as human beings, as well as praising God for all that he was as God. Psalms specifically designated for worship include each type of psalm: prayer (Pss. 5; 9), praise (Pss. 8; 19), messianic (Ps. 22), commitment (Ps. 31), confession of sin (Ps. 51), instruction (Ps. 77), and even imprecatory (Ps. 109).

Essentially, the liturgy we see in the Psalms teaches us to link all the events and meanings of our lives to God. We bring ourselves totally to him. We focus on who God is, and, in centering on God, we find our own experiences brought into perspective. This transformational aspect of worship is reflected in many psalms which trace the worshiper's transition from fear or anguish to peace and understanding.

Within the Psalms, then, we have a handbook for personal prayer and for corporate worship. The Psalms are a worship liturgy for the Old Testament people of God. By studying them, we can learn more about coming together and worshiping God in a rich and transforming way.

*Synagogue and congregation.* The temple was destroyed in 586 B.C. by the Babylonians. Although it was rebuilt in 520 B.C., the focus of the religious life of God's people had meanwhile shifted subtly. During the Captivity, the synagogue, as a place of Sabbath gathering, was invented. In this institution the Israelites gave their attention to Scripture and to prayer. While the rebuilt temple and the reestablished festivals were not ignored, weekly gatherings in local communities assumed increasing importance.

Among the Jewish people the act of gathering for study took on the character of worship, of being with God. Darby's translation of the *Mishnah* states, "If ten men sit together and occupy themselves in the Law, the Divine presence rests among them, for it is written, *God standeth in the Congregation of God.*"[2] The gathering of the community to occupy itself with God and his Word (which are inseparable) is central in this approach to worship.

For both the synagogue and early church settings, we have a fairly complete picture of the procedures followed. Synagogue worship began with an affirmation of faith, drawn from Deuteronomy 6:4–9; 11:13–21; and 28:1–11. Then three sets of prayers were repeated, with two of the three sets honoring and thanking God. Prayers were followed by a reading of the Law and then a sermon (see Luke 4:16–30). The sermon explained what had been read and applied it to the life of God's people. During Jesus' life on earth he participated in both synagogue worship and festival worship.

The New Testament letters demonstrate that the worship of the early church was greatly influenced by the synagogue pattern. While the first Jewish Christians also praised God in the temple, home gatherings of smaller groups became the norm as Christianity spread in and beyond the Holy Land. First Corinthians 12 and 14 list gifts intended to be exercised "for the common good." Chapter 14 identifies several elements of the worship service: revelation, knowledge, prophecy, a word of instruction (v. 6); prayer, singing, giving of thanks (vv. 13–17); and "a hymn, or a word of instruction, a revelation, a tongue or an interpretation" (v. 26). Further insights are provided in Colossians 3:16 and Hebrews 10:24–25. In addition, some Scripture passages may reflect a liturgy developed by the early Christians (Luke 1:46–55, 68–79; 2:14, 29–32; John 1:1–18; Eph. 2:20–21; Phil. 2:6–11; Col. 1:1–15; 2 Tim. 2:11–13; Rev. 4:8, 11; 7:12; 11:17–18; 15:3–4).

Even this brief survey provides insights we can use in thinking more carefully about corporate worship.

● Corporate worship involves the gathering of God's people to focus on him and on his expression about himself in the Word.

---

[2] *The Mishnah* (London: Oxford University Press, 1933), p. 450.

- Corporate worship involves praise, which is our response to God himself.

- Corporate worship may be enriched by consciously identifying with and participating in God's historic acts for his people.

- Corporate worship may be enriched and encouraged by liturgy.

- Corporate worship may be participative, involving the exercise of spiritual gifts as God's people lead each other to a clearer vision of God and to a deeper response to him.

Many approaches to corporate worship can be traced through church history. Yet we should be sensitive to our need as the people of God to come together to meet *him*. Patterns seen in each of the Testaments can provide guidance and help for reaching this objective.

## CORPORATE WORSHIP IN JESUS' LIFE

We know from the Gospels that Jesus, as a Jewish man who lived under the law, kept the festivals and customarily attended Sabbath services at local synagogues (Luke 4:15–16). As a worshiper, Jesus participated fully in the gathering together of God's people to be with God. While Jesus taught his disciples a new approach to personal prayer, he suggested no new patterns for public worship.

Jesus did, however, by his life, death, and resurrection, change the historic focus of worship. Rather than looking back, as did the festivals of Israel, to redemption from Egypt, Christian festivals look back to what God did for all persons in Christ. The Lord's Day, Sunday, marking the resurrection of Jesus, replaces the Sabbath, Saturday, which marked Creation, as the pivot of our week. The Lord's Supper which Jesus instituted is in fact a new *zikkārôn:* God's perpetual invitation to his people to identify with Jesus in his death and to participate personally by faith in all that event means to humankind.

In the same way, the incarnation, death, and resurrection of Jesus restructure our year, as Christmas, Good Friday, and Easter give festival structure to our faith. Finally, evidence in Acts makes it plain that the young Christian community, like the church today, practiced water baptism as a sign of initiation into new life in Christ, as circumcision was a sign of an Israelite's inclusion in Old Testament covenant relationship with God.

As we note the structure given our worship by the new content implicit in our faith, we need to be aware that the practices of corporate worship have remained consistent across the ages. Public worship, like prayer of the heart, is a drawing near to the Lord to be *with him*. Table 6 displays a number of striking parallels discussed in these two chapters on intimacy.

**Table 6. Intimacy with God**

| Element | Prayer of the heart | Public worship |
|---|---|---|
| *Distinctive* | Alone | With God's people |
| *Attitude* | Submission | "Bow down" |
| *Involves* | Remembering God's acts, Scripture | Remembrance (*zikkarôn*), Scripture |
| *Aids* | Images, symbols | Liturgy, festival |
| *Issues in* | Praise | Praise |

## GROWTH IN WORSHIP

The comment at the beginning of this chapter reflects a common criticism of evangelical Protestant worship. In many ways our corporate worship is sterile, lacking many features that are intended to bring a worshiping community into the very presence of God. In a significant sense most of us can do little to effect change in the pattern of worship in our local congregation. And change is all too often counterproductive: it disturbs so many in the congregation that it distracts from worship rather than promotes it.

Yet each of us can fasten on those elements in our church services which do aid worship. Each of us can come, personally and gladly, into the presence of God with the brothers and sisters who have come with us to honor our Lord. In worship, as in everything in the life of faith, the heart is more important than the form.

*Come to church to be with God.* Learn to think of Sunday morning not as a time for a "church service" but rather as an "event of meeting." We can come to church to meet God, not just friends. We can come to honor God, sure that, when even two or three assemble in Jesus' name, he is there (Matt. 18:20). Even if others around us seem to ignore his presence, we can concentrate on his being there—the focus and the goal of our assembly.

*Prepare the heart.* Visualize the meeting place as a sanctuary. When we enter, we can pause to pray. We can select one word from a verse or from the sermon topic to meditate on while waiting for the service to begin. We can relax, with head bowed, grateful to be there with Jesus.

*Participate.* Even in congregations where no opportunity is given for members to contribute spontaneously, we Christians can participate in the worship service. As we listen to Scripture we can mentally place ourselves in the situation described in a gospel or can imagine ourselves as an early hearer of an epistle's teaching. As we share in the Communion service, we can by faith see ourselves with Jesus in his death and with him in his resurrection. Listening intently and actively is one way that we can participate in any worship service.

*Respond to God.* We can respond to God in any service as well. When a hymn speaks of God in the third person, we can shift the pronoun to you and address him personally. We can let our hearts be carried along as we pray with the persons leading congregational prayer, making praise they offer our own. And we can focus carefully on the Word as it is preached, asking the Lord to help us sense what he has to say to us and letting the Holy Spirit open our understanding and guide us to the obedient response God wants us to make.

To live life in union with God demands moments of intimacy with him. We can find that intimacy in prayer of the heart and in worshiping him with a people who are his own.

**PROBE**

**exercises for personal development**
**case histories**
**thought provokers**

1. Visit services of at least three churches, or two churches and a synagogue. Go not to observe but to meet the Lord. Afterward, think about each experience. Did the services incorporate principles suggested in this chapter? How? What seemed to enhance worship for you? If you were to plan an "ideal" church worship service, what would you include?

2.  Read more deeply in the literature on worship. A good book to begin
    with is Robert E. Webber's *Worship, Old and New* (Grand Rapids:
    Zondervan, 1982). Webber's thorough bibliography will guide you to
    resources that touch on every aspect of historic and contemporary
    worship.

    Write a report on Webber's thesis (or that of another book on
    worship), including your own evaluation of that thesis.

3.  Study psalms that are identified by their superscriptions as intended
    for public worship. Write a ten-page paper, explaining what these
    psalms teach us about corporate worship and how their teaching
    might be incorporated into contemporary church services.

4.  Assume that you are chairman of your church's worship committee.
    Which of the following topics would you want to bring up for
    discussion? Which should be given priority? Write a one-page
    position paper on each issue you select as important, as a discussion
    starter for your committee.

    *Communion.* Jesus instituted the Lord's Supper by saying, "Do this in
    remembrance of me" (1 Cor. 11:24), thus casting Communion in the
    tradition of the *zikkārôn.* How can we help our members understand
    this concept and, through this service, actually participate in Christ's
    death?

    *Liturgy.* The Psalms and sections of the New Testament make it clear
    that liturgy has historically played a significant part in public worship.
    What role should liturgy have in our services? What does liturgy
    involve? How is liturgy intended to facilitate our public worship?

    *Congregational participation.* The New Testament pictures the gath-
    ered church worshiping God more spontaneously and freely than
    most of our congregations do. How can we make room for the
    exercise of the spiritual gifts of our people? What is the balance
    between participation and structure? How does participation relate to
    liturgy?

    *Worship as praise.* How do we maintain the focus of our worship on
    God himself? Is the music we use appropriately focused on God, or
    does it deal more with our human experience? Is prayer in congrega-
    tional settings more request or more praise? More a valid expression
    of needs, or more like prayer of the heart?

    *Structure.* What is the climax of our Sunday gathering? How should
    music, preaching, Scripture, liturgy, prayers of praise, etc. fit
    together if the focus of our gathering is truly on God himself and if
    our worship service is a shared "event of worship"?

6.  As you go to your church, begin to focus personally on that
    experience as a meeting with God. Plan ahead what you can do to
    focus on him and on meeting with him.

    Put your plan into practice, not just for a week or two, but for at least
    a year. After that year has passed, evaluate. What has happened in
    your own attitude toward Sunday services? Toward God?

# Section C: Sinfulness

The warning had been clear: Do not eat fruit from the tree of the knowledge of good and evil. But Adam and Eve did. From that moment death established its grip on the human race, and sin took root in human nature.

Early Genesis shows us many faces of death. There is biological death, slowly draining the vitality from an aging Adam and Eve and brutally ending Abel's youth. There is cosmic death, as nature itself is twisted into perverse shape and humanity is forced to wrest a living from the now-resisting ground. There is social death, as, eager to shift the blame, Adam points to God and then to Eve, saying, "The woman you put here with me—she gave me some fruit" (Gen. 3:12). Finally, there is spiritual death. The man, who had communed so naturally and gladly with his Creator, was suddenly afraid. He and Eve vainly struggled to cover their nakedness, ran from God as he approached, and cringed when they heard his voice.

We can never truly understand the full impact of the death Adam's action introduced into the world. We can never see the full reality of the sin that warps our personalities, distorts our relationship with others, and destroys our relationship with God. But we do know that, as we live our human life, we confront sin again and again—in ourselves and in others. While Christ opens up to us the possibility of living a holy life (see chapters 16 and 17), sin will tragically and repeatedly intrude.

To live a human life is to become aware constantly of shortcomings and rebellion. To live a human life in union with God means learning to deal with sin whenever it appears and to deal with it in God's way, responding to our own sins with confession and to the sins of others with a willing forgiveness which is modeled on Christ's own forgiveness.

# 10

## CONFESSION

An incident described in Luke 5 illustrates our problem. The fishermen had labored all night, letting down and pulling in their heavy nets. All for nothing. Now, in the early morning, they were hard at work on the shore, washing the nets and stretching them out to dry. Jesus was there, followed by the usual crowds. Then Jesus got into Simon Peter's boat and asked the muscular fishermen to push the boat out in the water. Jesus sat down and taught the crowds from the boat.

When Jesus finished teaching, he said to Simon, "Put out into deep water, and let down the nets for a catch" (v. 4).

Peter objected. "Master, we've worked hard all night and haven't caught anything. But because you say so, I will let down the nets" (v. 5).

The Greek word rendered "master" means "chief" or "commander." It implies a right to give orders. Out of respect for Jesus as a rabbi, an authority figure, Peter did as he said. The result was that the nets were suddenly filled with so many fish that two boats nearly sank under their weight.

Peter's reaction may seem surprising. Rather than show excitement or gratitude, Peter fell on his knees and said, "Go away from me, Lord; I am a sinful man!" (v. 8).

### SIN AND HUMAN EXPERIENCE

Peter's reaction was intuitive. The nets full of fish convinced him that Jesus was more than a rabbi whose learning he respected. Peter intuitively realized that he was in the presence of the Lord, and suddenly, like Adam, he was overwhelmed with a sense of his own sinfulness. That sense was so painful that Peter, again like Adam, desperately wanted relief from what he must have felt was the condemning presence of his God. Awareness of sin intensifies our feelings of alienation from God, which cause us to run from God, even as a sudden light sets cockroaches scurrying to seek the shelter of darkness (see John 3:20).

*Scripture's dark vision.* The Bible is blunt in its portrait of humankind as sinful. Scripture describes the devastating impact of Adam's sin on human nature and in careful detail explains how sin is expressed in our experience. The impact of sin on humanity is most graphically portrayed in Ephesians 2:1–3, which describes the human condition as one of living death.

> As for you, you were dead in your transgressions and sins, in which you used to live when you followed the ways of this world and of the ruler of the kingdom of the air, the spirit who is now at work in those who are disobedient. All of us also lived among them at one time, gratifying the cravings of our sinful nature and following its desires and thoughts. Like the rest, we were by nature objects of wrath.

The intuitive realization that, as sinners, we are rightly objects of God's wrath is the immediate cause of flight from God. When we sense that God is near, then, like Peter, we sense our moral misshapenness, realize our shortcomings, and remember our many acts of willful rebellion. The sudden vision of our God can fill us, as it did Peter, with fear and impel us to run and try to hide. This impulse is perhaps our first reaction when we discover some specific sin in our lives.

The Old Testament, like the New, uses many words to describe sin, including *guilt, fault, injustice, offense, transgression, unrighteousness, wickedness,* and many others. Three Hebrew words, however, sum up the major emphasis in the Old Testament: *ḥāṭā'* and its cognates are used some 580 times and suggest a falling short of the standard that God sets for human beings; *pešaʿ* describes rebellion, a willful revolt; and *ʿāwōn* indicates a twisting or deviation from an accepted standard. Each of these words implies the existence of a standard against which acts can be measured. For those with access to revelation, that standard is God's law. Yet even people without such access have standards. "They show that the requirements of the law are written on their hearts, their consciences also bearing witness" (Rom. 2:15). Every human being acknowledges some standard of right and wrong and also, in experience, repeatedly violates that same standard. We each fall short, rebel, or deviate from what we believe to be right.

The New Testament tends to sum up sin in two broad categories. One is expressed by *adikia* ("wrongdoing") and its cognates. Words in this group are translated in various ways, but all view such sin as willful human acts that harm others and violate the divine standard. The other category is expressed by *hamartia* and its cognates. Words in this group incorporate the full range of meanings of the three key Hebrew terms. In the New Testament, "sin" (almost always used to translate the *hamartia* word group) indicates our native moral misshapenness, our shortcomings, and our acts of conscious, willful rebellion.

In all these forms, sin rises up to find expression in our thoughts and actions. And the specter of our guilt makes our first, spontaneous reaction to God one of flight.

*The avoidance of sin.* No individual can live a human life without being aware of personal sin. We each know that we fall short of doing what we believe to be right. We each are aware of acting rebelliously. But this knowledge is painful, and so, through the ages, human beings have tried in various ways to deal with this moral dilemma as well as the need to accept ourselves and have at least some hope of divine favor.

Some try *pretense*. After eating the forbidden fruit, Adam and Eve were suddenly aware that they were naked. The Bible says, "They sewed fig leaves together and made coverings for themselves" (Gen. 3:7). The coverings were intended to support the first pair's denial: "Naked? No! Look, we're covered and perfectly respectable."

Pretense is most closely related to shame. We can pretend, but only if others cannot see us as we are. People who pretend suppose that they can deal with their sins and failures if only others do not look on and thereby force them to face what they want to ignore and to hide. By pretending, we can deny that our sins exist, and by focusing all our energy on work or pleasure or some other activity, we simply refuse to deal with them at all.

But if we are to pretend successfully, we have to suppress thoughts of God. God knows all, and no one can visualize being in God's presence and avoid the self-realization that he or she is a sinful person. No wonder Peter, suddenly aware of who Jesus was, begged, "Go away from me, Lord; I am a sinful man!"

Others handle sin through *denial*. In Romans 1, Paul traces the process of moral decay. Although God has made his existence plain, human beings may refuse to give thanks or glorify him as God. Rejection of the purifying knowledge of God leads directly to shameful and indecent acts. Filled with wickedness and evil and dominated by passions, such individuals know intuitively that what they do is wrong, but "they not only continue to do these very things but also approve of those who practice them" (v. 32).

How easy it seems to call the immoral "adult" and to laugh at purity as old fashioned. In the company of those who deny God, sin can be given new labels and identified, if not as right, at least as normal. Even homosexuality can be passed off as simply an "alternative life style." A denial of God leads inevitably to a denial that sin is sin and to deeper and deeper involvement in sinful acts.

Some try to deal with sin by making *excuses*—especially by shifting the blame. Adam first blamed God, then Eve, for his sin. Romans 2 teaches that, as people violate their standards of right and wrong, their conscience bears witness to that failure. In attempting to avoid facing the fact of sin, sinners think desperately of how to defend themselves against the charge of the guilt they feel (v. 15).

Some modern psychiatry is appealing because it takes this approach. It does not deny the reality of our sins and failures. It simply excuses them, arguing that such acts were caused by circumstances or by the influence of others earlier in one's life. But this defense traps us in a web of unreality. John makes it plain that, "if we claim to be without sin, we deceive ourselves and the truth is not in us" (1 John 1:8). No one attempting to live such a lie will experience fellowship with God (v. 6). We will be lost, wandering in darkness, because we will surely lose touch with God.

Still others try *self-accusation*. The Romans passage on conscience says that, while some try to avoid its pangs by defending themselves, others slip into self-accusation and self-contempt (Rom. 2:15). The Greeks tended to view conscience in a negative light, as relentlessly plaguing its owner with accusations concerning past failures. Under its pressure, individuals might become depressed and anxious, struggling helplessly against inner forces they could not control and against memories of a past they could not change. In the darkness of self-accusation, feelings of worthlessness and shame increase, and people may feel that they deserve to suffer or to die. Many who thus come to hate themselves believe that God must hate them too, and so their image of God is distorted by their own self-contempt. Feeling unworthy, the self-condemning person is most likely to turn away from God rather than approach him.

The ways that persons attempt to deal with sins are summarized in table 7. Living as a human being means that we will become aware of sin in our lives. But living in union with God means that we must learn to deal with our sins in his way. We must reject the futile ways that a lost human attempts to deal with sin and choose instead the path of confession.

**Table 7. Human Ways of Dealing With Sin**

| Response | Characteristics | Results |
|---|---|---|
| Pretense | Tries to hide sins and failures from others and from self. | Uncomfortable in the presence of God, who knows us as we are. |
| Denial | Assumes that sin is "normal," and relabels sinful acts to cloak them in respectability. | Increasing involvement in immorality; denial of the existence or relevance of God. |
| Excusing | Seeks some one or something to blame for own sinful acts and failures. | Leads to loss of fellowship with God; to inability to see or deal with reality. |
| Accusing | Blames self for sins and failures, to the extent of depression, anxiety, denial of personal worth and value. | Sense of guilt may lead to self-punishing behavior; inability to accept God's forgiveness or to believe that relationship with God is possible. |

*Confession.* Both the Old Testament and the New contain clear teaching on how the person who lives in union with God is to deal with his or her sins. Psalm 32 portrays the inner anguish the believer feels as he or she senses personal failure, tries desperately to avoid dealing with it and with God, and then finally surrenders.

> When I kept silent,
> my bones wasted away
> through my groaning all day long.
> For day and night
> your hand was heavy upon me;
> my strength was sapped
> as in the heat of summer.
> Then I acknowledged my sin to you
> and did not cover up my iniquity.
> I said, "I will confess
> my transgressions to the LORD"—
> and you forgave
> the guilt of my sin.
>
> (Ps. 32:3–5)

We do not know just what sin occasioned writing the Thirty-second Psalm. But we do know the background to another psalm on the same theme, a background that shocks us even now. David had committed adultery with the wife of one of his officers, arranged for the man to be killed in battle, and then added the woman, Bathsheba, to his harem.

We can imagine that David's actions must have shocked even him. How much the young David had loved God. How faithful the maturing leader had been in serving his Lord. How deeply an aging David yearned to honor God by building a temple in his honor. And yet, suddenly, David had taken one sinful step after another, rushing on until confronted by the prophet Nathan and, through Nathan, brought face to face again with God—and with himself.

We can sense David's anguish as he sees the reality of his sinfulness in an act that he could never approve. We can sense how painful it was to face the flaw in his own personality. Yet David did face his sin. He looked deep within himself, acknowledged what he found, and then, instead of trying to escape in pretense or denial or in excuses or self-accusation, David *turned to God* and appealed for spiritual cleansing, which only God can give.

Wash away all my iniquity
   and cleanse me from my sin.

For I know my transgressions,
   and my sin is always before me.
Against you, you only, have I sinned
   and done what is evil in your sight,
so that you are proved right when you speak
   and justified when you judge.
Surely I have been a sinner from birth,
   sinful from the time my mother conceived me.
Surely you desire truth in the inner parts;
   you teach me wisdom in the inmost place.

Cleanse me with hyssop, and I will be clean;
   wash me, and I will be whiter than snow.
Let me hear joy and gladness;
   let the bones you have crushed rejoice.
Hide your face from my sins
   and blot out all my iniquity.

Create in me a pure heart, O God,
   and renew a steadfast spirit within me.
                                    (Ps. 51:2–10)

This honest, confrontational approach to sin is taught in the New Testament as well. The rationale is explained in 1 John 1:5–2:2, in the context of which John writes about living in fellowship with God and with other believers (1:1–4). Such fellowship depends on walking in the light, as God is light. In this passage, "light" is not sinlessness, for John says that, if we walk in the light, the blood of Christ keeps on purifying us from every sin (v. 7). If we were sinless, we would not need continuing purification.

In the passage light and dark are contrasted and should be understood as living in and by reality versus living in and by illusion. God is light; he knows and deals with reality, with things as they truly are. To live in union with him, we must walk in the light, dealing honestly with the realities of our life.

John is very clear that a person who claims to be without sin is walking in darkness. In such a case, "we deceive ourselves and the truth is not in us" (1 John 1:8). Our sin—and our sins—must be faced. We cannot pretend, deny, or excuse. Then John tells us that we are to deal with the reality of who God is and not just the reality of who we are. God is forgiving and loves us completely. Fixing our eyes on God, we are to reject Adam's remedy of flight and, against all our instincts, are to come to God rather than cringe away. John says, "If we confess our sins, he is faithful and just and will forgive us our sins and purify us from all unrighteousness" (v. 9).

The word *confess* means simply "acknowledge." In itself it does not suggest sorrow or imply a promise "not to do it again." The Greek word *homologeō,* often translated "confess," indicates simply agreeing with God. In confession we formally acknowledge that he is right in considering something which we have thought or done to be sin. We, like David, come to the Lord, in utter honesty opening up our lives and, without excuse, presenting ourselves to him as we are.

John's promise is that, in so coming to God, we will find both forgiveness and cleansing. God forgives us, removing all our guilt. And God "keeps on purifying" us. In confession God's Spirit is given free access to our inmost being so that he can continue his work of rearranging our motives and desires, of reshaping our perspective and our will.

John makes it very clear that the promise of assured forgiveness does not lead to moral laxity. In fact, learning to deal with our sins realistically by bringing them to God is a hedge against sin. John writes about confession and forgiveness "so that you will not sin" (1 John 2:1). Our unacknowledged sins, which we hide or struggle to excuse, lead us on from one sin to another. When we have experienced forgiveness and as we know the Spirit's continual work within, our path leads away from sins and along righteous ways.

Confession, then, is the way God intends us to deal with our sins as we live in union with him. Because we are human, we *will* sin. But if each failure is brought to God, honestly evaluated, and confessed, we will experience the cleansing power of Christ's atoning blood.

## SIN AND JESUS' LIFE ON EARTH

We know that Jesus himself lived a sinless human life. He thus had no need for confession and cannot model this dimension of spirituality for us. But there is much in Jesus' experience that helps us as we face our own sins. For instance, Jesus was often criticized by the religious leaders because he ate with tax collectors and "sinners." The Gospels suggest that such people felt especially comfortable in Jesus' presence, in contrast to the condemnation they sensed from the Pharisees, who boasted of their own firm commitment to Old Testament law.

From Jesus, whose personal holiness all recognized, even sinners felt only a caring, accepting love. The writer of Hebrews emphasizes this point. He notes that a high priest must be chosen "from among men" so that he will be "able to deal gently with those who are ignorant and going astray, since he himself is subject to weakness" (Heb. 5:1–2). Although Jesus was without sin, he was fully human. He understands the pull of temptation. He knows the frailty of humanity. The same writer says that, because Jesus was tempted "in every way, just as we are," he is "able to sympathize with our weaknesses" (4:15).

Jesus does not condemn us now. He died to win the right to forgive sins, and he stands ready, as our high priest, to guarantee our access to the throne of grace. Because we know God as he has revealed himself in Jesus and because Jesus has died to pay the penalty of our sins, we have no need to hide from him when sins overtake us. Instead we can freely bring our sins to him, certain that he will forgive and that our lives—and we ourselves—will change.

## GROWTH IN DEALING WITH PERSONAL SINS

Living a human life on this earth means that we will at times be shaken by and surprised at our own sins. Living our human life in union with God means that we must learn to confess our sins, freely and fully, to the Lord. It is all too human of us, in John's words, to deceive ourselves. It is all too human to make excuses, blame another, or condemn ourselves rather than turn to God. For spiritual growth, however, we must develop sensitivity to sin and must learn the discipline of confession.

*Be sensitive to sins.* We typically attempt to ignore our sins and failures, or we excuse them or repress them. It is not typical to engage in self-examination, thinking carefully through our daily thoughts and actions in order to identify times when we fell short or acted wickedly. Yet self-examination can be a vital aid to spiritual growth. Hebrews points out that those who are mature have achieved that stature in part by training themselves to distinguish good from evil. Such training involves a "constant use" of Scripture's teaching about righteousness (5:11–14).

Self-examination, then, involves a study of righteousness

as it is revealed in the living and written Word, not so that it can be "believed" but so that we can use what we learn in distinguishing good from evil. This process may well begin by distinguishing the good from the evil in our own lives.

The goal of such self-examination is to sensitize us to sin. At first we may recognize sin after the fact. But as the process of self-examination is continued, we begin to recognize a thoughtless word, an uncaring act, or a rebellious urge *before* we sin.

One of the most serious of our spiritual failures is to drift through life, reflecting the values, attitudes, and morality of those around us, without scrutinizing everything in the light of God's Word. While self-examination may tend to discourage us at first, as we discover the many ways in which we all stumble (see James 3:2), the path of self-examination and confession will lead us toward righteousness.

*Confess sins, not sin.* The spiritual growth of many believers is stunted by a nagging sense of guilt that seems impossible to discard. All too often we may be aware of our sinfulness without being aware of specific sins. The Bible is bluntly honest about humanity: we are sinful beings, ruined in the Fall. But the Bible is not despondent about this situation. God in Christ has dealt with our sin. He has given us new life in Jesus, vitalizing us who knew only spiritual death. And God promises a progressive transformation that will, in eternity, be a perfected holiness that duplicates Jesus' own. As forgiven people, we can put sin and guilt behind us, released from its awful power by our Savior's blood.

We now have to deal with sins, not sin. We can handle a generalized guilt by affirming what God has done for us in Christ, but we must deal with specific sins and shortcomings by confessing them as they occur. Confession, then, is God's way for us to deal with those sins that we commit, even when we feel the most spiritual. In the act of acknowledging our sins as sins and coming with them to God, we continually live in vital union with God.

*Focus on God's nature.* Scripture repeatedly presents God as forgiving. Flight from God is more than recognition of personal failure: it is a denial of God's loving nature and of his concern for humankind. We can find greater freedom to come to God with our sins and failures by meditating on passages which speak of forgiveness. Among the passages that can clarify our vision are Psalm 32:5–6; 85:2; 86:5; 103:3, 12–14; Jeremiah 31:34; 1 John 1:9; Micah 7:18–19; and Acts 10:43.

We can also read and reread incidents in which Jesus meets persons who are identified as sinners. Only in the case of the religious leaders who would not acknowledge their sins was Christ anything but loving and accepting.

*Confess sins to other Christians.* It is particularly hard for some whose parents were harsh and unforgiving to sense the forgiveness which God extends to them. Such persons may confess sins but not *feel* forgiven. A continuing, nagging sense of guilt robs them of what David calls the "joy of my salvation" and makes them doubt their fellowship with God. Such doubts are particularly detrimental to spiritual growth.

In most Protestant traditions, people hesitate to confess their sins to each other. But this suspicion should be re-examined. James 5:16 certainly suggests that there is a role in Christian experience for confession to others. In my own experience with seminarians, I have found that hearing confession of sins and then affirming forgiveness can be a turning point in a person's life.

To say, "God forgives you, and I forgive you," affirms a spiritual reality and enables an individual to experience forgiveness in a flesh-and-blood way, conveying the reality of God's forgiveness through a brother or a sister in Christ. We *are* members of the body of Christ, and Jesus lives in us, doing his work in others through you and me. Confession of sins to others, and especially in groups, should not be overly encouraged. But in some cases confessing to another Christian can communicate the reality of forgiveness to individuals who could experience that forgiveness in no other way.

**PROBE**

**exercises for personal development**
**case histories**
**thought provokers**

1. The author suggests several typical reactions to sin, summarized in table 7 above. Think about your own way of reacting to sin in your life. What are you most likely to do when you become aware that you have sinned or fallen short? How does that reaction affect your relationship with other people? How does that reaction affect your relationship with God? How does it affect your feelings about yourself? Your motivations? Your next actions?

2. Read the story of the Prodigal Son (Luke 15:11–32). Put yourself in the prodigal's place, identifying situations in which you have departed from your Father's house this day in thought or act. Identify the emotions you felt as you left and as you finally recognized the error of your choice. Then, in your imagination, return with that son to your Father. Rehearse the confession you will make. Finally, envision God's response in the act of the prodigal's father. As you do, sense the joy of God's forgiveness and his acceptance flooding your own soul.

3. Can you set aside a few minutes, perhaps toward the end of each day, when you can engage in self-examination and confession? Ideally we should become aware of our sins and confess them as they occur. But most of us need a special, quiet time to open our hearts to the Holy Spirit, asking him to reveal any unintentional sins so that we can confess them and recognize them in the future.

4. Everyone will find helpful insights in a fine book by S. Bruce Narramore, *No Condemnation: Rethinking Guilt Motivation in Counseling, Preaching, and Parenting* (Grand Rapids: Zondervan, 1984). Narramore shows that condemnation makes a righteous life more difficult to live and considers the way in which experiencing forgiveness opens individuals to growth and change.

5. The tradition of many churches (for instance, Episcopalian and some Lutheran) includes a liturgy of confession in the Sunday morning services. Locate several of these liturgies. What seems to be their focus? What function do you think they perform? Would you like to have (or continue) a liturgy of confession in your own Sunday morning service? Why, or why not?

6. Analyze one of the three key passages on confession mentioned in this chapter (Pss. 32; 51; and 1 John 1). Trace the words used in the original languages and their meaning. Then write a ten-page commentary on the selected passage.

# 11

---

# FORGIVENESS

"So I said, 'Craig, that's the tenth time this month. It's fine to say you're sorry. But after ten times, I just don't believe you. I mean, if you really loved me, you wouldn't keep doing it again and again, would you? I'll forgive you this time. But I'm warning you: Don't let it happen again!'"

Such scenes are not really unusual, nor are moments when the pain from another's sin is almost unbearable. We live in a tangled world, sharing it with others whose inner being is likewise warped by sin. Others, too, fall short, strike out in anger, and act selfishly, thoughtlessly, and hatefully. The impact of sin is felt not only within us but as those around us sin in ways that bring us pain.

Living a human life means living with sin in others. Living a human life in union with God means learning to deal in God's way with expressions of sin in others. Simply put, that way is the way of forgiveness.

## FORGIVENESS IN SCRIPTURE

The concept of forgiveness is carefully developed in the Bible. Several Hebrew words are linked with the Old Testament's teaching on forgiveness and are at times translated as "forgive" in modern English versions. The verb *kāpar* means "make atonement" and refers to the removal of sin or of ritual defilement. The word *nāśā'* means "lift up" or "take away." The Old Testament affirms that God can take away the sin that makes us guilty before him. This removal of sin makes divine forgiveness possible (cf. Ps. 32:1–5). Finally, *sālaḥ* and its derivatives mean "forgive" or "pardon." This word group is used only of God's offer to pardon sinners (see Isa. 55:6–7), and it is linked with atoning sacrifices (cf. Lev. 4:20; 5:10; 6:7).

Three Greek words are translated "forgive" in our versions. *Aphiēmi* reflects the emphasis of *nāśā'* and teaches us that God does not simply overlook our guilt but literally takes away our sins, so that neither guilt nor sins exist. The related noun *aphesis* has the same emphasis, expressing remission of sins of humankind. The other word, *charizomai,* has a different emphasis. It simply means "be gracious," or "give freely." It is used of the canceling of a debt and is the word chosen in the New Testament to describe the forgiveness that God's people are to extend to others. There is no suggestion that this kind of forgiveness can take away sin. It suggests instead a deep sense of compassion, an awareness of the weakness of others, and a willingness to be gracious to them in their frailty.

*God's forgiveness.* God's forgiveness is a unique, transforming grace. It is focused in and through Jesus, won for us at the price of his own blood (Eph. 1:7). This theme is developed in Hebrews. The writer looks back at the Old Testament animal sacrifices and finds them inadequate. They might cover sins temporarily, but they could never really take away sin. The very fact that such sacrifices had to be repeated endlessly was a reminder to the Israelites that they had not been truly cleansed and so must continue to feel the guilt of their sins (Heb. 10:1–3). Yet these sacrifices testified to a final one to come: an ultimate sacrifice which would truly remove all sin and guilt. And now, the writer continues, "the blood of Christ, who through the eternal Spirit offered himself unblemished to God" (9:14), has brought that kind of forgiveness to us.

In Christ we are forgiven for all sin. Forgiven, we can be released from our nagging sense of guilt, from our bondage to sins past, and from our terrible inadequacies. Jesus' one sacrifice of himself was to "cleanse our consciences from acts that lead to death, so that we may serve the living God" (Heb. 9:14). In Jesus, "we have been made holy through the sacrifice of the body of Jesus Christ once for all" (10:10). The divine forgiveness is more than a legal transaction by which the sins charged to our account are marked "paid in full." The divine forgiveness is truly a cleansing and transforming grace. Conscience, like Satan, is the accuser of humankind. It constantly calls us to look backward, reminding us of our sins and failure. All our inadequacies are there, stored rank upon rank. All our shortcomings and acts of rebellion live in our memory, and all of them testify to our failure and guilt. All shout that we have been and are failures and that we must fail again if we try to live a holy life. Our past sins and past failures "lead to death" because they program our present, robbing us of hope and faith, predisposing us to fail again.

Then comes God's Word of forgiveness. As that word takes root in our hearts and we begin to believe, the message of forgiveness begins to "cleanse our consciences" from those past acts which lead to our present death. The cleansing word is summed up in the repeated promise "Their sins and lawless acts I will remember no more" (Heb. 10:17; see also 8:12). Through Christ's sacrifice our sins and lawless acts have been so perfectly removed that they simply are not remembered against us. And as we increasingly realize how complete God's forgiveness is and as we believe God's word, we experience a gradual inner cleansing as well.

The memory of those past sins that once filled our conscience and programed us for continuing failure begins to fade, and released from their crushing weight, we look forward to serve the living God. Experiencing God's forgiveness, then, means to accept the freeing grace of Jesus Christ. It means to believe that past sins are gone and to put each fresh outbreak of sin behind us by immediate confession. Experiencing forgiveness means release from the burden of our past and looking ahead in the confidence that our union with God promises us a new day that is bright, fresh, and holy.

*Reconciliation.* You and I can never take away sins as God does. But we can be gracious to others. We can offer them release from a guilt-forged bondage to us that is similar to release from bondage to conscience.

In 2 Corinthians 3–5, the apostle Paul writes about the transforming work of God's Spirit in the believer's heart. At the end of his argument, Paul explains why he can remain confident and positive, even though the many sins and failures of the Corinthians might seem reason for discouragement. Paul explains that anything which can be seen is, by nature, temporary and subject to change (4:16–18; 5:12). So Paul bases his approach to ministry not on what he observes in another person's life but on unseen, eternal realities. One of those realities is the compelling love of Christ (5:14). The power that changes human hearts is the link of love, initiated by God and awakened in the very core of the one who responds to his love with faith. These are persons for whom Christ died, with the goal that they "should no longer live for themselves but for him who died for them and was raised again" (v. 15). To Paul it is unthinkable that any purpose in Jesus' death will not be achieved. Even those as slow to respond to God as the Corinthians will indeed change and grow toward holiness. And so Paul regards anyone in Christ as a new creation (v. 17) and his ministry is designed to reconcile them, or bring them into harmony, with God.

But what does a reconciling ministry involve? Paul looks to God and sees in his gift of Jesus the pattern for his own ministry to his brothers and sisters. "God was reconciling the world to himself in Christ, *not counting men's sins against them.* And he has committed to us the message of reconciliation" (2 Cor. 5:19; italics mine).

The secret of reconciliation is not reminders of guilt and warnings about punishment but the message that, in Jesus, people's sins are no longer held against them. The reconciling word is *forgiveness,* because forgiveness can fill the heart with love and motivate a change toward righteousness (see 2 Cor. 5:21). And the reconciling method is *being gracious.* It is not counting other's sins. It is not holding other's sins and failures against them—even when those sins and failures cause us pain.

## JESUS' LIFE AND TEACHING

We cannot imagine what it must have been like for Jesus to live in our dark world. Everyone around him was flawed, hurting, and causing hurt. People heard his words of love and saw his acts of compassion and yet were unwilling to respond. John says, "He came to that which was his own, but his own did not receive him" (John 1:11). The rejection, the hatred, and the thoughtless acts of those Jesus had come to redeem must have been overwhelmingly painful.

Even those who did receive Jesus failed to demonstrate his values. As Christ and his followers traveled in Samaria, they came to a city that would not welcome them. James and John asked, "Lord, do you want us to call fire down from heaven to destroy them?" (Luke 9:54). Yet, in all their years with Jesus, they had never seen him use his power against a single soul.

And just days before Christ had to face the cross, the Twelve squabbled over who would have the best place in Jesus' kingdom. And a few hours before all of them ran away in terror from the crowd that came to arrest Jesus, Peter solemnly promised that he would die rather than desert the Lord, a promise echoed by all the others as well.

Jesus experienced every pain that one person can cause another, not just as God, but in his humanity. There is no sin, no insensitivity, no rejection, and no hostility that we can experience that Jesus Christ has not felt too. Yet in it all, Jesus continued to love. He continued to be gracious and refused to hold other's sins against them. On the cross, Jesus died crying out, "Forgive them, for they do not know what they are doing" (Luke 23:34).

It is no surprise that we see a stress in Jesus' teaching on forgiveness. Such an emphasis reflects his own tragic experiences as well as the experiences that each of us has with others in our sin-cursed world. I consider here three of Jesus' most important teachings on forgiveness.

*Forgive seven times* (Luke 17:3–10). Jesus said to his disciples, "If your brother sins, rebuke him, and if he repents, forgive him. If he sins against you seven times in a day, and seven times comes back to you and says, 'I repent,' forgive him" (vv. 3–4).

We can sense the stunned silence and imagine the disciples' unexpressed thoughts. "Lord, that's *hard* !" Finally they said aloud, "Increase our faith" (v. 5). They were saying, in effect, "Lord, if in this life we are to keep on forgiving people who sin against us again and again, repeating the same acts even after saying they repent, we'll need far more faith than we possess now!"

Jesus' response seems puzzling at first. He makes a remark about faith ("If you have faith as small as a mustard seed, you can say to this mulberry tree, 'Be uprooted and planted in the sea,' and it will obey you" [v. 6]) but then goes on to tell this illustration.

> Suppose one of you had a servant plowing or looking after the sheep. Would he say to the servant when he comes in from the field, "Come along now and sit down to eat"? Would he not rather say, "Prepare my supper, get yourself ready and wait on me while I eat and drink; after that you may eat and drink"? . . . So you also, when you

have done everything you were told to do, should say, "We are unworthy servants; we have only done our duty" (Luke 17:7–10).

The disciples had asked for more faith to enable them to forgive. Jesus said, in effect, that faith was fine for moving mulberry trees. Then in his story Jesus shifted their attention to the real issue: servants are supposed to do what they are told. Jesus, one whom the disciples rightly call "Lord," has told his followers to forgive and to keep on forgiving.

When Jesus' followers are sinned against repeatedly, they are to ask not for greater faith but simply for greater faithfulness. Our Lord has *commanded* us to forgive. Forgiving others is a matter not of faith, but of obedience.

*Forgive—and be forgiven* (Matt. 6:14–15). Jesus told his followers, "If you forgive men when they sin against you, your heavenly Father will also forgive you. But if you do not forgive men their sins, your Father will not forgive your sins." These words are disturbing. Does not our forgiveness depend on what Jesus has done for us rather than on ourselves? Is our forgiveness conditioned on our willingness to forgive others?

But Jesus is not dealing here with the way of salvation. He is describing reality. Jesus is pointing out that forgiveness is like a coin—it has two sides, extending and receiving. Just as a person cannot have only one side of a coin, so a person cannot grasp only one aspect of forgiveness. People for whom forgiveness is a reality will know forgiveness not simply as something they receive but as something they also extend freely to others.

Jesus' statement, then, is psychological rather than theological in character. If we are not forgiving, we will not really experience the freedom that being forgiven brings. The very attitude that sensitizes us to accept forgiveness from God will sensitize us to others and lead us to forgive them.

Both extending forgiveness and accepting it call for a special humility. There is no room in either for pride or self-deceit. We learn to look at the flaws in ourselves and in others with compassion, accepting, valuing, and affirming the person despite the sins that are so discouraging and harmful. Forgiveness is possible only when we have learned not to count trespasses against either ourselves or others, reflecting in our attitude the loving-kindness of our forgiving God.

*Live with compassion* (Matt. 18). In this important passage Jesus answers his disciples' question about greatness. Christ explains that greatness is rooted in a childlike faith which is demonstrated by an unhesitating response to Jesus' own words (vv. 2–5). This childlikeness can be maintained only as we live with each other in a simple, forgiving way which does not occasion sin.

Jesus tells three stories to illustrate. The first story is of a sheep that wanders away and is found by the shepherd (vv. 10–14). In living with others, we are to remember that we are all sheep, prone by nature to go astray. When one does go astray, we are to search until we find it, and then bring it back, "happier about that one sheep than about the ninety-nine that did not wander off" (v. 13).

What a stunning attitude! When the wandering one has returned, we are so quick to want to punish, or at least to make sure that he or she understands how much hurt has been caused. Rather than be happy, we tend to be angry, wanting the offending one to pay for our pain. Yet Jesus calls us to remember with compassion that we are all sheep and that, by nature, we all wander. When restoration comes, the joy of return is to erase any anger at past pain.

The second story reminds us that we believers are members of a family (vv. 15–22). As in any family, God's children at times sin against each other. When sins and hurts come, Jesus tells us to go to our brother and seek reconciliation so that forgiveness can flow.

How important the family relationship is! Hurts will come, but we are bound together in love by our common relationship to God our Father. We maintain that closeness of family as we forgive and, as this context also emphasizes, as we keep on forgiving each other again and again.

The third story uses yet another image (vv. 23–35). It speaks of servants who were responsible to a single master. One servant had an unpayable debt, amounting to several million dollars. When it came time to pay, the servant begged for more time. The master instead had compassion on him and actually canceled the debt.

This servant later met a fellow servant who owed him a few dollars. When the fellow worker could not pay, the first servant grabbed him and began choking him. Then he had the debtor thrown into prison until he could pay back every cent.

When these actions were reported to the master, the ruler called the first servant in. "You wicked servant!" the ruler railed. "I canceled all that debt of yours because you begged me to. Shouldn't you have had mercy on your fellow servant just as I had on you?" (vv. 32–33).

The application of the story is all too clear. God has forgiven our unpayable debt. He has dealt compassionately with us, asking us to pay nothing of what we owe but taking the burden of payment on himself in Christ. How readily we who have been forgiven so much should extend the forgiveness we have received to others, whose debt to us can hardly be compared to the debt we owe to God.

Jesus' instructions and teaching on forgiveness, then, emphasize several basic points, as summarized below.

| | |
|---|---|
| Luke 17:3–10 | Forgiveness is commanded. Forgiving others is an issue not of faith but of obedience. |
| Matthew 6:14–15 | Receiving forgiveness and extending forgiveness are linked in human experience. An attitude enabling one enables the other. |
| Matthew 18:10–14 | Forgiveness will always be needed, for human beings, like sheep, tend to go astray. Such individuals need to be sought out and reconciled, without recrimination. |
| Matthew 18:15–22 | Like siblings, we will sin against each other. Forgiveness—extended again and again—will maintain family intimacy and love. |
| Matthew 18:23–35 | We who have been forgiven such a great debt by God are to forgive those who sin against us, knowing that, however greatly we have been hurt, that debt cannot be compared to the debt we owe to God. |

## PRACTICING FORGIVENESS

There can be no doubt that anyone living a human life will be affected by the sins of others. And anyone living a human life in union with God will seek, as Jesus did, to forgive. But how do we practice forgiveness in our relationships with others?

Do we simply overlook others' sins? Do we say nothing

when we are hurt? Do we let people who sin against us "get away with it" again and again, or do we make them pay for (i.e., be responsible for) their actions? And what about sin in the church and church discipline? How is this issue related to forgiveness?

Figure 4 sums up our response when it seems that someone has sinned against us. The left side of the figure deals with perceived sins against us as individuals. The two options we have when someone's actions cause us hurt are either to forbear or to enter into a process of rebuke that leads to extending and accepting forgiveness.

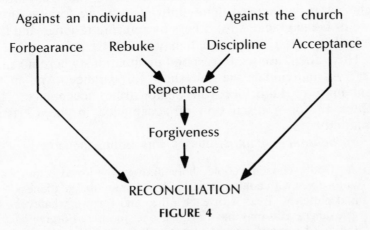

**FIGURE 4**

Dealing With Perceived Sins

"not counting men's sins against them" (2 Cor. 5:19)

The right side of the figure deals with perceived sins affecting the Christian community. Again there are two options. We can either show acceptance or enter into a process of discipline that leads to extending and accepting forgiveness. When we understand the choices open to us and the guidelines Scripture provides for making those choices, we gain important insight into how to live with sin in others in a godly, forgiving way.

*Perceived sins.* Sin, as we noted in chapter 10, is a complex reality. The biblical concept of sin includes willful, wicked acts and human fallibility; rebellion and falling short. At times the things that others do may be sin in the clearest sense of willful rebellion against a known standard of God, and they may also be wicked in the sense of doing intentional harm to another person. At other times the things that people do may be sin in its guise of unknowing failure or unintentional harm. At times the things we identify as sins may even be violation not of God's standards but of ours or of our own misapplication of a biblical teaching.

These possibilities mean that we and I need to be careful before labeling others' acts as "sin," even though an action may inadvertently hurt us. All too often the faults we ascribe to others lie in ourselves. We take a remark intended to be a compliment as an insult. We judge an action without understanding the motive. The unintentional and the ignorant act might better be excused than confronted, as we forgive (in the sense of being gracious to) others by refusing to judge and thus overlooking even actions that may cause us pain.

How, then, are we to respond in situations where no sin is clear? As individuals we can show forbearance. And in the community of faith, we can demonstrate acceptance. (See chapter 13 for a discussion of acceptance in the Christian community.)

*Forbearance.* Paul discusses this option succinctly:

> As God's chosen people, holy and dearly loved, clothe yourselves with compassion, kindness, humility, gentleness and patience. Bear with each other and forgive whatever grievances you may have against one another. Forgive as the Lord forgave you. And over all these virtues put on love, which binds them all together in perfect unity (Col 3:12–14).

In these verses we sense an attitude toward others which is associated both with forbearance and forgiveness. We are to view others with compassion and kindness. We remain humble, gentle, and patient. As these qualities take root in our personalities, we will be quick to forgive and ready to forbear.

The Greek word here means "tolerate; put up with." This response is often necessary because not every believer has been made beautiful by Jesus' touch—at least not yet. The young, the immature, and the struggling have not yet outgrown their imperfections, nor are they able yet to deal with them. And so, Ephesians 4:2 says, using this same word, "Be patient, bearing with one another in love." In many cases the person who lives a human life in union with God is simply to overlook the faults in others and to put up with the pain. When we do, we are to maintain toward them the reconciling attitude which God expressed in Christ of not counting their sins against them.

*Rebuke.* Not every sin is to be overlooked. Some sins have characteristics that call for confrontation. They may be sins that place an unbearable strain on relationships. They may involve regular violation of clearly stated biblical standards, that is, acts which God has unmistakably identified as sin and which thus disrupt the fellowship of the sinner with the Lord. Or they may be repeated sins of which the person seems to be unaware.

In such cases Scripture calls on us to come to our brother or sister, not with a condemning attitude, but with loving concern for his or her welfare. In such cases we come to extend forgiveness, knowing that, for Christians to grow, we need to be reconciled to God and to one another.

Both Testaments show us the process God intends us to use. "Rebuke your neighbor frankly" (Lev. 19:17), the Old Testament says. And Jesus expanded on this theme.

> If your brother sins against you, go and show him his fault, just between the two of you. If he listens to you, you have won your brother over. But if he will not listen, take one or two others along, so that "every matter may be established by the testimony of two or three witnesses." If he refuses to listen to them, tell it to the church; and if he refuses to listen even to the church, treat him as you would a pagan or a tax collector (Matt. 18:15–17).

The process points up an important parallel between the forgiveness God extends to us and the forgiveness we extend to others. Both require confession. Individuals who will not acknowledge that they have sinned will not turn to Jesus for forgiveness, and believers who delude themselves about their actions will not confess daily failures to the Lord. Walking then in darkness, unwilling to deal with the reality of their need, these sinners wander far from fellowship with God. But when a person does hear our rebuke, acknowledging, if not the fault involved, at least the hurt caused, then forgiving love can flow, and hurts can be healed.

Forgiveness is God's way of maintaining fellowship in the community of faith as well as in human relationship with him. The friend or family member or the Christian brother or sister who will not deal with the reality of his or her own faults will not accept forgiveness from others. Only when people acknowledge their faults can forgiveness bring its healing touch, and intimacy grow.

*Discipline*. The New Testament establishes a parallel process for church discipline. If a brother or sister habitually engages in that which Scripture identifies as sin, that behavior must be confronted (1 Cor. 5:1–12). The confrontation is designed to lead to repentance, to acknowledgment of the sin and to turning from it so that forgiveness can flow and reconciliation be experienced.

It is important to see church discipline as a reconciling gift. The Bible tells us that a person who practices sin lives out of fellowship with God. Yet such a person can be blinded by self-deceit, denial, or any of the other fruitless ways that human beings try to deal with personal sins. Christian brothers and sisters thus act on earth for God. We confront, identifying sin as sin. And if the brother or sister still will not respond, the church on earth acts out a heavenly reality. The people of God cut off the sinning person from fellowship so that he or she will experience on earth the loss of his or her intimacy with God.

Forgiveness, then, has two experiential aspects. One is that of toleration, of bearing with and overlooking sins in others. The other aspect is that of confrontation, of rebuking and ultimately disciplining others until confession and repentance open the door for forgiveness to flow. In essence, each of these aspects reflects the reconciling grace of God, who, in Christ, came "not counting men's sins against them" (2 Cor. 5:19).

## GROWTH IN DEALING WITH OTHERS' SINS

To live a human life is to be affected by the sins of others, even people we love the most. And to live our human life in union with God is to respond to such sins with forgiving grace. But how hard it is to forgive when we have been hurt! We can well understand the disciples' request, "Increase our faith!" But learning to forgive is not so much a matter of faith as it is an issue of obedience. We are to forgive, as Jesus commanded, and so grow in Christian spirituality. I consider here some suggestions for growth in responding with forgiveness to the sins of others.

*Examine yourself first*. When we are sinned against, our first reactions are likely to be hurt and anger. We feel violated and insulted; antagonism is aroused. Sins that affect us do more than touch us emotionally. They understandably also cause us to blame or to condemn. Sins do incur guilt. They do create a debt or obligation, which all of us sense intuitively.

The same passages that call on us to forbear and forgive first tell us to focus on our own inner response to those who harm us. First, "Get rid of all bitterness, rage and anger, brawling and slander, along with every form of malice," then "Be kind and compassionate to one another, forgiving one another, just as in Christ God forgave you" (Eph. 4:31–32).

The actions that have hurt us may well be sins against us. But our bitterness, our rage, our anger, our striking back, our malice—these responses are sins too! Before we can deal in God's way with sin in others, we need to be willing to identify the sin in our reactions to them. We need to confess our sin to God, freeing his Spirit to cleanse us and to fill us with God's own kindness and compassion. Whenever we feel bitterness or anger at another's acts, those feelings are God's invitation to turn to him and receive forgiveness so that we will be able to forgive.

*Consider forbearance before rebuke.* At times we will need to rebuke a brother or sister who has sinned against us. But in most situations forgiveness will take the form of forbearance.

When the sins of another have affected us, we must look first to God for inner healing and for the gift of his own compassion. God's Spirit must work in our heart, drawing the pain, releasing us from the memory, so that, like God, we will not hold on to the failings of the other person.

*Rebuke lovingly.* We are never to rebuke in order to punish, but only in order to reconcile. God deals with us not in anger but always in love. When we do rebuke another person, our goal is to help him or her identify an inner sin which only God can cleanse.

It is important to pray for a right attitude when we feel that we must rebuke another person or confront one with a sin. Confrontation is to be an act of love, and only when God has enabled us to act in love should we proceed.

*Forgive fully.* The forgiveness that God offers us and that we are to offer others is truly complete. He remembers our trespasses no more. He does not count our sins against us. The divine forgiveness makes the past irrelevant and holds out hope for a new, transformed tomorrow.

We are to offer similar forgiveness. Forgiveness reconciles us fully to one another, and as we forgive, hurts are healed and the past recedes from view. God himself graciously works this process in us as we experience our union with him.

**PROBE**

**exercises for personal development**
**case histories**
**thought provokers**

1. Table 8 suggests relationships between the way we are to deal with
sins in our own life and sins that affect us in the lives of others.
Glance over the table. Then study the following passages: Psalms 32;
51; Romans 14:3; 1 Corinthians 13:5; 2 Corinthians 3–5; Ephesians
4:32; Colossians 3:13; 1 John 1:4–2:1. How would you change, or
add to, table 8 as the author has developed it?

**Table 8. Response to Sin**

| Comparison | Sin in us | Sin in others |
|---|---|---|
| *Emotional reaction* | guilt, flight | hurt, anger |
| *Intellectual reaction* | pretense, denial, excuse, accuse | blaming, condemning |
| *Outcome* | guilt, alienation, stunt growth | guilt, alienation, stunt growth |
| *God's alternative* | confess | forgive, forbear |
| *Outcome* | forgiveness, cleansed conscience, growth | reconciliation, growth |

2. Consider your relationships with others. With whom do you feel
most comfortable? With whom do you feel least comfortable? Who is
most likely to hurt you? Why? How do you characteristically deal with
your hurts? What in this chapter applies most directly to you right
now?

3. This chapter began with the following vignette. After reading the
chapter, how would you evaluate the incident? How would you be
likely to respond to the person who said it?

"So I said, 'Craig, that's the tenth time this month. It's fine to say
you're sorry. But after ten times, I just don't believe you. I mean, if
you really loved me, you wouldn't keep doing it again and again,
would you? I'll forgive you this time. But I'm warning you: Don't let it
happen again!' "

4. First Corinthians 13:4–6 describes Christian love. Examine this
paragraph, and write a paper showing the relationship of love to
forgiveness as it is explained in this chapter.

Love is patient, love is kind. It does not envy, it does not boast, it is
not proud. It is not rude, it is not self-seeking, it is not easily angered,
it keeps no record of wrongs. Love does not delight in evil but

rejoices in the truth. It always protects, always trusts, always hopes, always perseveres.

5. Figure 5 represents your personal "toleration level." Scripture teaches us to forbear (tolerate our grievances) with others as well as to take initiative to confront and rebuke when necessary for us to experience continuing reconciliation with them.

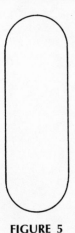

**FIGURE 5**

Personal Toleration Level

Indicate your personal toleration level by drawing a horizontal line at a level which you believe indicates your own capacity to live with others' sins in a godly, forgiving way.

List at least five things *below* the level that you currently tolerate in grace and love. Then list at least five things *above* that line which bother you so much that you cannot maintain the scriptural attitude of "not counting men's sins against them" (2 Cor. 5:19).

Compare your toleration level with that of others, and talk about the things you have listed above and below the line.

6. Look back at figure 5 and at the things you have listed above and below your toleration level. In your best judgment, should you deal with the things above the level by raising your toleration level (seeking God's grace to change your attitudes and reactions to others) or by rebuking those who do the things you have listed (helping them experience God's grace by dealing with a real fault or sin)?

7. Read through the Gospels and cut out any passages that deal with forgiveness. Tape them in a notebook and reread them carefully. What additional insights do you gain? What additional conclusions about dealing with others' sins can you draw?

# Section D: Lordship

Christians affirm that Jesus is Lord. We see the one who lived on earth as a human being, humbled even to the point of death, as our exalted and glorified Lord. With Paul the apostle we affirm that the risen Christ, seated at God's right hand, governs "far above all rule and authority, power and dominion, and every title that can be given" (Eph. 1:21).

We acknowledge Jesus' sovereignty in this present world, sure that our Lord is superintending not only the course of history but our very lives. We affirm Jesus as living Head of the church, which is his body, and with the New Testament we believe that we live "in" and "under" and "through" him.

We also believe that when Jesus comes again, he will openly exercise ultimate authority, demonstrating his sovereignty over all creation. Then, at the name of Jesus, every knee will bow and every tongue confess that Jesus Christ is Lord (Phil. 2:10–11).

In view of the testimony of Scripture that Jesus is Lord, it is clear that living a human life in union with God must involve relating to Jesus Christ as Lord. We are to experience Christ's lordship in our life, and perhaps most difficult, we are to release others to experience Jesus' lordship in theirs.

# 12

## CHOICE

Suddenly Carol's eyes lit up. "Oh, I know what you mean by 'hearing God's voice.'"

It was a Friday evening, and our home Bible study group was looking at what Jesus' lordship meant in our walk with God.

"Richard and I were just married and were sent to an army base in Texas. We'd heard there was no housing there, and we were really worried. So when we came to a house-trailer sales office about a hundred miles from the base, we stopped just to look.

"Well, talk about high-pressure salesmen! That man had us ready to buy a sixty-by-ten-foot trailer in no time. He promised us space near the base, and everything. But when we went in to sign, well, I just had this feeling, almost like a voice inside, saying, 'Don't do it. Don't do it.'

"I was a young Christian then and didn't know anything about the Holy Spirit or about God's guiding us. So we signed—and when we got to the base we found out there were all sorts of nice little houses to rent nearby, for just about nothing."

Carol's experience is not unusual. Most of us have had times when we felt a strong sense of inner direction. Some Christians ignore such feelings, uncomfortable with the idea of the supernatural. Others gradually become aware that the believer is called to live a supernatural life; that to live a human life in union with God involves a growing awareness that Christ is with us daily and that many of our choices in life are to be made at his express direction!

## "LORD" IN THE SCRIPTURES

*The Old Testament.* English versions of the Old Testament use LORD to translate the Hebrew form *yhwh,* the original pronunciation of which is uncertain but is approximated in the name *Yahweh.* Before we can grasp the implications of Christ's lordship in our Christian life, we need to have some awareness of the powerful significance of this Old Testament name.

The name is introduced and explained in Exodus 3. Moses at the burning bush asks God what he should say if the Israelites ask the name of the one who sent Moses to deliver them from Egyptian servitude. God tells Moses, "I AM WHO I AM," and instructs him to say that "I AM" has sent him (v. 14). And then the text adds that Moses is to say, "The LORD [i.e., *Yahweh,* a word which sounds like and probably is derived from the verb meaning "I am"] . . . has sent me to you. This is my name forever, the name by which I am to be remembered from generation to generation" (v. 15).

This revelation of the divine name is significant in two ways. First, it is not a *descriptive* name but a *personal* name. The Bible gives many descriptive names of God—Sovereign Lord, the Lord of Armies, God our Healer, etc. Such names express a quality or characteristic of God, much as we might speak of a person as a good teacher, a Boy Scout leader, or a first baseman on the church softball team. But speaking to Moses, God now unveils his personal name that, by identifying him uniquely and expressing a vital insight into his very essence, does more than describe. That personal name, Yahweh, rooted in the Hebrew verb "to be," can perhaps best be rendered as "the one who is always present." Our God is present at all times and in every place and situation.

Second, the unveiling of the name Yahweh to Moses is important historically. The people of Israel, enslaved then for generations, had known God by tradition. They knew that in the distant past God had spoken to their father, Abraham. They knew too that God had given Abraham great covenant promises and that one day some future generation would experience the blessings guaranteed to them by the divine oath. God was present to Abraham. God would one day be present again. But where was God while they suffered in Egypt, powerless and without hope?

And then God spoke to Moses, unveiling his name, and in a stunning series of miracles, the Lord demonstrated his reality, his power, and his presence with his people.

This name, God said to Moses, "is my name forever, the name by which I am to be remembered from generation to generation" (v. 15). God is to be known and experienced by his people as "the one who is always present."

God's presence will seldom be as obvious to the world as it was during those days in Egypt. But God's people are to know by faith that, obvious or not, God is here. He is with us always, in our own here and now.

*The New Testament.* The Greek word translated "lord" is *kurios.* In ordinary speech the word was a term of respect, like our *sir* or an earlier *master.* But the translators of the Old Testament into Greek used the word *kurios* to translate the Hebrew term *Yahweh* (LORD). This choice lifts *kurios* beyond the ordinary and, when used in a religious context, infuses it with the vital and powerful meaning of the Old Testament name.

In some cases, then, the Gospels use *lord* and even refer to Jesus as "lord" in nothing more than the ordinary sense (see Matt. 8:2; Luke 9:59). But in other cases, as in Jesus' own use of *Lord,* this word clearly identifies Christ with the always present one of Old Testament revelation (see Matt. 12:8; Luke 20:42–44; also John 20:28).

After the resurrection of Jesus, the church immediately affirmed that "Jesus is Lord." In this confession the church fully identified Jesus of Nazareth with the Yahweh of the Old Testament. Paul, apparently repeating an established confessional statement, looks at Jesus in his self-humbling before the cross and then affirms:

> Therefore God exalted him to the highest place
>     and gave him the name that is above every name,
> that at the name of Jesus every knee should bow,
>     in heaven and on earth and under the earth,
> and every tongue confess that Jesus Christ is Lord,
>     to the glory of God the Father (Phil. 2:9–11).

The term *Lord* has two major emphases in the Epistles. First, we are repeatedly reminded that Jesus is the *Lord* Jesus Christ. Paul notes that, although we once viewed Christ from a worldly point of view (that is, in his humanity as a human being), we now stand in awe of him as Lord (2 Cor. 5:11, 16). The primary use of Lord in the epistle is to identify Jesus and to remind us that the one we knew as a man is truly God and, as Lord, is present with us in power.

Second, we see the lordship of Jesus exercised in his

relationship with believers. Paul is not concerned about the opinion of others, for Jesus is Lord and only he is competent to judge (1 Cor. 4:4). The apostle's work is "in the Lord" (9:1), accomplished though his presence and power and done in his name. Our hope is in Jesus as Lord (Phil. 2:19), and the Lord acts to rescue us in our need (2 Tim. 3:11).

In essence, the Christian's acknowledgment of Jesus as Lord is, first, an affirmation of Christ's full deity and, second, an expression of expectation. To live a human life in union with God is to practice the presence of God, for the Jesus in whom we believe is Lord, the one who *is* present with us, now! We are to count on his intervention as well as to respond always to his leading.

## LORDSHIP IN JESUS' LIFE

To understand what it means to practice God's presence, acknowledging him as present with us, we need only to look at Jesus in his relationship with the Father. This relationship is expressed in statements such as these from the Gospel of John.

> I tell you the truth, the Son can do nothing by himself; he can do only what he sees his Father doing, because whatever the Father does the Son also does. For the Father loves the Son and shows him all he does (5:19–20).

> I do nothing on my own but speak just what the Father has taught me. The one who sent me is with me; he has not left me alone, for I always do what pleases him (8:28–29).

The responsiveness of Jesus to the will of God was so complete that Christ could say, "When a man believes in me, he does not believe in me only, but in the one who sent me. When he looks at me, he sees the one who sent me" (12:44–45). Furthermore,

> Anyone who has seen me has seen the Father. How can you say, "Show us the Father"? Don't you believe that I am in the Father, and that the Father is in me? The words I say to you are not just my own. Rather, it is the Father, living in me, who is doing his work (14:9–10).

In these sayings of Jesus it is clear that practicing the presence of God, living in vital union with God as one who is present, involves both *communication* and *obedience*. Jesus knew the Father's will. And he responded obediently.

When Christ goes on to speak of the believer's experience of union with *him,* both factors are emphasized. Jesus promised that "anyone who has faith in me will do what I have been doing" (John 14:12). The union that Jesus experienced on earth with the Father, which enabled him to know and respond to the Father's will, is something that we are to experience too. The Holy Spirit is the living bond between Jesus and us, enabling us to know God's will and to act in obedience.

Speaking to this point, Jesus focused on the significance of choice and the importance of obedience.

> Whoever has my commands and obeys them, he is the one who loves me. He who loves me will be loved by my Father, and I too will love him . . . , and we will come to him and make our home with him. He who does not love me will not obey my teaching. These words you hear are not my own; they belong to the Father who sent me (John 14:21–24).

For Jesus, then, knowing the will of God and doing it were vital to living his human life in union with the Father. This same relationship of knowing and doing Jesus' will is vital if we are to live our human life in union with Jesus as Lord.

## HEARING THE LORD'S VOICE

The Bible makes it clear that the believer is expected to know the will of God and to recognize the voice of the Lord when he or she is spoken to. Jesus told his followers, "My sheep listen to my voice; I know them, and they follow me" (John 10:27).

The concept of the voice of God is explained most clearly in an extended argument in the Book of Hebrews (3:7–4:13). The writer begins by quoting from Psalm 95, which looks back on the events occurring as the generation that Moses led from Egypt was poised on the edge of the Promised Land. But they refused. And so the Holy Spirit speaks to subsequent generations, saying,

> Today, if you hear his voice,
>     do not harden your hearts
> as you did in the rebellion (3:7–8).

This theme is repeated throughout the passage. Believers are warned against a "sinful, unbelieving heart that turns away from the living God" (3:12) because the present time too is called "Today" (v. 13). In our today,

> . . . if you hear his voice,
>   do not harden your hearts
>   as you did in the rebellion (v. 15).

The writer argues that the present time clearly is "today," for not only the Exodus generation heard and responded to God's voice. In David's time too God said,

> Today, if you hear his voice,
>   do not harden your hearts" (4:7).

For all, then, there is a today in which God's voice is heard, because God is, by his very nature and name, the *one who is present*. God is here, with you and me, just as he was "here" to the generation that hesitated to enter the Promised Land when God said "Go."

The word *today* is important in understanding this passage in Hebrews that speaks of God's voice. The concept of rest, which is used in this passage in three senses, is likewise central.

First, in the historic setting, *rest* was entry into the Promised Land (3:11, 18). When that first generation rebelled against God's voice, they were turned back into the wilderness, where they wandered until death overtook them. God swore they would "never enter his rest" because they disobeyed.

Second, *rest* describes God's seventh-day rest following the six days of Creation. The writer says, "There remains, then, a Sabbath-rest for the people of God; for anyone who enters God's rest also rests from his own work, just as God did from his" (4:9–10). Now, God's rest clearly is not inactivity. In fact, God has been and remains vitally involved in all that happens in our world. But while active, God's involvement is not "work." In fact, from the Creation itself, a universe was set in motion in which every contingency was planned for. There is nothing that can happen which God has not foreseen and taken into account. The work of creation is complete, and all now proceeds as God's plan and purpose unfolds.

Third, in the present, *rest* is an experience of resting from one's "own work, just as God did from his" (4:10). It involves our entering into the flow and process of God's plan, taking the place that he has chosen for us. It means that we are to learn to listen for and to obey God's voice and so be guided into his will.

*Work* for us in this context is to attempt to find our own way through life, to struggle to make unaided decisions and to hope for the best. But because Jesus is Lord, present with us, and because he does communicate his will to us, the true struggle of the spiritual man or woman is not to determine the next step but to sense and to do the will of God.

Practicing the presence of God, then, involves realizing that Jesus, the true Word, is "living and active" (4:12). Because "nothing in all creation is hidden from God's sight" (v. 13), our Lord is able to guide us toward what is good and beneficial and away from all that is harmful and wrong. Christian spirituality, living our human life in union with God, means practicing the presence of Christ as Lord by sensing his voice and responding obediently to him.

## PRACTICAL GUIDELINES

Both Jesus' own words and Hebrews 3–4 suggest that living in union with God involves sensitivity to his contemporary voice. This "voice" of God is divine guidance. It is a word spoken within us, confirming a particular choice or decision as his will for us as an individual. While the idea of a supernatural conviction bothers some who look for a more rational approach to Christian decision making, we need to remember that Christian spirituality *is* supernatural and that the name by which God intends to be known from generation to generation is *Yahweh*—the one who is truly present. We have the promise of Jesus that those who are his sheep "follow him because they know his voice" (John 10:4).

Growth in Christian spirituality means learning to listen for, recognize, and obey the voice of Jesus as he directs our path. But given the supernatural element, some observations may help defend us against our own immaturity.

*Jesus' voice will not contradict Scripture.* Very few absolute prohibitions are expressed in the Bible. And most of the positive requirements are expressed as principles that must be applied in differing situations. Yet we can be sure that Scripture is fully authoritative. It provides a trustworthy check on our subjective impressions, for we know that God will not speak today contrary to what the Bible says.

*Some may not hear Jesus' voice.* The Hebrews passage says, "Today, *if* you hear his voice. . . ." God has made each of us special. He has given us each every capacity of personhood.

We have minds and emotions, differing talents and abilities, and various values and goals. Most of our decisions will be made in a "natural" way, growing out of our interests and abilities, made as we apply the capacity that God has given us to think and understand. It is not necessary for Jesus to speak to us concerning the great majority of the choices we make. Probably the color of socks we choose will never be of concern to the Lord (although it may concern a spouse!). And even in some life-shaping decisions, we may have no special sense of divine direction.

The essential element, the Hebrews passage emphasizes, is to live in the awareness that Jesus is present, that Jesus is Lord, which means that we take each step and make each choice *relying* on the divine presence. We remain always open to hear what Christ may be saying in us. And we go on living our life, using the capacities God has given us to make the choices that we believe will be pleasing to him.

Again, this "natural" process is closely linked to the written Word of God. The more familiar we are with that Word, the more we understand of God and his desires, the better our decisions and choices will be. In many cases, general guidance, through the principles and precepts of the written Word, will be the only guidance we require.

*Jesus' voice is heard in many ways.* Mature Christians do not expect to hear a literal voice speaking to them. Instead, the "voice" is simply the inner conviction that God wants us to make a particular choice.

At times Scripture serves as the means by which God gives special direction. A verse or phrase will seem to speak directly to us and our situation. At times God's voice will be recognized in a word of advice from a Christian friend. At other times, a conviction will grow while we are in prayer, or perhaps a sudden thought will emerge in the midst of a busy day. The important truth is that Jesus has said that his sheep *do* recognize his voice. Jesus *is* present with us, and we are to live in the conviction that he will speak words of guidance to us that we recognize as his.

*Jesus' voice is to be obeyed.* Spiritual growth takes place as we hear, recognize, and respond to Jesus as Lord. We are to respond to the written Word of Christ, and we are to respond to the quiet, inner voice as we sense his direction in our today. Our experience of the presence of Christ in our life is contingent largely on our obedience. Jesus said, "Whoever has my commands and obeys them, he is the one who loves me. He who loves me will be loved by my Father, and I too will love him *and show myself to him*"(John 14:21; italics mine).

As we sense the voice of God, we must treat him as Lord, acknowledging Jesus as the one who is present. Only by obedience to his voice do we truly acknowledge Jesus as Lord.

To live a spiritual life, then, means to live our human life in union with a God who is Lord and who is actually present with us. Because God is with us now, he speaks to us in our today. When we hear his voice and obey, we experience the rest that God has promised his people, and we experience Jesus in a fresh and vital way.

## PROBE

**exercises for personal development**
**case histories**
**thought provokers**

1. Many of the Corinthians were critical of the apostle Paul. They questioned his motives, condemned his choices, and, in general, challenged all he did and said. In response, the apostle wrote the following:

   > Men ought to regard us as servants of Christ and as those entrusted with the secret things of God. Now it is required that those who have been given a trust must prove faithful. I care very little if I am judged by you or by any human court; indeed, I do not even judge myself (1 Cor. 4:1–3).

   Paul's thrust here is that, as a servant of Christ, he is responsible only to prove faithful to Jesus. He is not responsible to give an account to his critics or to any court. How do you think that this passage relates to our exploration of the lordship of Jesus and to hearing his voice? Can you locate other passages in Paul's letters or in Acts which suggest that the apostle viewed himself as directly led by and responsible to obey only the voice of the living God?

2. Sometimes Christians surrender to the lordship of others rather than to the lordship of Jesus. That is, they listen to the voice of others in making personal choices rather than seeking direct guidance from God. Discuss whether you have ever let others exercise lordship over you. How did it happen? Why? When you were doing it, were you aware of any inner voice speaking against this course? How did you deal with it?

3. The author suggests that Scripture is important in learning to hear the "today" voice of the Lord. He notes that (1) familiarity with Scripture helps us understand God's values and general principles that guide decision making and (2) the voice of Christ as Lord will not propose any action that contradicts the clear teaching of Scripture.

We need to evaluate our reading of the Bible so that we include approaches designed to sensitize us to Scripture as an expression of God's living voice. One of the best ways is to *read for the divine perspective,* that is, to read in order to understand how God thinks, what he values, what attitudes are appropriate to godliness, what purposes are in harmony with his goals, etc. A simple and effective means of gaining this perspective is to *outline chapters.* Read a Bible chapter over several times and then write down major thoughts as main points in an outline, filling in as many subpoints as necessary. When you are confident you have understood the flow of thought, go back and write down a summary statement on God's perspective and on how his perspective can be applied as you view your own life situation.

4. No matter how well we understand God and his perspective as these are revealed in Scripture, in many situations we will sense a need for divine guidance. Typically these situations involve personal choice. And typically there is no clear or specific principle in Scripture that can be applied to guide us.

   Here is a sample list of such choices. See how many more you can add from your own experience.

   - Should I go to _____ College?

   - Should I try out for cheerleading?

   - Should I buy a new car now?

   - Should I change jobs?

   - Should I keep on dating _____ ?

5. Growth in spirituality is encouraged by developing increased sensitivity to Christ's contemporary voice. It is good to begin praying daily for sensitivity, that you will be open to hear the Lord when he speaks to you. Surrender complete lordship to Jesus, committing yourself to respond to him rather than to other persons or things that have influenced your choices. It is good, when uncertain about a decision, to pray for specific guidance. It is helpful also to develop an "obedience diary," simply to record times and situations in which you sense God's voice, reporting what happens as you do or do not respond obediently.

   Begin at least one of these practices and follow through with it for a minimum of three months. Then evaluate your progress and ways in which seeking to practice the presence of Jesus has affected you personally.

# 13

## FREEDOM

She was understandably upset when she came to talk with the pastor. Her former husband was begging her to remarry him and had even promised to start going to church.

Every time she talked with one of her friends, she got different advice. "You've got to remarry him," one of them said. "After all, God doesn't recognize divorce, so if he wants you back, you've got to go." But the next friend she checked with quoted, "Do not be unequally yoked together with unbelievers."

Finally, completely confused and deeply disturbed, she came to ask her pastor what she should do. The pastor listened to her story. Then he very carefully explained the different passages friends had shared with her and suggested a few others that might contain general guidelines.

As he talked, she became more and more agitated. Finally she burst out, "Look! You're the pastor. You're supposed to *tell* me what to do!"

The pastor tried to explain that this situation called for personal guidance. "Jesus is present with you," he said. "You need to let Jesus show you what he wants you to do."

Furious, the young woman got up and left the church, angry because her pastor would not tell her what to do. After fuming for two whole days, she decided that perhaps she *should* pray and ask Jesus what to do.

As she prayed, she felt she was certain of God's answer. At peace at last, she came back to her pastor and told him, "Jesus doesn't want me to marry him—at least not now."

Some might be upset with the pastor in this true story. But at least he honored the lordship of Christ. For if Christian spirituality means living our human life in union with God and responding to his voice in our today, and if Jesus speaks to us, then he can and will speak directly to others. We should never play Lord but must extend to others the freedom to respond personally to Jesus Christ.

## JESUS' LORDSHIP OVER OTHERS

In an extended passage the apostle Paul explores the significance of the lordship of Jesus over others in the fellowship of faith. This significant passage teaches us to extend freedom to others by accepting them and their personal choices.

> Accept him whose faith is weak, without passing judgment on disputable matters. One man's faith allows him to eat everything, but another man, whose faith is weak, eats only vegetables. The man who eats everything must not look down on him who does not, and the man who does not eat everything must not condemn the man who does, for God has accepted him. Who are you to judge someone else's servant? To his own master he stands or falls. And he will stand, for the Lord is able to make him stand.
>
> One man considers one day more sacred than another; another man considers every day alike. Each one should be fully convinced in his own mind. He who regards one day as special, does so to the Lord. He who eats meat, eats to the Lord, for he gives thanks to God; and he who abstains, does so to the Lord and gives thanks to God. For none of us lives to himself alone and none of us dies to himself alone. If we live, we live to the Lord; and if we die, we die to the Lord. So, whether we live or die, we belong to the Lord.
>
> For this very reason, Christ died and returned to life so that he might be the Lord of both the dead and the living. You, then, why do you judge your brother? Or why do you look down on your brother? For we will all stand before God's judgment seat. It is written:
>
> > "'As surely as I live,' says the Lord,
> > 'Every knee will bow before me;
> >     every tongue will confess to God.'"
>
> So then, each of us will give an account of himself to God.

Therefore let us stop passing judgment on one another. Instead, make up your mind not to put any stumbling block or obstacle in your brother's way. As one who is in the Lord Jesus, I am fully convinced that no food is unclean in itself. But if anyone regards something as unclean, then for him it is unclean. . . .

So whatever you believe about these things keep between yourself and God. Blessed is the man who does not condemn himself by what he approves. But the man who has doubts is condemned if he eats, because his eating is not from faith; and everything that does not come from faith is sin.

We who are strong ought to bear with the failings of the weak and not to please ourselves. Each of us should please his neighbor for his good, to build him up. . . .

May the God who gives endurance and encouragement give you a spirit of unity among yourselves as you follow Christ Jesus, so that with one heart and mouth you may glorify the God and Father of our Lord Jesus Christ.

Accept one another, then, just as Christ accepted you, in order to bring praise to God (Rom. 14:1–15:7).

In looking at this extended passage, we note several emphases. First, Jesus died and rose again that *he* might be Lord. As Lord, Christ is not only our master but is also the master of other believers. We have no basis for judging someone else's servant; a servant is bound to obey his own master, not a fellow servant.

Second, the specific issues Paul refers to are defined as "disputable matters." That is, the passage deals with the question of personal choices that individuals make in response to their perception of what the Lord wants them to do. On these matters Scripture does not clearly say, "This is sin," and thus there is room for disagreement among Christians. Here we must make a careful distinction. Many support their personal choices by *reasoning from* Scripture. No doubt in Rome the vegetarians and meat eaters each argued their persuasion and gave a "biblical" rationale. But nowhere does the Bible give a command regarding eating meat.

Most of the issues in human life are disputable in this sense. And so most of the choices and decisions which Christians are called on to make must be subjective personal decisions, made in a sense of responsibility to Jesus as Lord rather than made in obedience to a specific written command.

This is not to say that one choice or another is not more in harmony with Christian teaching. In fact, Paul says clearly, "I am fully convinced that no food is unclean in itself" (Rom. 14:14). But here, even that harmony is not relevant. The larger issue is that each person must have the freedom, and bear the responsibility, of choosing *as an act of faith.* The choices we make are to be made in obedience to God's will, as we understand that will. And who is to say that God's will for one servant is necessarily his will for another? The issue, as Paul sees it, is not so much whether a person is "right" as whether he or she acts in faith (v. 23).

Whenever we move into the realm of personal decisions about matters which are by nature disputable because there is no specific word on the matter in Scripture, we move into the realm of Christ's personal lordship. And in this realm, each servant of the Lord is responsible to choose what he or she believes will please Jesus Christ—*and that person is not subject to the judgment or criticism of others for that choice!*

This truth is difficult for us to grasp. We find it hard to understand why a choice that seems so "right" to us (and undoubtedly is right for *us*) is not also "right" for others. But Paul's instructions are clear. We are not to "look down on" and "must not condemn" others for their choices (14:3). "Each one should be fully convinced in his own mind" (v. 5). We are to "stop passing judgment on one another" (v. 13) and instead to encourage and build others up as fellow members of the body, being sensitive to their convictions. "So," Paul says, "whatever you believe about these things keep between yourself and God" (v. 22). We are to act on our convictions, showing sensitivity to others, but retaining and giving each other freedom to relate to Jesus, not to other human beings, as Lord. Paul concludes his argument with these words: "Accept one another [i.e., welcome each other warmly into full fellowship], then, just as Christ has accepted you, in order to bring praise to God" (15:7).

Other passages stress the same message. Paul, identifying himself as a servant of Christ (and thus responsible to please the Lord, not his fellow servants), says of the criticism he has experienced in Corinth,

> Now it is required that those who have been given a trust must prove faithful. I care very little if I am judged by you or by any human court; indeed, I do not even judge myself.

> My conscience is clear, but that does not make me innocent. It is the Lord who judges me. Therefore judge nothing before the appointed time; wait till the Lord comes. He will bring to light what is hidden in darkness and will expose the motives of men's hearts. At that time each will receive his praise from God (1 Cor. 4:2–5).

No human court has jurisdiction over what Jesus as Lord says to one of his servants. No person has the right to judge whether or not another is responding to the voice of God.

A little earlier Paul laid the groundwork for this position and made a striking statement. He speaks of the Holy Spirit, given to reveal the hidden things of God, first in words and then within the person who has the Spirit. In this context Paul writes, "The spiritual man makes judgments about all things, but he himself is not subject to any man's judgment" (1 Cor. 2:15).

Making one's life choices involves a spiritual process, and no one is capable of judging the rightness or wrongness of another's personal decision making. We know that, while the Old Testament points out the impossibility of any human being *discovering* "the mind of the Lord," in the Spirit, believers "have the mind of Christ" (1 Cor. 2:16).

Jesus is Lord, the one who is present. He speaks in our today, and we who are his people recognize and respond to his voice. Because of this spiritual reality, we are each personally responsible to Jesus as Lord, and we must give others freedom to make their personal decisions as acts of obedience to him, without being condemned or looked down on by us.

## JESUS' TEACHING

Jesus often insisted that his followers relate to each other nonjudgmentally. For instance, Jesus said, "Do not judge, or you too will be judged. For in the same way you judge others, you will be judged, and with the measure you use, it will be measured to you" (Matt. 7:1–2). This warning is given to the community of faith. If we judge others, others will judge us. The community God intended to be distinguished by love will then become bickering and antagonistic and will merely reflect the world. But if we use a measure of love rather than judgment, we will contribute to the spirit of unity and love that is to mark a congregation "so that with one heart and mouth [we] may glorify the God and Father of our Lord Jesus Christ" (Rom. 15:6; cf. Luke 6:37–38).

Jesus claims an authority to judge, stating that the Father has "entrusted all judgment to the Son" (John 5:22). Since Jesus is in charge of *all* judgment, there is no area in which we, individually or together in ecclesiastical courts, have a right to judge our brothers. The reason is explained in John 8. Jesus told religious leaders who claimed the right of judgment in Israel, "You judge by human standards" (v. 15). Only Christ, who knows the heart, is able to make right determinations about others (vv. 15–18). Human beings are simply too limited, by their nature, to be able to make accurate assessments of others and of their responsiveness to the Lord.

A final story illustrates God's attitude. After the Resurrection, the disciples were together on the seashore, and Jesus had asked Peter, "Do you love me?" Embarrassed and ashamed, Peter tried to change the subject. Looking at John, who was standing nearby, Peter asked, "Lord, what about him?" (John 21:21). Jesus answered, "If I want him to remain alive until I return, what is that to you? You must follow me" (v. 22).

What a clear statement! Lord, what about our brothers and sisters? What about the choice *he* made or the things *she* is doing? The answer of Jesus to such questions remains the same. "What is that to you? You must follow me."

## DEVELOPING A NONJUDGMENTAL ATTITUDE

Living a spiritual life is to live our human life in union with God. Such a life clearly demands responsiveness to Christ as Lord, both in making our own choices and in avoiding reacting to others, who are, like us, personally responsible to Jesus for their choices. Our personal spiritual growth must be expressed in the development of a nonjudgmental attitude toward others.

Having a judgmental attitude is one of our most common sins. We look at others and, without really thinking, impose our standards on their behavior and evaluate their choices from our perspective.

"How can they spend money eating out, on their income? I'd never do anything like that!"

"You'd think she'd at least keep the kitchen clean."

"I thought young Hank came forward at the missionary conference to dedicate his life to the Lord. How come he's going back on his vow and starting work at IBM?"

"I think his sleeping so late is just irresponsible. He's got to learn to get up early and get to work!"

"Ever since I heard about that, I've had serious doubts about his Christian commitment."

"He should have got a job two years ago, instead of fooling around with his painting. I don't want to see anyone in need. But I've got to say that now they're in just the trouble they deserve."

We could easily add additional examples of criticizing others. All of us tend to make just such judgments and evaluations of others. We can even argue that our evaluations are "right." We keep a clean kitchen to cut down on the germs, and a neat house is so much nicer to live in. If we make a spiritual commitment, we try to keep it. We do not waste money eating out, because it is much cheaper—and better steward-ship—to make good meals at home. Our values seem right to us; our convictions, the ones that should be held by all Christians who seek to be responsive to Jesus.

Actually, we should have such convictions. And we should try to live by them. But it is wrong of us to assume that the convictions we hold should be the convictions of every Chris-tian, and we are wrong to look at the practices of others judgmentally.

Imagine for a moment that those others choose to eat out often because it is the only way the couple can find time to be alone together. Suppose that keeping a clean kitchen is con-sciously sacrificed to get extra play time with the children or to get naps desperately needed because of health. Suppose the one who sleeps late is a "night person," who works on his projects when we are in bed. What if the response at that missions conference *was* a heartfelt commitment to Christ—and that Jesus wants young Hank at IBM instead of in Africa? Suppose the decision to paint was in response to a sense of calling—an act of obedience to Jesus as Lord that was carried out at high personal and family cost.

Now, none of the above suppositions may fit the case. In fact, the behaviors described may have actually been expres-sions of self-will, immature or ignorant choices, and not in any way a mature response to Jesus' lordship. They may be just as irresponsible as we believed when we uttered our criticisms.

The immaturity of others, however, does not give us the right to stand in judgment. In Paul's words, we have no right to look down on them or to condemn them. Jesus is Lord, and as his servant, each Christian must give an account to him, not to us. Indeed, Jesus is "able to make him stand" (Rom. 14:4).

When we begin to grasp the implications of Jesus' lordship in our own life and see its implications for others, we have grasped a vital key to our growth in the spiritual grace of acceptance.

First, we acknowledge that passing judgment on others is sin. We become alert for any condemning thought or attitude, aware of any thought or word that suggests looking down on others. We stop trying to rationalize or justify such thoughts. We acknowledge them to be sin, confess them, and let God cleanse us of this way of thinking about and relating to others.

Second, we make no issue of our own personal convictions. We stop trying to persuade others that our values or way of looking at disputable matters is "right." Romans says, "Whatever you believe about these things keep between yourself and God" (14:22).

Third, we acknowledge the debt of love we owe others, as Paul stresses in Romans 14. We all live with others who have convictions that differ from ours. We live with others who are immature and have not yet learned to sense and hear the voice of God in their today. To all such persons we owe love and acceptance and a sensitivity to their situation. We may need to express these attitudes by surrendering our freedom to do something that we are convinced is all right for us, if such action may do them harm.

Finally, we accept other Christians, no matter how they may differ from us in the disputable things in life. The Greek word translated "accept" in Romans 14 and linked with the lordship of Jesus in others' lives is *proslambanō*. The *Expository Dictionary of Bible Words* identifies this word as

> a significant relational term. It means to actively accept into one's society or circle of friends. We might well translate it "welcome," for it is used in the NT to communicate the warm sense of welcome to be given to fellow believers by a local community of faith (p. 8).

We are not simply to put up with people whose differences may bother us. We are not simply to stop our habit of judging such persons by our own values and standards. We are to seek out their company actively, opening our lives to them in friendship. We are to bond ourselves to them in love so that, in a supernatural unity not based in being like each other but based instead in Christ, we might together glorify God.

Table 9 sums up the implications of Jesus' lordship for us personally and for our relationships with others.

## Table 9. Implications of Jesus' Lordship

| Relation | Personal Meaning | Interpersonal Meaning |
|---|---|---|
| To Christ | Listen for and obey Jesus' voice (Heb. 3–4) | Recognize that Jesus speaks as Lord to others too, that others have the mind of Christ |
| | Keep convictions between oneself and Christ | |
| To others | Make judgments spiritually that are not subject to anyone's judgment (1 Cor. 4:3) | Do not condemn or look down on others for their choices (Rom. 14) |
| | | Actively welcome others into fellowship |

## PROBE

**exercises for personal development**
**case histories**
**thought provokers**

1. There are limitations on the nonjudgmental acceptance taught in this chapter. These limitations have to do with church discipline, which, according to 1 Corinthians 5, is to be exercised when a fellow member of the body practices what is clearly identified in Scripture as sin.

   Write a paper in which you define the limits on nonjudgmental acceptance—and the limits on church discipline.

2. "Passing judgment" is characterized by two different attitudes, according to Romans 14. One is described as "condemning," and the other as "looking down on." Understanding these two attitudes gives us an opportunity for a cleansing self-judgment.

   Write down two lists of names. On the first list include family and close friends. On the second one include others whom you know but not as well.

   Begin regularly to pray through these lists, taking one name each time. Follow this simple process:

   1. Meditate on Christ's acceptance of and love for you until you sense praise welling up in your heart.

2. Choose a word or phrase in Romans 14:1–15:7 for further meditation, recognizing it as a word from the Lord.

3. Focusing on one person on your list, ask God to reveal any judgmentalism in your attitude toward him or her. Confess any fault you are shown, and thank God for cleansing.

4. Pray now for the welfare of the person you have been considering, and thank God for exercising lordship in his or her life.

3. Memorize Romans 14:1–15:7. Meditate on the passage regularly until God engraves the truth of these verses on your heart.

4. As the illustration at the beginning of this chapter suggests, the lordship of Jesus has significant impact on Christian counseling. Complete one of the following assignments, each of which requires analysis of current views of counseling.

1. Select one popular school of Christian counseling and evaluate its practices in terms of its recognition of the lordship of Jesus in the life of counselor and counselee.

2. Reproduce as closely as possible a recent session where you were counselor or counselee. Evaluate the session, and then rewrite the session as you think it should have been conducted.

3. Interview three to five local pastors and write a report on their counseling practices. See if you can develop a simple questionnaire that will, without giving away its purpose, determine how the pastor as counselor demonstrates the conviction that Jesus is Lord in the counselee's life.

# Section E: Mortality

Adam had not understood. Perhaps if he had, he would have refused Eve's offer of the forbidden fruit. But Adam did not refuse. He ate, and with that act of disobedience, darkness fell, and death shrouded the human race.

Adam and Eve met death at the end of their biological life. But they had become all too familiar with it long before. Death is a constant companion to humankind, known in every pang of suffering. God said to the woman, "I will greatly increase your pains" (Gen. 3:16), and told Adam that he would gain his living only "through painful toil" (v. 17).

Much later Paul wrote with yearning of the restoration that lies ahead:

> We know that the whole creation has been groaning as in the pains of childbirth right up to the present time. Not only so, but we ourselves, who have the firstfruits of the Spirit, groan inwardly as we wait eagerly for our adoption as sons, the redemption of our bodies. For in this hope we were saved. But hope that is seen is no hope at all. Who hopes for what he already has? (Rom. 8:22–24).

Yes, restoration and release do lie ahead. But we know them only as a hope. Today, to live a human life means to know all the suffering to which mortal individuals are heir. To live a human life in union with God means to meet suffering in an attitude of submission and to respond to the suffering of others with Christlike compassion.

# 14

## SUFFERING

When old Jack Whitsen called my friend Dr. Paul Johnson, Jack almost broke down. He went through his familiar litany of complaints and then, his voice quivering, asked, "Why is God doing this to me? What have I done that's so wrong?"

The question is a common one. Paul knew that, sooner or later, he would hear it from Jack. Jack was one of those folks who are irritating witnesses. Whenever he came into the doctor's office, he would start talking to other patients in the waiting room. When he found that a person did not believe exactly what he believed, he would loudly confront them. "God has people he blesses," Jack would say, making it very clear that the other's sickness or injury proved that they simply were not one of them. Finally Dr. Johnson, hearing that loud, hostile voice condemning others, had to forbid Jack to "witness" in the office.

Jack suffered from a number of complaints, ranging from aches and pains to tension and anxiety. As Jack grew older, his visits to Paul's office became more and more frequent. Jack, so right in his own eyes, finally cried out that most common of questions, "Why is God doing this to me? Why me, God? Why *me*?"

This was Paul's opportunity, and he took it. He said to Jack just what he had said to himself some years before, when, stricken suddenly with cancer, Paul had at first asked, "Why me?" As forcefully as he could, Paul Johnson said to Jack, "Why *not* me?"

## THE MYSTERY OF SUFFERING

The notion that suffering is something unusual and that a person living a human life in union with God should somehow be immune to suffering does have biblical roots. Job and his three friends struggled with this problem as Job, whom God himself called "blameless and upright, a man who fears God and shuns evil" (Job 1:8), was struck with a series of dreadful disasters. The inner anguish experienced by Job and the growing hostility of Job's three friends are rooted in the conviction that God is a just judge. Since God is a moral being, with responsibility to judge his universe, it follows that he must punish evildoers and reward the good.

The timing and nature of the disasters that befell Job made it clear that some supernatural agency was involved. Job's suffering, then, was taken as evidence that God was punishing him, and he therefore must have done evil.

Job struggled against this conclusion, because his conscience was clear. Yet Job had no other explanation for what was happening, because Job too believed in a moral and just God. And it seemed to Job, as it did to his friends, that a God who would permit the good to suffer was acting unfairly.

Finally, in a pain-filled dialogue in which Job resisted the unrelenting accusations of his friends, a younger onlooker, Elihu, offered a partial solution. Human suffering is not *always* punishment. Sometimes God uses suffering in human life to instruct.

Elihu's contribution did not answer the question of why Job was suffering. But it did release Job and his friends from the trap of their limited reasoning about God. Yes, God is a moral judge who punishes evil and rewards good. But suffering is not always punishment. God may have a beneficial purpose in permitting even the good to know pain.

While our concept of God is one source of the notion that the good should not suffer, another source is seen in the Mosaic Covenant. This covenant (contract, agreement, promise, or oath) spelled out the conditions under which God would bless the nation Israel. If the people of God, as Moses said to them, "fully obey the LORD your God and carefully follow all his commands" (Deut. 28:1), they are promised a series of blessings. Their land and herds will be fruitful. Their enemies will be defeated. Every project will succeed, and "the LORD will grant you abundant prosperity" (v. 11). On the other hand, if the people were disobedient, poverty, plague, disease, defeat, and drought would come (vv. 15–29).

The notion that individual blessing and trial, like national blessing and suffering, hinged on living in obedient relationship with God was deeply ingrained in Hebrew thought. We see it in the question of Jesus' disciples on seeing a man who was blind from birth: "Rabbi, who sinned, this man or his parents, that he was born blind?" (John 9:2). We can imagine their blank, puzzled looks when Jesus answered, "Neither this man nor his parents sinned, but this happened so that the work of God might be displayed in his life" (v. 3).

We recognize the same pattern of thought in another incident, reported in Matthew 19. Jesus said to his disciples, "I tell you the truth, it is hard for a rich man to enter the kingdom of heaven" (v. 23). In absolute astonishment the disciples asked, "Who then can be saved?" (v. 25). The disciples assumed that wealth was the blessing of God and indicated that the rich were especially close to the Lord.

This thinking has a legitimate basis in the covenant, but it is not complete. Had the disciples and others paused to remember the prophets, they would have realized that these godly individuals were seldom rich or even popular. While in the normal course of events the godly were blessed under the law, there remained many exceptions in which suffering came not because of sin but "so that the work of God might be displayed" in a human life.

Perhaps even more significant is the fact that suffering has been the portion of humankind since Adam's fall. To be human is to be vulnerable and to know pain. From the beginning, the glory of God has been displayed, not in any immunity to suffering which God has granted his own, but in the unique good which God has worked in us through suffering.

*Suffering in the Old Testament.* Many different Hebrew words express the idea of pain and suffering. Some of them emphasize intensity, indicating that suffering can be agony or anguish. Others are synonyms that speak of suffering in a general way and usually can be used interchangeably, including words translated "affliction," "distress" or "trouble," and "sorrow."

These words encompass both bodily pain and mental anguish, with the latter considered to be more serious. Generally the Hebrew words for suffering draw attention to how tragedy affects human beings, not to the tragedies themselves. The devastating element is not so much the death or the illness but the doubts, fears, and trembling we experience as the pattern of our lives is broken and our hopes for the future are dashed.

The primary image which the Old Testament associates with human pain is that of childbirth. God said to Eve, "I will greatly increase your pains in childbearing; with pain you will give birth to children" (Gen. 3:16). And God said to Adam, "Through painful toil you will eat" (v. 17). This conjunction of pain and childbirth is theologically significant. Pain is traced back to the Fall. But pain, like the travail of childbirth, contains a promise. Out of suffering, a new life will be born. Out of suffering, God intends to bring good.

*Suffering in the New Testament.* The Greek language also contains a number of words for pain and suffering. One common term, *lypē,* is used in the Septuagint to render some thirteen different Hebrew words. In our New Testament versions this one term is translated "distress," "grief," "sorrow," and "pain" (both physical and emotional).

Most instances of the word *suffering* in the New Testament are translations of the Greek verb *paschō.* Strikingly, most uses of this word refer not to our suffering but to the death of Jesus and to events associated with it. In the strongest possible language we are reminded that Jesus suffered according to God's specific will (Matt. 16:21; Luke 17:25; 24:26; Acts 17:3) and that his suffering was in harmony with the prophetic word (Mark 9:12; Luke 24:26; Acts 3:18; 1 Peter 1:11).

The Greeks, who saw suffering as the grinding outcome of an impersonal fate, and the Jews, who saw suffering as evidence of God's displeasure, could hardly grasp this idea. In Jesus we see a suffering that is planned and purposive, a suffering not just human but divine. And because of Jesus we realize that we must develop a different perspective on suffering.

To live a human life in union with God is not to live without pain. To live such a life is to suffer, but to suffer "so that the work of God might be displayed" in our life.

## THE SUFFERING OF JESUS

*Old Testament Prophecy.* The image of a suffering savior was not unknown in Judaism. Many rabbis before Jesus' birth had identified Isaiah 53 as a messianic passage. There the prophet describes a servant who is sent by God. This servant of the Lord will be "a man of sorrows, and familiar with suffering" (53:3). Although he is completely innocent, God will "crush him and cause him to suffer" (v. 10). This suffering also draws on the image of giving birth: "After the suffering ["travail," KJV] of his soul, he will see the light of life and be satisfied; by his knowledge my righteous servant will justify many, and he will bear their iniquities" (v. 11).

This passage expresses clearly a biblical perspective on the suffering of believers. Servants of God may be "familiar with suffering," although innocent of wrongdoing. But after the suffering, and out of it, God's servants will emerge into light, aware that their suffering was redemptive. The Bible clearly contains a deeper, more significant strain of teaching on suffering than that which is suggested in the law as the normal course of events or that which is suggested in our reasoning from the morality of God.

*Jesus as sufferer.* We typically think of Jesus' suffering in theological terms, as his death for us. This view is appropriate, for the New Testament's use of *paschō* focuses our attention on the cross and the events leading up to it. We who see the focus of the ages in the cross of Christ and the shedding of his blood as redemption for humankind understandably think of his suffering in theological terms.

But in our exploration of Christian spirituality, it is important to see Jesus *as sufferer,* and his experience as a human event. Perhaps the key passages which help us to see Jesus in this light are those which describe Christ in Gethsemane. There, in great anguish, Jesus said to Peter and James and John, "My soul is overwhelmed with sorrow to the point of death" (Matt. 26:38). Luke adds this description: "Being in anguish, he [Jesus] prayed more earnestly, and his sweat was like drops of blood falling to the ground" (Luke 22:44).

All the torment and terror that humanity might experience focused in Jesus in that time of looking forward to the cross, knowing that a moment would come when the sinless Son of God would know the ultimate agony of being made sin for us (2 Cor. 5:21). Yet, in the moment of his anguish, Jesus reaffirmed his submission to God: "Not as I will, but as you will" (Matt. 26:39). In the time of his suffering, Jesus surrendered himself to the will of God.

Looking back, the writer of Hebrews says that "he offered

up prayers and petitions with loud cries and tears to the one who could save him from death, and he was heard because of his reverent submission'' (Heb. 5:7). He was heard, but he experienced no relief from the suffering. He was heard, but the agony of his death was itself the doorway to God's answer and to new life.

Peter describes Jesus' attitude this way: "When he suffered [at the hands of evil men] he made no threats. Instead, he entrusted himself to him who judges justly'' (1 Peter 2:23). Jesus surrendered himself to God, confident that God is just and that what God intended to accomplish through his pain was good.

*The example of Jesus' suffering.* The New Testament looks back on the death of Jesus as the key to our salvation. But the suffering of Jesus is often referred to as an example for believers, providing a new perspective on the meaning of suffering in human experience. Perhaps the central passage here is 1 Peter 3:8–4:6.

Peter begins this section with a call to do good and quotes from Psalm 34 to show that, because God does truly superintend the events of our lives, the one who would "see good days" must do good. He sums up the general course of a human being's life by his rhetorical question, "Who is going to harm you if you are eager to do good?" (3:13).

But then Peter deals with the exceptional case. He looks at a situation in which a person suffers "for [doing] what is right" (3:13). The Greek construction makes it clear that such suffering is considered unlikely, but clearly possible. Peter then tells the believers how to respond. Those who do right but yet suffer for it must (1) not be anxious or terrified, (2) acknowledge that Jesus is Lord, (3) be ready to explain the positive and expectant attitude this position enables them to display, and (4) continue to do good and so maintain a clear conscience.

Peter then argues that suffering for good is a manifest evidence of God's active will (3:17). He points to Jesus as an example, noting that Jesus, who did nothing wrong, suffered instead of the unrighteous who deserved it. Yet God used that suffering "to bring you to God" (v. 18).

In this passage, then, Peter holds Jesus up as a model and example. Jesus is the eternal proof that God uses the suffering of his servants redemptively. If, as we live a godly life, we suffer, we need not be fearful or anxious. We are to see in our suffering the hand of a sovereign God, and submitting to the Lord, we are to let God use our suffering as he chooses in order to bring forth his good.

## GROWTH THROUGH SUFFERING

In Scripture we see that to live a human life is to live subject to suffering and to pain. But in Jesus, we learn that to live a human life in union with God is to experience *purposive.* suffering which, by God's grace, gives birth to something good.

We are speaking here not of suffering that comes as a result of personal sin but of suffering that comes as we walk with the Lord, living close to him. *The Expository Dictionary of Bible Words* sums up its discussion of suffering as follows:

> The Christian, redeemed by Jesus, has been delivered, but not from earthly suffering. Rightly approached, "suffering produces perseverance; perseverance, character; and character, hope" (Ro 5:3–4). Confident of our inheritance through Jesus' resurrection, we rejoice "though now for a little while [we] may have had to suffer grief in all kinds of trials" (1 Pe 1:6). . . .
>
> Moreover, suffering should be viewed as fellowship (*koinōnia,* "participation"). Jesus suffered for his commitment to doing the will of God. A similar commitment on our part leads to a uniquely "Christian" suffering, which is linked with the completion of Jesus' mission on earth and which is in fact an aspect of fellowship (a close relationship) with our Lord (e.g., 1 Pe 4:1, 13; Php 3:10). Thus, truly Christian suffering is also purposive: it is for the sake of Jesus, his kingdom, and his righteousness (e.g., Ac 9:16; Php 1:29; 2 Th 1:5; 1 Pe 2:19; 3:14; 4:14, 16, 19) (p. 476).

Suffering, then, is something those who live a human life in union with God should expect. But this truth seems hard for many of us to grasp. Some even go so far as to teach that God intended Christians to be delivered from all sickness and pain. The promise of deliverance, they say, is guaranteed in the Atonement and may be claimed by faith. If only a person has enough faith, he or she will be released from every trial to which the rest of humanity is subject.

This teaching is attractive. But it is not true. It overlooks the mystery of the pain-filled good and the fact that even Jesus was subjected to the cross. If he suffered, why not me? In fact, the Bible says, "Christ suffered for you, leaving you an example, that you should follow in his steps" (1 Peter 2:21).

The teaching that Christians are exempt from suffering violates even our common sense. We parents constantly hear the cries and complaints of our children when we deny them something or insist on other things that cause them a momentary pain. We say no to their demand for candy. And we make them take bad-tasting medicine. As adults we know what they do not understand, that such pain is for their good, a part of growing up, a contribution to their maturity. Why, then, should we ever suppose that God, the good Father, would indulge our whims or permit us to avoid pains that are essential for our spiritual maturity? We, who insist our children submit to our wisdom and do what we say is good for them, should submit gladly to the wisdom of our God and accept what comes to us from his hand.

Both Testaments present suffering not only as something that is rooted in the human condition but as something that God uses for good in the lives of his people. And both use words for suffering which point out that the mental anguish involved is of greater significance than painful events. The wonderful gift of God to believers is that, through trust in him, Christians drain much of the anguish from pain and can find their relationship with the Lord a source of inner peace and joy.

How, then, as we live our human life in union with God, are we to deal with our own times of suffering? First, we must accept Peter's advice to his readers: "Do not be surprised at the painful trial you are suffering, as though something strange were happening to you. But rejoice that you participate in the sufferings of Christ, so that you may be overjoyed when his glory is revealed" (1 Peter 4:12–13). This invitation to welcome suffering seems strange, but it is repeated in James. "Consider it pure joy, my brothers, whenever you face trials of many kinds" (James 1:2). For the Christian, suffering is not an evil. It is simply a pain-filled good, and we are to learn to express thanks to God for suffering and the good we trust it will bring.

Second, we are to submit consciously to the Father's will. We can beg for relief as Jesus did or as Paul did when he was afflicted with what he calls a "thorn in the flesh" (2 Cor. 12:7). But we must also express our desire that God's will be done, confident that his will is good, pleasing, and perfect (Rom. 12:2). As we submit, we come to the attitude that the apostle Paul adopted.

Three times I pleaded with the Lord to take it away from me. But he said to me, "My grace is sufficient for you, for my power is made perfect in weakness." Therefore I will boast all the more gladly about my weaknesses, so that Christ's power may rest on me. That is why, for Christ's sake, I delight in weaknesses, in insults, in hardships, in persecutions, in difficulties. For when I am weak, then I am strong" (2 Cor. 12:8–10).

When I am weak, I surrender to God's will, and when I am at the end of my resources, I rely on God's power.

What will enable us to trust God in this way? What will release us from the fears and terrors associated with human vulnerability to suffering and pain? Only our conviction that Jesus is Lord. Only our belief that he who loved us and suffered for us has been raised to the place of all power.

## PROBE

**exercises for personal development**
**case histories**
**thought provokers**

1. The following verses contribute to a biblical perspective on suffering. Each is worth committing to memory for later meditation.

   We also rejoice in our sufferings, because we know that suffering produces perseverance; perseverance, character; and character, hope (Rom. 5:3–4).

   It is commendable if a man bears up under the pain of unjust suffering because he is conscious of God. . . . If you suffer for doing good and you endure it, this is commendable before God. To this you were called, because Christ suffered for you, leaving you an example, that you should follow in his steps (1 Peter 2:19–21).

   When he [Jesus] suffered, he made no threats. Instead, he entrusted himself to him who judges justly (v. 23).

   Since Christ suffered in his body, arm yourselves also with the same attitude, because he who has suffered in his body is done with sin. As a result, he does not live the rest of his earthly life for evil human desires, but rather for the will of God (4:1–2).

   Dear friends, do not be surprised at the painful trial you are suffering, as though something strange were happening to you. But rejoice that you participate in the sufferings of Christ, so that you may be overjoyed when his glory is revealed (vv. 12–13).

   The God of all grace, who called you to his eternal glory in Christ, after you have suffered a little while, will himself restore you and make you strong, firm and steadfast (5:10).

Now if we are children, then we are heirs—heirs of God and co-heirs with Christ, if indeed we share in his sufferings in order that we may share in his glory. I consider that our present sufferings are not worth comparing with the glory that will be revealed in us (Rom. 8:17–18).

2. Psalm 73 reports the envy of Asaph, who compared the prosperity of the wicked with his own personal struggles and pain. The first part of the psalm reports the writer's thoughts and feelings (vv. 1–16). A turning point comes when he relates his experience to God and has the sudden insight that the prosperity of the wicked is "slippery ground" (vv. 17–20). With this insight he realizes that his envy and his view of suffering were "senseless and ignorant" and that his pangs have actually made him more aware of God (vv. 21–28). His troubles have been a pain-filled good and have caused him to realize that "it is good to be near God" (v. 28).

Develop a sermon or a lesson plan showing how you might communicate the message of Psalm 73 to those who are presently undergoing suffering.

3. What are you suffering now for which you can thank God and consciously submit to his will?

Remember that it is not wrong to express pain to God or to ask for relief. In your pain, however, it is important that you consciously submit to God and that you find comfort in your relationship with the Lord and the conviction that even the greatest of human agony is intended as a pain-filled good.

# 15

---

# COMPASSION

I remember how uncertain I felt when a close friend from our Bible study group lost his brother, a Missionary Aviation Fellowship flyer, in West Irian. I went to visit Paul and, as I knocked on the door, did not know how I should feel or act. Were Paul and his brother close? Paul had never mentioned him. How did Paul and his family feel about the death? Should I be formal? Or give him a hug?

Looking back, I see how badly I handled that visit. I was reserved, holding back my feelings, watching for clues in Paul's behavior that would tell me how he felt. But I saw no clues there, and so, after an uncomfortable few minutes, I left, without knowing anything of his pain and with him wondering if I really cared.

Jesus never had my problem. He always knew what to do. One day when a leper hesitantly approached and, on his knees, said, "If you are willing, you can make me clean," Jesus looked at the man, isolated from others by the nature of his disease, and was "filled with compassion" (Mark 1:40–41). Then "Jesus reached out his hand and touched the man," saying, "I am willing" and "Be clean" (v. 41).

Jesus might have healed with a word. The disease would have fled without the touch. But Jesus knew that, as much as this man needed the healing of his body, he needed equally the healing for his soul. He needed a sign of release from the rejection and the horror his disease generated in others.

With his touch Jesus healed the inner man. With his touch

Jesus welcomed the leper back into the human family, affirming him as loved and valued as a person. Jesus' touch restored his dignity and showed an acceptance of him as an individual, no matter how repelling his disease.

## SUFFERING AND COMPASSION

When we experience suffering, we are to welcome it as a pain-filled good. We are to submit to God's will and, as Jesus, to commend ourselves to a God we trust. This attitude, which goes far beyond resignation, sees in suffering an opportunity to experience deeply the meaning of our union with God.

In sharp contrast to our response to personal suffering, when we see the suffering of others, we are *not* to treat it as a good. We are to treat it as an evil and are to respond, as Jesus did, with compassion.

*Compassion in the Old Testament.* Two Hebrew words are often translated "compassion" in our versions. One is *ḥāmal,* which is also rendered "have pity" or "spare." This word expresses an emotional response that results, or may result, in action to meet another's need. For example, *ḥāmal* moved Pharaoh's daughter to draw the baby Moses from the Nile and raise him as her own. The other Hebrew word is *rāḥām* ("love deeply"). Such deep love also moves one to have mercy or to be compassionate. This word and its derivatives occur 133 times in the Old Testament, nearly three-quarters of which indicate God's love for human beings.

*Compassion in the New Testament.* Three different Greek words are translated "compassion." The least important, *oiktirmos,* is seldom found. The word most used in the Greek is *eleos,* which is usually translated "mercy" rather than "compassion." Originally *eleos* indicated only the emotion aroused by contact with a suffering person. By New Testament times the concept had been broadened and, with the emotion, suggested a compassionate response: a person who felt for and with a sufferer would be moved to offer aid.

This word is linked with Jesus in two ways. First, we often meet persons in the Gospels who cried out to Jesus, "Have mercy on me" (e.g., Matt. 15:22; 17:15). In such cases Jesus responded and met the need. Second, Jesus often encouraged his followers to be merciful. The merciful, according to Jesus, are blessed (5:7), and Christ's followers are commanded, "Be merciful, just as your Father is merciful" (Luke 6:36). The religious leaders of Jesus' time were criticized by the Lord because they were preoccupied with the minutiae of Old Testament law and "neglected the more important matters of the law—justice, mercy and faithfulness" (Matt. 23:23).

Numerous incidents show that those who live in union with God will identify with the need and will respond to the suffering of the oppressed (e.g., Matt. 9:9–13; 12:1–7; 18:21–33). Mercy is something God extends generously to us. And mercy is a quality which God seeks in those who live in union with him.

The last Greek word translated "compassion" is the verb *splanchnizomai*. This word and its related noun form are found just twenty-three times in the New Testament, almost always in important contexts. Originally, *splanchnizomai* referred to the inner parts of the body and gradually came to indicate the seat of such emotions as love, pity, and compassion. This word has special significance because the Gospels use it in speaking of Jesus' having compassion on someone in need.

When Jesus is moved by compassion, the event is often the turning point in another's life. It was thus for the leper who was healed by Jesus' touch. As Christ traveled and saw the milling crowds, he "had compassion on them, because they were . . . like sheep without a shepherd" (Matt. 9:36). Shortly afterward, Jesus gave his disciples power to heal and sent them throughout the land (Matt. 10:1–42). The compassion Jesus felt for the crowds moved him to take an action which changed many lives.

The active aspect of compassion is also seen in two parables of Jesus. Matthew 18 tells of a king who was owed an unpayable debt. When the debtor begged for time, the king was so moved by pity (*splanchnizomai*) that he canceled the debt. In Luke 15 we read of the Prodigal Son. When he finally came to himself, the son was ready to accept a place as a hired man with his father. But the father was "filled with compassion for him" (v. 20) and welcomed him home as a son. In both cases, the compassion one person felt for another, like the compassion Jesus felt for those who came to him, moved him to action that changed the course of life for the sufferer.

From Scripture we see very clearly that the godly response to the suffering of others is a compassion that stimulates action designed to change the life of the sufferer. While we face our own suffering with trust, submitting to God's good will, we are never complacent about the suffering of others. We never hesitate or have theological doubts. We react with a concerted effort to relieve human pain.

## GROWTH IN COMPASSION

To live a human life means not only to suffer but also to touch the lives of many sufferers. To live our human life in union with God means to respond to them with compassion. Two things seem to make it hard for us to open our lives to those who suffer: the amount of pain we can bear and the amount of revulsion we feel.

Ever since childhood it has been hard for me to watch a missions film or to see scenes of starvation in Africa; it hurts to look at the victims of terrorism, strewn in some bloody airport lobby. There is too much pain there, too much hurt. I want to look away, to insulate myself, to close my heart to people who are, after all, strangers. It is much more comfortable for me to close my heart. I have enough pain in my life—as everyone does—so that opening myself up to feel with the hurting seems just too great a burden to bear.

Yet, when I find myself creating inner barriers to emotion, I have to remember that Jesus did not live this way. Christ looked at the crowds and at individuals, and he felt their suffering. Jesus let his heart fill with a compassionate love, which led him to caring action. Jesus did not hold back but opened himself to the suffering of others, even when his empathy led only to futile tears, as when he wept over Jerusalem (Matt. 23:37–39).

There is also something in suffering that repels. I can identify with those who drew back in horror from leprosy, for I confess similar feelings about AIDS and the sin of homosexuality. It is such a temptation to dismiss that dread disease, generated in the promiscuity of the homosexual community, as a divine judgment and thus to try to justify my feelings. But the only emotion that is truly justified by the sight of *any* suffering is compassion.

AIDS may well be a divine judgment on the guilty. And in the innocent who contract it, AIDS may be a modern statement that the innocent in a society which sanctions sin will suffer too. But I am not called by God to judge sinners. As Paul writes, "What business is it of mine to judge those outside the church? . . . God will judge those outside" (1 Cor. 5:12–13).

Instead, as one who lives in union with Jesus and who seeks to express his life in this world, I can only care about the suffering. I must learn to put aside my defenses and open my heart to pain. I am to feel with and for my fellow human beings. I am to have compassion.

Each of us knows pressures such as these that lead us to build emotional barriers to block out the suffering of others. Yet if we are to grow in spirituality and to live our human life in union with God, we must learn to feel with others, and we must begin to respond to them. I list here three suggestions for learning compassion.

*Sense the pain of others.* We can consciously choose to open ourselves up to feel with and for others. When we read a newspaper or watch TV, rather than automatically insulating ourselves against those who are suffering, we can open ourselves up. We can stop and seek to sense their pain. Instead of dismissing them as "others," we can identify with them. As we begin to sense and feel their pain and feel frustration because there seems nothing for us to do, we *can* pray. Opening ourselves up to others' pain and making it a habit to pray when we feel their suffering is a vital step in developing Christian compassion.

*Visit ones who are suffering.* We need to expose ourselves to personal contact with the suffering. We can visit suffering people in our church. We can go to the hospitals and the prisons, or help at the shelters for unwed mothers or battered wives. Again, there may not be much that we can do. But a touch, a word, may mean as much to a sufferer as Christ's touch meant to the leper. As we grow in compassion, we will also be led by God's Spirit to appropriate ways to help.

*Give to meet needs.* In the Old Testament, giving was regulated by the law. Each person put aside a set percentage of his or her income. These funds were used institutionally for the support of those serving God in the temple. Another tithe was collected every third year for local distribution to the poor. In the New Testament, however, there is no temple or priesthood to support. Instead, giving to meet human needs receives heightened emphasis. Giving is *koinōnia,* "sharing," and sharing flows out of an awareness of the suffering and needs of brothers and sisters in Christ.

We can trace this emphasis throughout the New Testament. The earliest Christians practiced "selling their possessions and goods [to give] to anyone as he had need" (Acts 2:45). James insists that a person who sees a brother or sister in need must do more than offer good wishes. If he or she "does nothing about his physical needs, what good is it?" (James 2:16).

John, the Apostle of Love, says,

Jesus Christ laid down his life for us. And we ought to lay down our lives for our brothers. If anyone has material possessions and sees his brother in need but has no pity [compassion] on him, how can the love of God be in him? Dear children, let us not love with words or tongue but with actions and in truth (1 John 3:16–18).

Compassion may not lead you or me, as it has Mother Teresa, to a lifetime of self-giving in India. But opening ourselves to the suffering of others, identifying with them, and beginning to respond will undoubtedly involve a personal cost. We will be moved by compassion to give ourselves and then to give of our means. In the giving we will lose nothing; we will only gain. For in feeling with, and responding to, those who suffer, we will discover who we were intended to be in Jesus Christ. We will discover more of what it means to live a human life in union with God.

We human beings are vulnerable to suffering. It is part of the human condition, and no one living will avoid pain. Living a human life means that we must and will suffer. Living a human life in union with God means that we come to understand and respond to suffering in a godly way, seeing it as pain-filled good in our own lives and acting with compassion to relieve it in the lives of others.

### Table 10. Suffering

|  | Our own | Of others |
|---|---|---|
| Misunderstood as | Punishment | Punishment |
| To be seen as | Pain-filled good | Pain-filled good |
| God | Sovereignly involved | Sovereignly involved |
| Our response | Pray<br>Submit to God<br>Keep on doing good | Have Compassion<br>Act to relieve the suffering |

**PROBE**

**exercises for personal development**
**case histories**
**thought provokers**

1. Take five minutes a day for at least two weeks simply to expose yourself to the pain of strangers. Select a newspaper article that describes suffering. Read it carefully, then pause to feel with and for the persons involved. Let Jesus' own compassion fill you and overflow in prayer.

2. Read though one of the Gospels thoughtfully. Look for incidents in which Jesus comes into contact with a person who is suffering.

   How does Jesus speak with those who are suffering? Can you sense his tone of voice? How do people express their anguish? What responses does Jesus make to such people?

   You might find it helpful to cut out the passages you located and collect them in a booklet that puts each incident—and your written observations—on a separate page.

   Return to this booklet often, to read and meditate, asking the Holy Spirit to fill you with Jesus' own compassion for those in pain.

3. The New Testament's central passage on giving is 2 Corinthians 8–9. It emphasizes that Christian giving (*koinōnia*, "sharing") flows from an awareness of the needs of others, balanced against the believer's ability to meet his or her own needs. This passage makes it very clear that awareness of the suffering and needs of others is a prime stimulus to giving.

   Suppose that you were on the stewardship committee of your church. From 2 Corinthians 8–9 and the concept of compassion, can you develop a workable stewardship program for you church?

4. Work with others to define the behavior and words that communicate compassion to others. What might the author have done to communicate to the Paul mentioned at the beginning of this chapter? Have you ever known anyone who you sensed had compassion on you? What helped to communicate this attitude to you? See if you and others can draw up a list of "practices that communicate compassion" that might prove helpful to a person like the author, who failed in this incident to show caring.

5. Begin to expose yourself to the needs of others in your community. Work with others to develop a list of "places that Christians should visit" to develop sensitivity to suffering, and seek God's direction for compassionate ministries.

# Section F: Holiness

The sullen Cain was angry. What was wrong with the fruit and vegetables he offered God? They were the best he had, and he was proud of them. Why should he have to trade his fruits to Abel for a lamb and bring God an animal sacrifice?

Then the Lord spoke to Cain. "If you do what is right, will you not be accepted?" (Gen. 4:7). These words tell us two things. God had previously instructed the first family in what constituted an acceptable sacrifice. And human beings who seek to live in union with God must "do what is right," for our God is a holy God. Those who wish to walk with God must walk in holiness.

Holiness is itself a mystery. In the Old Testament the "holy" is the realm of the sacred, of persons and places and things set apart to God, who is himself the essence of the holy. God's holiness is shown in two primary ways: in the divine judgment that flames to consume sinners and in the moral demands expressed in God's law which unveil the divine character. The second aspect is emphasized in the New Testament. God has given us his Holy Spirit. God's people are his "saints"—literally, his "holy ones." The glory of God's own purity is to shine through the character of human beings who live in union with God.

# 16

---

# PERSONAL
# MORALITY

I was more than a little shocked. There she was, in a seminary classroom, hotly defending the right of young people to live together.

When I asked, "But what about moral standards?" she responded contemptuously. "Morality isn't about sex. Morality is about unjust wars and poverty. Morality is about South American dictators and persecution. Morality is about politicians who lie to us. Morality is about companies that raise prices in black areas because the people can't go outside their community to shop. That's what morality is about."

Her words were uttered in the late 1960s and did not necessarily reflect the view of the seminary where she and I were studying. Those were Viet Nam days, when people were questioning and doubting absolutes rather than accepting them. And those were days when "Morality" was a public rather than a private issue. Then sex, like so many other "personal" things, was assumed to be a matter of indifference to a God caught up in concern about Watergate and napalm and inner-city life.

Actually, it has never been easy to argue morality from Scripture. In the New International Version, for example, the word *moral* appears only once (James 1:21), and *morality* does not appear at all. People who want proof texts on moral and immoral behavior have to look beyond those terms. But when we do go deeper, we find that the Bible does have much to say about personal morality, in both a negative and a positive sense.

## MORALITY IN THE SCRIPTURES

To build a biblical understanding of morality, we need to
see its association with the broad biblical concepts of evil and of
holiness.

*Morality and evil.* The notion of evil is expressed throughout the Old Testament in the term *ra'* and its cognate words.
This word group is used in two primary ways. First, any act that
violates God's intentions for human beings is "evil." This
aspect of evil assumes that God alone is capable of making
moral judgments. The error of my classmate in limiting morality
to social issues and in ruling out personal ethics was simply that
the God who has spoken out about social evils has defined good
and evil in the personal arena as well.

It is clear from Scripture that moral wrongs are to be
measured not by human standards but by what is "evil in the
eyes of the LORD" (Deut. 4:25; cf. Num. 32:13; Judg. 2:11;
2 Sam. 3:39). It is also clear that the God who is the moral
measure of all things has unveiled his standards. As the prophet
Micah says, "He has showed you, O man, what is good" (Mic.
6:8). In God's written revelation he has made plain what is right
and what is wrong, providing objective standards against which
to measure our private as well as our public acts.

But *ra'* has an additional meaning, for it also describes the
consequences of doing what God says is wrong. When people
make wrong moral choices and do what is "evil in God's eyes,"
the consequences are tragedy, distress, and emotional as well as
physical harm.

This fact suggests something of the beauty of the good. God
does not simply impose meaningless standards on humanity.
God, in defining moral good and evil, expresses his love, for the
way of good is the way to life and peace, while a rejection of the
good leads human beings to misery and pain. Moses said to
Israel, after reviewing God's law, "See, I set before you today
life and prosperity [*tôb*, "good"], death and destruction [*ra'*,
"evil"]" (Deut. 30:15). The good that is represented in God's
standards means prosperity; the evil that is its dark reverse
means death and the destruction of human hopes.

*Morality and holiness in the Old Testament.* The Old
Testament links morality not only with good and evil but also
with holiness. Holiness itself is linked in Scripture with two
aspects of God's nature. The first is God's essential and awe-
inspiring splendor as the Holy One. This aspect of God's nature

is expressed in bursts of divine judgment, flaming against those who dishonor him or his name. His splendor is implied in the fire on Mount Sinai and in the quaking of the earth when God gave Moses the law. It is displayed in acts of judgment against those who dishonored God. When two of Aaron's sons disregarded the ritual regulations governing the worship of God, fire consumed them for treating him with contempt. The Lord then announced, "Among those who approach me I will show myself holy; in the sight of all the people I will be honored" (Lev. 10:3). The Holy One is splendid, to be approached with awe and wonder and to be honored in every way.

The second aspect of God's nature that is linked with holiness in the Old Testament is the moral. In Leviticus 19:2, for example, Moses is told, "Speak to the entire assembly of Israel and say to them: 'Be holy because I, the LORD your God, am holy.'" The commands that follow this injunction are not ritual but are moral. They speak of idolatry, theft, lying, fraud, slander, and revenge. Their positive force is summed up in the chapter's command to love one's neighbor, and again and again the commands are punctuated with the reminder, "I am the LORD." In this Old Testament passage and in many others, God's holiness is wedded to his moral character. Morality is an expression of holiness, and holiness is in essence moral.

The splendor of God, as revealed when he lashes out against sinners, is intended to underline the significance of morality. Anything associated with God is of ultimate concern to human beings. The punishment of ritual violations reminded Israel of this fact; he must be honored at all costs. As God is to be treated with utmost respect, so his call to personal holiness demands our careful attention.

To live a human life brings us again and again into situations in which moral choices must be made. To live a human life in union with God requires that our choices be holy, reflections of the holiness of our God.

*Morality and holiness in the New Testament.* Holiness in the Old Testament, besides being linked with God's intrinsic glory and with God's essential morality, is also linked with separation.

Anything designated as "holy" in Israel was shifted from the realm of the secular to that of the sacred. Holy things— whether persons, places, days, or objects—were so different from the common that there could be no association between them and the ordinary aspects of daily life. The nation itself, a holy people set apart to God, was to isolate itself from other peoples, and no marriages could take place between an Israelite and an unconverted pagan. In time, "separation" seemed to many Jews to be the essence of holiness, and keeping the details of the divine law was more important than morality.

But with the New Testament era a dynamic new emphasis is introduced. Holiness is *essentially* moral, but morality calls for both separation from sin and an active involvement with sinners and with the world. The Old Testament concept of separation as a rigid distinction between the secular and the sacred gives way to a powerful new morality. This change is important, because Christians live not as a separate nation but scattered through every society and culture. Paul wrote the Corinthians about what this scattering implies.

> I have written you in my letter not to associate with
> sexually immoral people—not at all meaning the people of
> this world who are immoral, or the greedy and swindlers,
> or idolaters. In that case you would have to leave this
> world (1 Cor. 5:9–10).

Rather than treating holiness as something which isolates God's people from others among whom they live, the New Testament unveils a concept of holiness as a dynamic morality which expresses this aspect of God's character in contact with, rather than by isolation from, the common and profane. This concept is important. Believers are to be separate from evil but not from evil people.

Morality and holiness are still intimately linked, but personal morality calls for active involvement in the ordinary and the secular dimensions of human experience. Morality still implies separation from evil acts. Like the Old Testament, the New contains prohibitions. For instance, believers are to reject decisively "sexual immorality, impurity, lust, evil desires and greed" (Col. 3:5). But New Testament moral and holiness teaching emphasizes positive qualities. Paul continues,

> Therefore, as God's chosen people, holy and dearly loved,
> clothe yourselves with compassion, kindness, humility,
> gentleness and patience. Bear with each other and forgive
> whatever grievances you may have against one another.
> Forgive as the Lord forgave you. And over all these virtues
> put on love, which binds them all together in perfect unity
> (Col. 3:12–14).

New Testament holiness is a powerful, dynamic, positive morality. It is displayed as we live involved lives in the real world, even though our "real world" is a secular and often sinful society. This theme is repeated so often in the New Testament that it is impossible to mistake. For instance, Ephesians 4:17–30 contains a list of characteristics of the immoral life. Then Paul concludes,

> Get rid of all bitterness, rage and anger, brawling and slander, along with every form of malice. Be kind and compassionate to one another, forgiving each other, just as in Christ God forgave you.
>
> Be imitators of God, therefore, as dearly loved children and live a life of love, just as Christ loved us and gave himself up for us as a fragrant offering and sacrifice to God.
>
> But among you there must not be even a hint of sexual immorality, or of any kind of impurity, or of greed, because these are improper for God's holy people (Eph. 4:31–5:3).

So my classmate was wrong about personal morality. Personal morality *is* taught in Scripture. But in much of our thinking about personal morality, we too are apt to be wrong. We all too often think of morality in terms of negative restrictions. We seldom see morality in terms of a holiness which is dynamic and positive and calls for active involvement with the sinners of our world. Christian holiness and personal morality do involve a complete rejection of all things that God says are evil. But they also involve a complete commitment to a caring, loving way of life.

## HOLINESS IN JESUS' LIFE

The religious leaders of Jesus' time were disturbed by the young rabbi. The Pharisees particularly were upset and antagonistic, in large part because they did not understand Jesus' kind of holiness. He did things they saw as unlawful and immoral.

We need to remember that the Pharisees saw "holiness" in the light of the Old Testament emphasis on strict separation between the sacred and the secular. And so when Jesus healed on the Sabbath, a day the Pharisees believed must be set aside for rest, they were angry. They challenged Jesus with the question, "Is it lawful to heal on the Sabbath?" (Matt. 12:10).

These men had no answer when Jesus replied simply, "If any of you has a sheep and it falls into a pit on the Sabbath, will you not take hold of it and lift it out? How much more valuable is a man than a sheep! Therefore it is lawful to do good on the Sabbath" (Matt. 12:11–12). Jesus' dynamic concept of holiness, which measured it by doing good, was new and unsettling.

Another time Jesus went to a party at the house of Levi, a tax collector, who had invited "many tax collectors and 'sinners'" to come and meet the Lord (Mark 2:15). When the Pharisees saw Jesus mixing with these guests, they asked Jesus' disciples why he ate with such undesirables. Their idea of holiness called for isolation from those whom they judged immoral, for they were sure they themselves would be polluted by such contact. But Jesus later told them, "It is not the healthy who need a doctor, but the sick. I have not come to call the righteous, but sinners" (Mark 2:17). Again we see the essential conflict in concepts. To Jesus, the morality of holiness was active, demanding that he reach out to bring health and wholeness to sinners. To the Pharisees, the morality of holiness was defensive, a careful avoidance of things and persons which might pollute them.

The same conflict is illustrated in another incident. A Pharisee had invited Jesus to eat with him. As they were reclining at the table, a "woman who had lived a sinful life" slipped in (Luke 7:37). Weeping, she began to wet Jesus' feet with her tears and dry them with her hair, as she poured an expensive perfume on them. The Pharisee was scandalized. He thought, "If this man were a prophet, he would know who is touching him and what kind of woman she is—that she is a sinner" (v. 39). Implicit in his thought was the assumption that a truly holy person would quickly draw back at a sinner's touch.

Again Jesus confronted this assumption. He spoke of two men who had debts canceled, the one a great debt and the other a lesser one. Which would most love and appreciate the gracious lender? The Pharisee answered that it would be the one who had been forgiven most. Jesus then turned to the woman and said, "Your sins are forgiven. . . . Your faith has saved you; go in peace" (Luke 7:48–50).

To Jesus, the sinner's touch was neither repugnant nor impure. Jesus was secure in his own holiness. Nothing outside could contaminate him, for he remained committed to God and, in that commitment, reached out to show sinners the beauty of holiness. God's moral character, expressed in judgment in the Old Testament, is expressed as well in loving forgiveness in the New.

Jesus' holiness, then, was expressed not by withdrawal but by involvement. It could not be corrupted by contact but was so dynamic and powerful that contact with it could actually transform the sinner. Jesus' holiness was rooted in his union with God and his commitment to please God and was expressed not only in rejecting evil but in actively doing good. In Jesus, who lived his human life in perfect union with God, we learn the true nature of holiness and of personal morality.

## GROWTH IN PERSONAL MORALITY

Living a human life brings us into countless situations in which we must make moral choices. Some of these choices will involve temptation to do evil; some, the opportunity to do good. Living our human life in union with God means both that we will refuse evil and that we will reach out to do good. Today we need to model our notion of personal morality not on the Pharisees, who saw morality only in the negative as withdrawal from evil, but on Jesus, whose moral life was marked by an active, positive reaching out to do good.

Peter calls for just such a balanced holiness. Throughout 1 Peter, the negatives and the positives of personal morality are held in careful balance. We can chart Peter's vision of holiness and personal morality as follows:

| *Negatives* | *Positives* |
|---|---|
| Do not conform to the evil desires you had when you lived in ignorance (1:14). | Just as he who called you is holy, so be holy in all you do (1:15). |
| Rid yourselves of all malice and all deceit, hypocrisy, envy, and slander of every kind (2:1). | Crave pure spiritual milk, so that by it you may grow up in your salvation (2:2). |
| Abstain from sinful desires, which war against your soul (2:11). | Live such good lives among the pagans that, though they accuse you of doing wrong, they may see your good deeds and glorify God on the day he visits us 2:12). |

We are to reject the old desires and to abstain from evil. But true morality, true holiness, must also be expressed in positive good, characterized by good deeds that bring glory to God as they reveal the inner nature of his holiness.

Table 10 summarizes the teaching on holiness in various sections of Scripture. While the moral element of holiness was always expressed in the divine law, the emphasis *as understood by Israel* was on the ceremonial, or ritual, aspect of holiness. This aspect was rightly understood as calling for a separation of the secular and the sacred, but not to the extent that the positive moral qualities also taught in the law should be disregarded, as often happened in Israel (cf. Matt. 23:23–24).

### Table 11. Biblical Holiness

| Aspect | Old Testament | Jesus | Epistles |
|---|---|---|---|
| Requirements | Ritual and moral | Moral | Moral |
| Emphasis | Ritual | Moral requirements | Moral requirements |
| Expression of emphasis | Separation | Doing good | Refusing evil; doing good |
| Quality of revelation | Splendor | Beauty | Beauty |
| Mode of revelation | Judgment on violators | Forgiveness | Christlikeness |
| Effects | Moral and ceremonial separation | Transformation of sinners; revelation of God's beauty and love | Transformation of sinners; revelation of God's love and true goodness |

With Jesus, however, the emphasis shifted to the moral element always present in the idea of holiness. That moral element was further defined as Jesus lived his human life in union with God, as an active involvement in doing good. Jesus' holiness' was of such a nature that he could associate with sinners without contamination. Indeed, the beauty of his holiness was such that, rather than feeling condemned, sinners were drawn to him. The dynamic holiness of Jesus, expressed as he went about doing good, unveiled the beauty of God in a powerful, fresh way and drew people to him.

Christian holiness is seen everywhere in the New Testament to be modeled on Christ. The Old Testament's ritual elements are put aside, and with them the expression of holiness as separation or isolation. Like our Lord, the believer who lives a human life in union with God is called to do good in active involvement with others in this world. I consider four suggestions for developing an adequate morality, in view of morality's roots in holiness.

*Examine one's concept of moral action.* The Pharisees' view of morality was inadequate. It stressed the ritual and mistook isolation from evildoers as separation from evil acts. To the Pharisees, the needs of the cripple that Jesus healed on the Sabbath were unimportant, as were Jesus' motives for sharing a meal with tax collectors and sinners. All too often our view of needy people is colored by the distorted image of the Pharisee. We too may sum up holiness and morality as some list of dos and don'ts and never see it as a positive dynamic which impels us to reach out in love. We may isolate ourselves, emotionally if not physically, from the modern sinners whom Christ yearns to touch through our own positive and caring deeds.

If such has been our approach to personal morality, we need to continue to reject evil. But we need to break out of the self-imposed boundaries of a "separation" mentality.

*Focus on positive morality.* Paul describes the spirit of the law as one of love. He writes,

> Let no debt remain outstanding, except the continuing debt to love one another, for he who loves his fellow man has fulfilled the law. The commandments, "Do not commit adultery," "Do not murder," "Do not steal," "Do not covet," and whatever other commandment there may be, are summed up in this one rule: "Love your neighbor as yourself." Love does no harm to its neighbor. Therefore love is the fulfillment of the law (Rom. 13:8–10).

Christian morality is active and positive. Like the holiness which it expresses, Christian morality is a dynamic force, compelling us to reach out to others and to do good.

Jesus himself helps us to understand the full implications of the command Paul has quoted. When asked a question about the obligation to love one's neighbor, Jesus told the story of the Good Samaritan, a man willing to take risks to help an enemy. How powerfully Jesus' own life demonstrated this principle. The love that led Jesus to enter our world, to associate with sinners while here, and, ultimately, to die for a humanity which was his enemy reveals the true nature of personal morality. We are neither holy nor moral, even though we resist doing evil, if we have not chosen actively to do good.

*Follow Jesus' style in relationships.* We need to visualize Jesus, comfortable and laughing as he lunches with sinners. We need to sense his friendliness, his warmth. We need to see Jesus accepting the touch of the prostitute in that Pharisee's home, responsive to her need, despite the condemnation of those who watched. We need to realize, as we meditate on what Jesus did, that sinners hold no threat to the holy. The person who lives in union with Jesus is hardly attracted to gross sins.

*Befriend the person nearby.* We need to reexamine our attitude toward individuals with whom God has placed us in contact. Has the filthy mouth of a co-worker so offended us that we draw back instead of reach out? Has the immoral life style of an acquaintance led us to condemn rather than to care? If so, we need to remember that Christian morality teaches us to reject sin but at the same time to befriend the sinner so that the beauty of holiness can be seen in us.

Living a human life brings us constantly into situations and relationships in which moral choices must be made. The person who lives a human life in union with God will refuse evil but will also reach out to do good.

## PROBE

**exercises for personal development**
**case histories**
**thought provokers**

1. Explore the Bible's statements of the negatives of personal morality. Look at this list, drawn from Ephesians, Colossians, and Galatians. How many of them has your relationship with Jesus enabled you to overcome?

| | |
|---|---|
| sexual immorality | debauchery |
| impurity | hatred |
| greed | fits of rage |
| obscenity | selfish ambition |
| lust | envy |
| evil desires | drunkenness |
| anger | orgies |
| malice | slander |
| filthy language | lies |

First steps toward personal morality will be taken by rejecting such sins. You can be thankful and glad as you do overcome them. But do not fall into the trap of supposing that Christian morality involves only avoiding such sins.

2. Here is a list of positive moral qualities, drawn from the same three New Testament letters. Their presence is a mark of Christian spirituality. Which of them has God been building into your life and relationships?

truthful speech          love
kindness                 peacefulness
compassion               kindness
forgiveness              goodness
self-sacrifice           faithfulness
humility                 gentleness
patience                 bearing with others
doing good

These positive moral qualities are to be expressed in our relationships with others, both within and outside the body of Christ. Christian personal morality is marked by the presence of these positive qualities as well as the absence of the negative ones.

3. From the list in point 2 above, select one or two of the positive qualities that you want to develop further in your life. Try jotting down every way that you can envision each of the two qualities expressed. Try to picture how each might shape your relationship with different individuals.

As you build an image of a quality, begin asking God to express himself through that quality in you. Meditate on Jesus and on how his life expressed the quality you seek. Trust God's Spirit to express his holiness in and through you in this special way.

4. In most cases when *holy* appears in the New Testament, it is in the name of the Holy Spirit. And in most cases where the Spirit is mentioned, the word *holy* accompanies it. The *Expository Dictionary of Bible Words* explains,

This title is more than a reference to the Spirit's deity; it is more specifically a reference to the nature of his work.

Old Testament cultic holiness focused attention on holy persons (priests), places (the temple, Jerusalem), and things (the altar, the temple furniture, etc.). In the New Testament the sacred is no longer seen in places or things. The focus of the holy shifts dramatically to persons. "Don't you know," Paul writes emotionally, "that you yourselves are God's temple and that God's Spirit lives in you?" (1 Cor. 3:16). In the New Testament, holiness is linked with the Spirit's working and with the product of his work within human beings. The Spirit is the Holy Spirit because he himself is the source of the holy. Thus New Testament holiness is always rooted in a relationship with Jesus and with the Spirit, whom Jesus sends to be within every believer (p. 341).

Look up references to the Holy Spirit in the Epistles. What do you learn from studying the context of such passages about Christian holiness and personal morality?

5. Read through the Gospels and cut from them incidents which show Jesus' relationships with persons and which suggest to you his unique approach to holiness and personal morality. Make up a booklet by pasting each gospel incident on a sheet of paper and jotting down your own observations. Use the booklet in your personal meditations to make yourself more sensitive to the dynamic quality that infuses Christian morality.

# 17

## DOING JUSTICE

I remember hearing this story from a Southern Baptist friend one day in Nashville.

> It seems there was a river flowing past a town where Christians lived. Down that river came a growing stream of bodies—some were dead; others were terribly injured. The Christians, deeply moved by the suffering, set a watch for the living. When an injured person floated by, they rescued that one and nursed him or her back to health.
>
> But soon a debate developed. Some wanted to send an expedition upriver, to see if they could discover the cause of the tragedy and stop it at its source. Others were firmly convinced that their Christian duty was done when they rescued individuals.

This story, my friend said, is a parable of the modern church. We see persons crushed and hurt by injustice, and some of us try to help them. "But," my friend asked, "shouldn't we attack sources of the injustice that causes poverty and oppression? Aren't we to be concerned with society as well as individuals whose lives touch our own?"

The issue divides Evangelicals. Many respond to needy individuals but are uncomfortable with social action. Yet there is a biblical imperative, seen often in the Prophets, to do justice. Doing justice, like personal morality, is an expression of the one who lives in union with God. Does doing justice require social as well as personal response to need?

## JUSTICE IN THE SCRIPTURES

Two Hebrew words express the concept of justice. The first, *mišpāt,* is found over four hundred times. It might be rendered, "doing what is just and right according to one's rights and obligations under law." The second word is *ṣāḏaq,* which implies, first, that moral and ethical norms exist and, second, that one's actions are in harmony with those norms.

An "unjust" act is one that is out of harmony with established norms. Those norms, which in Scripture are expressed in God's law, define a person's rights and obligations. Both the standards themselves and the individual's behavior as judged by the standards are justice issues.

*Justice for individuals.* Old Testament teaching on justice clusters around the twin concerns of God's law: (1) just individuals and (2) structures that are essential for a just society. Two Old Testament passages help us sense the nature of justice in both contexts, individual and societal. In the first passage, Isaiah speaks against the religiosity of individuals who seem eager to approach God but who oppress their fellows.

> "On the day of your fasting, you do as you please
>     and exploit all your workers.
> Your fasting ends in quarreling and strife,
>     and in striking each other with wicked fists.
> You cannot fast as you do today
>     and expect your voice to be heard on high.
> Is this the kind of fast I have chosen,
>     only a day for a man to humble himself?
> Is it only for bowing one's head like a reed
>     and for lying on sackcloth and ashes?
> Is that what you call a fast,
>     a day acceptable to the LORD?
>
> "Is not this the kind of fasting I have chosen:
> to loose the chains of injustice
>     and untie the cords of the yoke,
> to set the oppressed free
>     and break every yoke?
> Is it not to share your food with the hungry
>     and to provide the poor wanderer with shelter—
> when you see the naked, to clothe him,
>     and not to turn away from your own flesh and
>     blood?

"... If you do away with the yoke of oppression,
  with the pointing finger and malicious talk,
and if you spend yourselves in behalf of the hungry
  and satisfy the needs of the oppressed,
then your light will rise in the darkness,
  and your night will become like the noonday"
(Isa. 58:3–10).

We see the same theme in Jeremiah.

" 'This is what the LORD says: Do what is just and right.
Rescue from the hand of the oppressor the one who has
been robbed. Do no wrong or violence to the alien, the
fatherless or the widow, and do not shed innocent blood in
this place' " (Jer. 22:3).

Jeremiah goes on to commend a godly king, who

"  ... did what was right and just,
  so all went well with him.
He defended the cause of the poor and needy,
  and so all went well.
Is that not what it means to know me?"
  declares the LORD.
"But your eyes and your heart
  are set only on dishonest gain,
on shedding innocent blood
  and on oppression and extortion" (vv. 15–17).

In the *Expository Dictionary of Bible Words* the idea of
doing justice is summed up as follows:

Justice is an interpersonal concept in the Old Testament.
Doing justice has to do with how human beings treat one
another, individually and in society. The norm or standard
that defines just behavior is a moral and ethical one. It is
derived from God's character and is expressed in those
commands of the law and exhortations of the prophets that
reveal how God expects his people to relate lovingly to
those around them (p. 370).

The individual, then, does justice by feeding the hungry but also
by doing away with the yoke of oppression. Meeting the needs
of the oppressed is to be accompanied by a commitment to
rescue those who are being robbed by oppressors.

*Social justice in the Old Testament*. The prophets insistent-
ly call individual believers to a concern for justice in both an

interpersonal and a social level. But the law most clearly defines the nature of a just society, identifying the issues with which "doing justice" is concerned on a society-wide level.

When we examine the law we are struck by the number of mechanisms that God designed to protect individuals from injustice and oppression. These mechanisms are strikingly relevant to our own society, for they suggest approaches to social issues that might be adapted to our own time.

I review here five of these means of protecting individuals and creating a just moral society.

First, the law provided for *preservation of capital*. One of the problems in our society concerns the concentration of capital, and thus economic power, in the hands of a few. While modern laws protect individuals from the kind of exploitation practiced under the "robber barons" of capitalism in the last century, many still have observed that the poor have less opportunity and access to the benefits of our society than the wealthy. There are still institutionalized forms of oppression.

Wealth in Old Testament times was based on the land and on what the land could produce. The law decreed that land was to remain perpetually in the family of its first settlers: "The land must not be sold permanently. . . . Throughout the country that you hold as a possession, you must provide for the redemption of the land" (Lev. 25:23–24). This regulation refers to a provision that, in case of need, a family might sell the *use* of its land for a period of time. The value of the property was to be computed, based on the projected value of the crops between the time of sale and the Year of Jubilee, which came every fiftieth year. In that year, people were not to work the land, and every family was to repossess its heritage, its land.

The significance of this regulation is that, although people might make bad choices and squander their wealth, there was always capital for the next generation—wealth in the form of land to be reclaimed during the Year of Jubilee. Thus every fiftieth year the real wealth of the nation, its land, was redistributed, giving the poor the means to make a fresh start.

Second, the law allowed *voluntary servitude*. The Old Testament recognized that many poor people were poor not because of oppression but because of their own inadequacies. So the law established a unique training mechanism for the unsuccessful or those who could not find work. This mechanism involved selling one's personal services to a fellow Israelite.

This system is defined in Deuteronomy 15:12–18 and Leviticus 25:39–55. The person who sold his or her services was to be paid an initial purchase price. The sale of services was for a limited time. At the end of the seventh year of service, a Hebrew servant was to be released. The law specified, "When you release him, do not send him away empty-handed. Supply him liberally from your flock, your threshing floor and your winepress" (Deut. 15:13–14).

We probably should look at this program as one of apprenticeship. A poor man who could not meet his financial obligations, for example, was given money to pay his creditors. He bound himself to serve the person who had thus purchased him. But during the seven years of service, the servant would learn skills from the more successful person who had bought him. By the time of release, he would be able to make it on his own. And when released, he was to be supplied "liberally" by his former master with the resources he needed for a fresh start.

It is clear, from the initial cost to the purchaser and the expense of release, that the servants benefited most from this transaction, for, even while they learned, their needs were met in the household of their benefactor. And when finally trained and able to contribute most to their owner, they were released.

Third, the law established *interest-free, forgivable loans*. Leviticus 25:35–37 and Deuteronomy 23:19–20 outline the making of interest-free loans to fellow Israelites. Such obligation was to be canceled each sabbatical, or seventh, year (Deut. 15:1–3). Persons in debt had to attempt to repay the amount borrowed, yet, if they could not do so, their debt was not to weigh them down forever. In a sense, the sabbatical year's release was parallel to bankruptcy in our society.

The law does make it clear that a person borrows as a last resort—not to get a luxury item but to keep a roof over one's head. Loans are extended as a response to this kind of need. And the law defines the appropriate attitude of the person who has funds and sees another in need.

> If there is a poor man among your brothers in any of the towns of the land that the LORD your God is giving you, do not be hardhearted or tightfisted toward your poor brother. Rather be openhanded and freely lend him whatever he needs. Be careful not to harbor this wicked thought: "The seventh year, the year for canceling debts, is near," so that

you do not show ill will toward your needy brother and give
him nothing. . . . There will always be poor people in the
land. Therefore I command you to be openhanded toward
your brothers and toward the poor and needy in your land
(Deut. 15:7–11).

Fourth, the law guaranteed *access to necessities*. During
regular harvests, landowners were to go through their fields
only once. All that had been missed or that fell on the ground or
that was late in ripening was to be left for the poor, who were
permitted to enter the fields to glean whatever they could (Lev.
19:10; 23:22). In addition, every seventh year the land was to be
given a sabbath; no crops were to be planted. Whatever did
grow in the fields or on the trees was set aside for the poor, who
again could freely enter the fields and harvest what they found
(Exod. 23:10–11).

It is noteworthy that this structure called on the poor to
work for what they gathered. There was no demeaning "charity," but the needy had the right to take what they could gather.

Finally, the law provided for *organized charity*. A number
of different tithes were ordered by the law. Most were collected
annually and used for the support of the priests and the Levites
who ministered in the temple. Deuteronomy 14:28–29, however, tells of a special tithe to be collected every three years. A
tenth of all that the land produced was to be stored locally and
to be used for "the aliens, the fatherless and the widows."

This brief survey makes it clear that Old Testament
teaching regarding social justice involves both the godly individual and the society itself. The law established social structures
such as interest-free loans and the right to glean in harvested
fields. But making these structures work depended on godly
individuals willing to loan freely and to open their gates to the
working poor. The law established structures for the redistribu-
tion of capital and for apprenticeship training. But again the
function of these structures depended on the existence of godly
individuals who would respond appropriately to the poor and
exhibit a personal commitment to doing justice.

*Doing justice in the New Testament.* The exhortations of
the prophets for God's people to do justice on an individual and
societal scale have few echoes in the New Testament. They
hardly need repetition, however, for the words of the prophets
establish for all time God's concern with justice and his anger at
injustice in all its personal and social forms.

But there are reasons for the relative silence of the New Testament. Israel, the Old Testament's faith community, was also a nation. As such, Mosaic Law rightly established a social and legal framework within which God's people should live. The church, the New Testament's faith community, is not a nation. Instead the church is the assembly of God's people, of all times and places. Christians live in a variety of societies, under many different secular laws. Thus, rather than spelling out the structure of a just moral community (which Israel had already modeled), the New Testament deals primarily with how the individual lives in love with other persons in the church and with persons outside it.

Yet even in this context, the New Testament deals with the plight of the poor and speaks of how believers are to respond. This teaching is focused in the New Testament concept of giving, which is in essence a sharing of resources, even as in Old Testament times the well-to-do were to share with their poorer brothers and sisters through tithes, loans, opening their fields to gleaning, etc. In the New Testament, the church is often seen as a worldwide community, and Christians in need in various parts of the world are to have those needs met by the generosity of believers who live in wealthier lands (see Rom. 15:25–28; 1 Cor. 16:1–4; 2 Cor. 8:1–7; Gal. 2:10). In these passages we see that famine or persecution stimulates the collection and forwarding of funds from more prosperous areas, intended to meet the survival needs of Christian brothers and sisters.

The New Testament also makes it clear that individuals are to respond to the needs of others with whom they have contact (James 2:14–16; 1 John 3:16–18). This obligation is reflected in certain structures that the New Testament suggests were built into local churches rather than the society as a whole. Thus there was an organization of widows who were supported by the church and who in turn ministered to younger women (1 Tim. 5:1–16). Poor believers were also helped in an organized way (Acts 6:1–7). Some were even willing to sell their possessions to give "to anyone as he had need" (2:45).

The philosophy of New Testament giving is spelled out in 2 Corinthians 8–9. Here giving is clearly assumed to focus on meeting human need rather than supporting institutions. The underlying concept is that those who are destitute should have their basic needs met by other believers. At another time, then, those who have received will be the ones to give. Paul writes,

"Our desire is not that others might be relieved while you are hard pressed, but that there might be equality. At the present time your plenty will supply what they need, so that in turn their plenty will supply what you need" (8:13–14). Although believers are to "do good to all people," there is a special sense in which we are to reach out to show concern for "those who belong to the family of believers" (Gal. 6:10).

In summary, individuals are constantly called in Scripture to have compassion on others in need and, in tangible ways, to help the poor and the oppressed. This standard becomes the measure of justice, in its basic sense of doing what is right. But the God who calls individuals to care also shows in Old Testament law and in New Testament church life that doing justice is facilitated by the existence of social structures designed to protect the poor and alleviate oppression.

From the patterns established in the Old and New Testaments, doing justice is both a personal and a social issue. To live a human life in union with God may well involve us in doing justice on both levels.

## JESUS AND JUSTICE

In view of modern liberation theology, it is important to note that Jesus was not a social reformer. He did not need to be. Jesus was born into a society theoretically founded on a divine law which incorporated justice in its very structure. The problem Jesus faced was not to create a new society but to call Israel back to the legal foundation already laid.

Thus we hear Jesus, toward the end of his ministry, scathingly indict the Pharisees:

Woe to you, teachers of the law and Pharisees, you hypocrites! You give a tenth of your spices—mint, dill and cummin. But you have neglected the more important matters of the law—justice, mercy and faithfulness. You should have practiced the latter, without neglecting the former. You blind guides! You strain out a gnat but swallow a camel (Matt. 23:23–24).

Even more compelling, however, was Jesus' own commitment to act on behalf of the poor and the oppressed. When John the Baptist sent followers to find out if Jesus truly was the Messiah, Christ answered simply, "Go back and report to John what you hear and see: The blind receive sight, the lame walk, those who have leprosy are cured, the deaf hear, the dead are raised, and the good news is preached to the poor'' (Matt. 11:4–5).

Jesus was not a modern-day revolutionary. But he was a spiritual revolutionary. Jesus called people back to the love of God and to that doing of justice which love compels.

Like Jesus, the person who lives a human life in union with God will respond to those who have needs and will reach out to help. And very possibly, the person who lives his or her life in union with God may be called to deal with the "more important matters of the law—justice, mercy and faithfulness" in a society-wide and institutional way, rather than simply on a personal level.

## GROWTH IN DOING JUSTICE

Every human society is warped by sin and will be marked by injustice, oppression, and the presence of the poor. Even Israel, despite the striking design of institutions intended to shape a just, moral community, constantly fell short. In the grip of self-centeredness, the people of Israel ignored the sabbatical year and the Year of Jubilee. They loaned to their brothers, but only at exorbitant interest. And when the wealthy occupied the land of others, they refused to give it up.

Yet the existence of such structures provided a base for persons like Nehemiah to recall the people of Judah to the way of justice (Neh. 5:3–12). When standards of just behavior have been institutionalized in a society, not only are there expanded opportunities for doing justice, but there is also a witness to the nature of what is right and just.

As Christians we are to share God's concern for justice in our private lives. But we are also to share God's concern that principles of justice be established in society. The holiness of God, which expresses itself in a commitment to do good to all, may also find expression through the Christian's involvement in concerns of social justice.

*Doing justice in society.* Justice demands that we show concern for the poor and the needy with whom we come in contact. This concern may be expressed in a gift or loan. To train the unemployed, a businessman may set up an apprentice-ship program within his business. Likewise, businessmen must not inordinately profit at the expense of labor, and laborers must do an honest day's work.

But individuals can also help change social conditions by involvement in the political process. It was largely through the efforts of committed Christians that slavery in England and in the United States was abolished. Christian involvement led to the passage of child-labor laws and the establishment of hospitals for the poor. Through Christian concern, Sunday schools were established, not for religious training, but to teach poor children how to read and write.

Today great social evils remain to be redressed. Our prison system needs reform—perhaps on the model of Old Testament law, which views crime as an offense against the individual and calls for restitution. In contrast, our system views crime as an offense against the state and makes little or no provision for recovery of damage by the victim.

In our society, the unborn still cry out for recognition of their value as human beings. The poor still live hopeless lives. The government continues to subsidize the growing of tobacco, while giant corporations profit from slow suicide by cigarette. Drunk driving is still condoned, even though more people have been killed by drunk drivers than have died in all the wars the United States has ever fought. Injustice, unfortunately, is still woven into the warp and woof of even our blessed society.

In many nations there is no significant way that an individual can work to bring about change. But in our open system, the individual can have an impact. We can lobby legislators, set up organizations, run for office, speak out, and publicize. Christians concerned with justice can have an impact on the structures of society itself.

It may appear strange to link spirituality, which to many seems a deeply personal issue, with personal morality and social justice. But it is not strange at all. Spirituality is, at heart, living a human life in union with God. A human life is lived in a social context in which persons are each faced with moral choices and are part of a larger society. A human life lived in union with God is a life in which godly personal choices are made and in which responsibility for the condition of society is accepted.

*Doing justice in the congregation.* Congregations have certain direct responsibilities for mercy and justice. These obligations are primarily for the alleviation of needs that exist within the congregation and for the help of believers worldwide who are hardpressed (cf. Rom. 15:25–28).

We see in the New Testament no drive to organize the

church as an instrument of social change. Yet we do see a powerful dynamic in its teaching, which ultimately led to the transformation of social institutions. For instance, Ephesians speaks of the relationship between slaves and masters.

> Slaves, obey your earthly masters with respect and fear, and with sincerity of heart, just as you would obey Christ. Obey them not only to win their favor when their eye is on you, but like slaves of Christ, doing the will of God from your heart. Serve wholeheartedly, as if you were serving the Lord, not men, because you know that the Lord will reward everyone for whatever good he does, whether he is slave or free.
>
> And masters, treat your slaves in the same way. Do not threaten them, since you know that he who is both their Master and yours is in heaven, and there is no favoritism with him (6:5–9).

The impact of Christianity on society came primarily from the personal transformation of those who functioned within existing social roles. The slave was taught to serve from the heart; the master, to respect and treat the slave as a brother. Even such an evil system as slavery could thus provide a context in which mutual Christian love could be expressed.

On the basis of the Old Testament's call for social justice and the example in the New Testament, we can say that the church does need to "meddle." We need to teach Christian love and its expression in every social situation. We need to structure the congregation for the care of its members. And we need to affirm the right and calling of individual believers to be involved as citizens in doing justice in their land.

## PROBE

**exercises for personal development**
**case histories**
**thought provokers**

1. Evaluate whether, as an individual, you are more drawn to express concern for victims of social injustice or to seek cures for the causes of social injustice.

   For instance, would you be more likely to help out in a residence where unwed mothers could stay and have their babies placed for adoption, or would you be more likely to gather signatures on a petition for constitutional protection of the unborn? Would you be more likely to counsel and help an individual, or to picket an abortion clinic?

Each of these approaches (caring for victims, seeking a cure of causes) may be a valid way to "do justice" today. Understanding your own temperament and gifts can help you be sensitive to opportunities God may send your way to be personally involved in the cause of justice in our land.

2. The author mentions several "justice" issues that are of concern in United States society, including criminal justice reform, abortion, poverty, tobacco, and drunk driving. What other issues might you add?

Make a list of issues which you think represent injustice in our present society. Think carefully about each item. You may not be called to any intense involvement, but there are simple steps you can take to express concern.

First, select one issue on your list for which you feel particular concern. Write a letter to your representative in Congress, or to your local newspaper, expressing that concern. Second, begin to pray for persons who are affected by the issue you chose. Open your heart to them, and open yourself to God that he may lead you to deeper involvement if he chooses.

3. You may want to consider involvement with existing groups that have organized to work with needy persons or to change the conditions which cause injustice. For instance, you may want to become a part of Charles Colson's Prison Fellowship, which works in prisons, helps former convicts become reestablished in society, and also lobbies for prison reform.

Check with your pastor or other church leaders for similar groups in your community that are focused on some specific issue.

4. Are you a "just" individual? Review the responsibility of persons to others as defined within the institutions established in Old Testament law. How do your relationships with others reflect the justice described in these institutions? How might you grow as a person "doing justice" in your personal relationships with others?

Look ahead at a typical day you expect to spend this coming week. Write out, in detail, what you will do, who you will see, etc. In the process, identify ways that you will live your human life in union with God by doing justice in those ordinary relationships of your life.

# Section G: Commitment

It was simple for Adam and Eve. As they wandered in the garden God designed for their pleasure, they faced only one crucial decision: would they, or would they not, eat the fruit of the tree of the knowledge of good and evil?

God's will for human beings was summed up in a single command. Holding fast to the Lord was a matter of simple obedience to his expressed will. Beyond that requirement, the first pair were free, in their innocence, to respond as they pleased to each other and to the world in which they lived.

With the first act of disobedience, innocence was lost. In today's tangled world, a host of attractions appeal to people's sin-warped nature, tugging and pulling at everyone. Yet, believers today are also called to hold fast to the Lord in a commitment that is to be at once complete and challenging. Today too a word from God is heard, directing us to follow what is right and warning us to avoid what is wrong. But today, strangers to innocence, we find the choice of commitment to God's way is far more difficult.

Still now, as in the original creation, to live a human life in union with God demands commitment. And for us, commitment means to live our daily life as disciples of Jesus and as servants of our fellow human beings.

# 18

## DISCIPLESHIP

When Jack told me he wanted a "discipling" ministry, I was unsure just what he meant. Most of my students were looking toward local church ministries or toward missions or teaching. But Jack had in mind something very different.

As we talked, his vision became clearer to me. He wanted to spend his life working with just a few persons. Those few must be serious about their faith, willing to meet with him weekly, and willing to follow a rigorous program of study and outreach.

I met Jack again some years after his graduation. He was following his dream. His focus during all that time had been on just eight or ten persons, each of whom he met with individually, each of whom he was "discipling" as he developed study materials that he hoped others could use some day to do what he was doing now.

I appreciated Jack's commitment and his willingness to sacrifice for his vision. And I had to commend him for being faithful to Jesus as Lord as Jack understood his call. But at the same time, I could not help being just a little uncomfortable, because I doubted whether what Jack was so committed to should properly be called "discipling."

### DISCIPLESHIP IN SCRIPTURE

The word *disciple* dots the pages of the Gospels but is absent from the Epistles. Even in the Gospels it has different meanings. The Greek word translated "disciple" is *mathētēs* and means literally a "learner." In New Testament times it was used in several senses. First, it identified followers of particular schools or traditions. It is often used in the Gospels in this sense—e.g., of the disciples of the Pharisees (Matt. 22:16; Mark 2:18; Luke 5:33) or the disciples of John the Baptist (Matt. 11:2–7; Mark 2:18; Luke 5:33; John 1:35–37; 3:25).

Second, *mathētēs* identifies the twelve men whom Jesus chose to be with him in the traditional relationship in which a rabbi in Israel trained others. Typically we think of these twelve as "the disciples."

Third, the same word is used in the New Testament to describe a wider circle of adherents to the movement led by Jesus. In some contexts the word *disciple* seems to have the sense of "believer" (John 8:31; 13:35; 15:8). But not all who are called "disciples" in the Gospels had made a firm commitment to Jesus. In fact, many who were initially attracted to Jesus and saw themselves as his adherents "turned back and no longer followed him" when they were confronted by difficult teachings (6:66).

After the Resurrection we do have one special use of *disciple* by Jesus himself, which makes it clear that the weaker, general senses of this word are irrelevant to Christian faith today. The living Christ told his followers, "Go and make disciples of all nations" (Matt. 28:19). In defining his term, Jesus forever dismissed the notion that a disciple can be nothing more than a loose adherent to Christ or his church. For Jesus said that disciples were to be taught "to obey everything" that he had commanded (v. 20). Discipleship today is a matter of full commitment and obedience to our Lord.

*Discipleship in Israel.* In Jesus' day, discipling was a clearly defined and well-understood process. The Jews held a deep respect for Scripture and were convinced that a person must be trained carefully to interpret and teach it accurately. Training was particularly important because a rabbi, or teacher, was expected to master not only the biblical text but also the oral and written traditions which explained the text. Only after thorough training would a person be viewed as a rabbi himself or be able to teach with any confidence. This assumption explains the Jews' amazed reaction to Jesus' public teaching, "How did this man get such learning without having studied?" (John 7:15).

In Christ's time, "study" referred to a man's attaching himself to a rabbi and learning from that rabbi as a disciple. Such a disciple left his home and moved in with his teacher. He served the teacher in every way and treated the teacher as an absolute authority. The disciple's goal was not only to learn what his rabbi knew but also to become like his master in character and piety (cf. Matt. 10:24; Luke 6:40). Rabbis in Jesus time were delighted to have disciples. While the rabbi was responsible for providing food and lodging for his disciples, the presence of disciples meant that his own distinctive interpretations of Scripture would be transmitted to future generations. When Mark says that Jesus chose twelve men "that they might be with him" (Mark 3:14), he is simply describing the typical training process of that time.

*Jesus' discipling goal.* As we read through the Gospels we frequently see reflections of the normal process by which a rabbi made disciples. The Twelve went everywhere with Jesus. They watched what he did, and they listened to what he said. Often after a public teaching the disciples gathered around Jesus and asked him for private explanations. At times Jesus followed up his public teaching by questioning his disciples. As time went by, Jesus sent his disciples on preaching and healing missions. He taught them to pray. He rebuked them and encouraged them. He explained his plans and purposes in special sessions of private instruction. Jesus acted throughout in the well-established role of a rabbi, training disciples who in turn would teach others what he had taught them.

Jesus himself placed special emphasis on one of the goals of traditional discipleship: "A student [*mathētēs,* "disciple"] is not above his teacher, but everyone who is fully trained will be like his teacher" (Luke 6:40). This statement agrees with the classic goals of discipleship in Jesus' time. The rabbi wanted his interpretations of Scripture passed on to future generations. But disciples considered the rabbi's character and holiness as important as his knowledge. A disciple yearned to be holy and felt that, if he might only become like his teacher, he would be a truly holy man.

Jesus told the Twelve that, when the Holy Spirit came, they would be guided into all truth as his teachings would be brought to mind (John 14:25–26). But Jesus stressed the fact that, when matured, the disciples were to be like him. This theme is further amplified in the Epistles. God's purpose and goal in salvation is that we become like our Lord. John looks ahead and says, "We shall be like him [Jesus], for we shall see him as he is" (1 John 3:2). Paul proclaims Christlikeness as our eternal destiny; God has predestined us "to be conformed to the likeness of his Son" (Rom. 8:29). But even more wonderful, the New Testament teaches that a progressive transformation toward Christ's likeness is possible now!

We see this teaching throughout the Epistles. "Put on the new self, created to be like God in true righteousness and holiness" (Eph. 4:24). "Put on the new self, which is being renewed in knowledge in the image of its Creator" (Col. 3:10). "We . . . are being transformed into his [Jesus'] likeness with ever-increasing glory, which comes from the Lord, who is the Spirit" (2 Cor. 3:18). These verses and others maintain and amplify the focus of discipleship on personal transformation. God intends that those who become disciples by full commitment to Jesus gradually become like Christ himself.

*The disciple's choice.* In Jesus' day his followers, like the other inhabitants of Judah, shared the common understanding of the discipleship process by which teachers were trained. Jesus followed this process in his ministry with the Twelve. But as the relationship with his intimate followers grew, Christ focused on a particular choice that disciples must make. We see that choice described in Matthew and also in John.

Near the end of his public ministry, Jesus sent the Twelve out to listen to the comments about him among the crowds. The disciples returned with a discouraging report. No one doubted that Jesus was a great man. People even ranked him with Elijah or Jeremiah or one of the other prophets. But for years now Jesus had been preaching and teaching—and still the people of Israel failed to acknowledge his deity.

Then Jesus turned to the Twelve. "What about you?" he asked. "Who do you say I am?" (Matt. 16:15). Peter answered for them. "You are the Christ, the Son of the living God" (v. 16). These men who were so close to Jesus knew him to be God in the flesh. But with that knowledge came a new responsibility.

From that time on, Jesus began to speak to the Twelve about his cross and actually shifted the focus of his ministry. He spoke less to the crowds and more to the disciples. He spoke less of the kingdom and more about his coming suffering. In the incident reported in Matthew 16, Jesus said to his disciples,

> If anyone would come after me, he must deny himself and take up his cross and follow me. For whoever wants to save his life will lose it, but whoever loses his life for me will find it. What good will it be for a man if he gains the whole world, yet forfeits his soul? Or what can a man give in exchange for his soul? (vv. 24–26).

The words are familiar. But we may miss their deeper meaning. When Jesus spoke to his followers he probably used Aramaic, and his words need to be understood in a way that is consistent with that language's patterns of thought and expression. In Aramaic, *soul* (Gk. *psychē;* Heb. *nepeš*) is commonly used to refer to one's person and is translated as a reflexive pronoun (*oneself,* etc.). Thus "Praise God, O my soul" is simply a way of expressing a deep desire to praise God with one's whole being. The word *soul* does not imply a separation of the human being into material and immaterial parts, as in later Greek and Christian thought.

The translators of the New International Version express this understanding in verse 25, for the Greek word translated "life" (in "wants to save his life") is *psychē,* which in the next verse is rendered "soul." If we consistently treat each occurrence of *psychē* as a reflexive pronoun, used emphatically to identify the person himself or herself, the passage reads as follows, which is probably what the Aramaic-speaking disciples understood Jesus to say:

> If anyone would come after me, he must deny himself and take up his cross and follow me. For whoever wants to save himself will lose himself, but whoever loses himself for me will find himself. What good will it be for a man if he gains the whole world, yet forfeits himself? Or what can a man give in exchange for himself?

This understanding makes special sense if we remember the goal of making disciples. The disciple, when fully trained, is to be like his or her teacher. Discipleship calls us to lose our old self, exchanging it for a new self that reflects the very character and nature of our Lord.

A person who meets Jesus must make a choice. He or she can hold on to the old self or can lose the old self. Individuals who hold back will lose the new self they are called to become in Christ. But people who are willing to lose the old self, surrendering what they were in order to find the new, will be transformed. To reach the goal of discipleship, the follower of Christ must make a total commitment to him.

Jesus said, "If anyone would come after me, he must deny himself [i.e., the old self] and take up his cross and follow me." I note that Jesus does not call for us to take up *Christ's* cross. Christian discipleship does not mean martyrdom. Jesus calls on his followers to take up *their* cross. In Christian theology Christ's cross is the key to our salvation. It is the focus of history, representing the moment that the sins of all the ages crushed life from the Son of God. But the cross had an additional significance to Jesus. To Jesus, living his human life in union with God, the cross was the ultimate test of self-denial and of surrender to the Father's will. In Gethsemane Jesus looked ahead with dread and yet prayed, "Not as I will, but as you will" (Matt. 26:39). In that moment of ultimate stress, Jesus models the disciple's choice. He took up the cross of the Father's will when that will called for self-denial.

The issue remains the same for each of us. As we live our human life, we reach crossroad after crossroad. All too often the desires and motives of the old self tug and pull at us. At such moments the disciple says, with Jesus, "Not as I will," and in this way takes up his or her cross. With each daily cross we choose to bear, we take another step away from an old self we yearn to lose toward that new and Christlike self we yearn to become.

The disciple's choice is a choice to do the will of God when our will and his will conflict. The choice to bear the daily cross brings us closer and closer to the disciple's goal.

The issue that is slightly masked in Matthew 16 is clearly stated in John 8. Christ, speaking to Jews who believed in him, said, "If you hold to my teaching [lit., "remain in my word"], you are really my disciples. Then you will know the truth, and the truth will set you free" (John 8:31–32).

Here we see that obedience brings us into the realm of truth—and in John's writings "truth" is to be understood as reality. To know the truth means to experience life as it really is, as God intended it to be.

True freedom is to be released from the illusions which trap a fallen humanity in sin and misery, to be released from blind, sinful choices that lead only to death. The disciple who chooses God's will and who lives by the words of Jesus will know by personal experience a new world of fellowship with God, a world made glorious by inner transformation toward Christ's likeness.

Both Matthew and John draw our attention to a disciple's commitment. The important aspect is not the training process itself but the goal of Christlikeness. To achieve this goal, the personal commitment of those who know Jesus is essential. Only commitment to Christ will lead us daily to take up our cross (Luke 9:23). Only personal commitment to Christ will move us to do God's will when that will is in conflict with the passions and desires of the old self. Only commitment to Christ will lead us to live by Jesus' words and so shake off the old as we move toward the newness we are promised in him.

## JESUS AS A DISCIPLE

In his training of the disciples Jesus broke little new ground. He followed the pattern deeply embedded in Judaism, selecting twelve men, and for the years of his public ministry, Jesus shared his life with them.

Yet at the appropriate time, Jesus confronted the Twelve with the necessity of personal, daily commitment. To become like him, they must lose the old self, putting its passions and desires aside, surrendering self-will to God's will whenever these are in conflict. The pain of such choices makes the cross an appropriate image. The old in us must die, and death has its pangs. But in Christ death gives way to life, and the self we lose will be replaced by a personality that is fresh and new.

While most writers on discipleship have tended to look at Jesus as the model discipler, it is more helpful to see him as the model disciple. Jesus, living his human life in perfect union with God, always made the disciple's obedient choice. It seems so easy as we watch him in the Gospels. His will and the Father's are always in such harmony.

And then we come to Gethsemane, where we see everything that is human in Jesus drawing back in anguish from the cross. And there, despite the pain, we see Jesus choose the Father's will.

This choice is the real and ultimate meaning of discipleship. Disciples surrender their old self to do not their will but God's. Like Jesus, in this act the disciples lose themselves. But also like Jesus, the surrendered disciples gain a new self. The resurrection power that burst forth to raise Christ from the dead brings life to our mortal bodies, and through the power of God we experience a personal transformation toward the likeness of our Lord.

## THE DISCIPLESHIP PROCESS IN THE EPISTLES

The word *disciple* appears frequently in the Gospels. It is used less often in Acts and is absent entirely from the Epistles. How can we explain this omission?

It is clear from the whole New Testament that the goal of discipleship—transformation of the old into the new—is a major Christian theme. We are consistently told, "Put off your old self, which is being corrupted by its deceitful desires; . . . to be made new in the attitude of your minds; and . . . put on the new self, created to be like God in true righteousness and holiness" (Eph. 4:22–24). When the passions and desires of the old in us come in conflict with the will of God, we are to choose the will of God so that the old self might be lost as we find ourselves renewed.

The difference in the Epistles, which explains the disappearance of the language of discipleship, is the process which facilitates personal transformation. Toward the end of his ministry Jesus even went as far as to tell the crowds and his followers, "You are not to be called 'Rabbi,' for you have only one Master and you are all brothers" (Matt. 23:8). The old relationship of a single teacher, superior to his little cluster of devoted followers, is ended. The training process implicit in the term *discipleship* is replaced by another.

There are several images in the Epistles that replace the Gospels' image of disciples gathered around a rabbi. The Epistles portray the Christian community as a family. Relationships in the Christian community are marked by the kind of intimacy appropriate to those who are in fact brothers and sisters. In an important Ephesian prayer Paul identifies a relationship between transformation and "family" living. Paul asks God that the Ephesians may be strengthened by the Spirit in their inner being, so that, "being rooted and established in love," they may have power, "together with all the saints," to grasp the full extent of Christ's love and to experience that love as they are "filled to the measure of all the fullness of God" (Eph. 3:17–19). In this context, the love in which believers are to be rooted and established as a ground in which to grow is neither God's love for them nor their love for God. It is family love, the intimacy of a community that experiences an inner transformation together.

Another Epistles' image casts the Christian community as a body. Believers, bonded together as members of a living organism, minister to and nurture one another. Growth into Christ, individually and as a whole body, takes place as the body "grows and builds itself up in love, as each part does its work" (Eph. 4:16).

Such images are strengthened by the New Testament's emphasis on giftedness, which teaches that each person is capable of contributing to the growth and spiritual vitality of other believers (1 Cor. 12:7). The vital importance of family and body relationships underlies the constant New Testament emphasis on the importance of loving one another and such exortations as we find in Hebrews 10:24–25: "Let us consider how we may spur one another on toward love and good deeds. Let us not give up meeting together, as some are in the habit of doing, but let us encourage one another—and all the more as you see the Day approaching."

In Judaism the discipling process drew a few individuals in a cluster around a rabbi, who was recognized as an authority. The disciples acknowledged him as their master, submitted to him, learned from him, and sought to imitate him. In this way Jesus trained the Twelve. But almost immediately the church rejected the traditional discipling process in favor of another. The new process drew believers together in an intimate, loving relationship as brothers and sisters, members of a single living organism. The new process acknowledges no human being as "master," reserving that title for Jesus, who continues to teach his people through the Holy Spirit who lives within us. In the new process, each believer is gifted by the Spirit with a spiritual gift which enables him or her to contribute to others, and in the context of loving community, each spurs the others on to full commitment to Jesus Christ.

The transformational goal of discipleship has never changed, nor has the challenge of discipleship to reject the old in favor of doing God's will, even when his will can be characterized as a daily cross. But the old process was rightly discarded in the church. The new process, which facilitates Christian transformation, depends on the vitality of the family and body relationships experienced by those follow Jesus Christ together.

## GROWTH IN DISCIPLESHIP

Today the issue of discipleship remains. We must lose ourselves to become ourselves and must choose God's will over our own. And the goal is unchanged: we are to become like Jesus. But we are not to carry over the process of disciple making we see in the Gospels into the church. We are instead to build those family and body relationships the New Testament emphasizes, realizing that through them we are strengthened to choose the will of God and challenged to go on to even deeper commitment.

### Table 12. Discipleship

|  | GOSPELS/CHRIST | EPISTLES/CHURCH |
| --- | --- | --- |
| Goal | Transformation | Transformation |
| Key | Take up cross<br>(Obey Jesus' word) | Put off old/<br>put on new man<br>(Obey Jesus' word) |
| Process | One Rabbi<br>Small group<br>Autocratic relationship | No "Rabbi"<br>Local fellowship<br>Family and body<br>relationship |

In various practical ways, we can strengthen ourselves to choose the daily cross and take daily steps toward Christlikeness.

*Surrender fully to God.* We need to make a basic commitment which goes beyond acceptance of Jesus as Savior. We need to surrender ourselves consciously to God. We need to surrender our will, determining to take up our cross in imitation of Christ.

*Develop sensitivity to choices.* We need to express our basic commitment in daily life, developing our sensitivity so we will recognize our daily crosses. The key to sensitivity is awareness of moments of psychological conflict between the self we currently are and the self we yearn to become.

All of us have moments when we sense God's will and are aware of conflict. We may have an impulse to speak to a friend about spiritual things. But immediately we feel conflict and hesitate to speak. We worry about what he or she might think. We are uncertain about what to say and afraid that, if questioned, we will not have an adequate answer. In that moment of inner conflict, we have entered a mini-Gethsemane and have identified a cross that we can bear only by responding to the Spirit's promptings.

Or perhaps we hear of a person in need and sense a spontaneous urge to help. But then we hesitate. We begin to calculate and to think of the things we want for ourselves or the time we might have to spend. Again we have entered a mini-Gethsemane. Our inner conflict of desires has helped us to identify another daily cross, which we can take up only by choosing what we believe to be the will of God.

We could mention other common experiences. We face a choice, and always, when the disciple's daily cross is involved, we feel an inner conflict between desires to do and not to do what we sense God wills. It is important to make the initial commitment of the disciple of submission to God's will. But that initial commitment must find daily expression in the choices we make when inner conflict indicates our cross.

*Build relationships with other believers.* If we are to grow as disciples, we need to build growth-promoting relationships with other believers. The daily choice of commitment is easier for us when we live close to others who share our determination to follow Christ. Our growth is facilitated as we learn from one another, love one another, and encourage, rebuke, and correct one another. Intimate family relationships, characterized by brotherly and sisterly love, are the context for that process which the New Testament shows will lead to personal inner renewal.

## PROBE

**exercises for personal development**
**case histories**
**thought provokers**

1. At the beginning of this chapter the author mentioned a former student and said he was uncomfortable with the student's approach to "discipling." First, give reasons, drawn from the Gospels, why this young man might have taken his approach. Second, give reasons, drawn from the Gospels and Epistles, why the author was uncomfortable with the approach.

2. The author suggests that a sense of inner conflict is often a key to recognizing situations in which a believer is to take up the "daily cross" that Jesus spoke of in Matthew 16. The feelings associated with such experiences—especially when you think you know what you should do—may be God's inner voice alerting you to the need to deny yourself so that you can discover your new self.

This concept is so important that it is worth exploration. Probably the best way is to keep a journal. Each evening, write about incidents during the day when you sensed conflict. In writing, describe the situation, record your feelings, and report your actions. Did you recognize the situation as a mini-Gethsemane? Did you consciously express to God your willingness to do God's will? Did you have a sense of what God wanted you to do? Did you choose to do it, or not?

In exploring such situations, the results of your action or inaction are not as important as what was happening inside you. Remember that the goal of discipleship is transformation to Christlikeness, which takes place only as we continue to choose to obey God's will. Your goal in keeping a journal is to help you become more sensitive to situations that represent your daily cross so that you will begin to choose consistently to deny yourself in favor of doing God's will.

3. In discussing the discipling process, the author pointed out that discipleship training in Judaism was clearly defined. Indeed, Jesus followed the common model in training the Twelve. But the discipling process intended to lead to likeness to one's true Teacher, Jesus, is different for the church. The church, as family and as body, is itself a transforming community. Believers are encouraged in their daily commitment to Jesus as they build warm, loving, intimate relationships with other believers as brothers and sisters. In the context of this kind of relationship, spiritual growth and growth in discipleship take place.

This fact demands that each of us carefully evaluate our relationship with other Christians. Do we experience the kind of family relationship of which Scripture speaks?

To explore this question, look up the phrase *one another* in a concordance. Then look in every New Testament context where this phrase appears. From them develop a picture of the kind of relationship God intends you to have with other Christians.

Then evaluate your own relationships with fellow Christians by what you have found. Are your relationships marked by the kinds of interaction described in Scripture? Or for growth as a disciple, do you need to build closer, more intimate Christian friendships?

4. If you find that you lack the kind of relationships with others that are appropriate to Christian discipling and discipleship, study my three books listed below, which deal with the complex issue of how modern congregations can become transforming, discipling communities. Then write a brief plan showing how you will go about building deeper Christian relationships in your own life.

*A Theology of Christian Education* (Grand Rapids: Zondervan, 1975), chaps. 19–25.

With Clyde Hoeldtke, *A Theology of Church Leadership* (Grand Rapids: Zondervan, 1980), chaps. 15–23.

With Gib Martin, *A Theology of Personal Ministry* (Grand Rapids: Zondervan, 1981), chaps. 9–12.

# 19

## SERVANTHOOD

"If you let them," she was saying, "people will take advantage of you."

I had to agree. In this very imperfect world of ours, many people will thoughtlessly impose on our hospitality, will take and take and never give back in return.

"I mean," she went on, "you've got to be assertive. Stand up for your rights. I don't mean be selfish or anything, but a person has got to take care of herself first, right?"

It is an important question. Do we have to take care of ourselves first?

Some Christians have been crushed by guilt when doing anything for themselves. They have been taught to sacrifice every personal goal and desire in an effort to please others. But is the self-denial that Jesus taught self-abnegation?

Still, there is a basic selfishness expressed in my friend's view that does not quite fit with the gospel. In this imperfect world, others still are important to God. And the person who lives a human life in union with God will often take the role of a servant.

### SERVANTHOOD IN SCRIPTURE

To understand Christian servanthood, we need to note both the overlap and the distinction maintained in the Bible between servants and slaves.

*In the Old Testament.* The root of the Hebrew word

*'ebed* (translated as "servant" and "slave") simply means "work" or "serve." An intensive form of the related verb *'ābad* means "enslave," or "force into service." But the normal verb form is used of serving God as well as of work in general. According to context, the work can be menial, performed under threat, or it may be a significant service freely and joyfully offered.

Another verb, *šārat,* also means "serve," but its focus is clearly on ministry. The service it indicates is always viewed as important, because the person served is of high rank, because the service implies a close personal relationship between the servant and the one served, and because the service itself is viewed as truly important. In *šārat,* the person serving another is busy with matters of real significance. It follows, then, that "servant" is a position of high status. Servanthood in this vital biblical sense does not demean, but instead exalts, the servant. While other Hebrew words are at times translated by "servant" in our Old Testament, these two primary words define the concept.

*Isaiah's "servant of the Lord."* The most significant teaching on servanthood is found in Isaiah's discussion of a person he identified as the servant of the Lord. In the second half of his book, Isaiah speaks of Israel as a servant who failed to accomplish God's purposes (Isa. 41:8–10; 42:18–19; 43:9–10; 44:1–3; 45:4; 48:20). Then in a series of Servant Songs, the prophet goes on to identify another servant—the Messiah.

Four major passages deal with this servant and his ministry. Isaiah 42:1–9 teaches us that he will be filled with God's Spirit (v. 1). He will walk humbly among the bruised and worthless of the earth (vv. 2–3) and will establish justice (v. 4). God himself will guide and protect his servant (vv. 5–6). Finally, in a stunning and unexpected act, the servant will become the means by which God releases life's captives (v. 7).

Isaiah 49:1–6 is an announcement by the servant of his credentials. He has been shaped and called by God and sent upon a mission that will display God's glory (vv. 1–3). He may appear to be a failure (v. 4), but the servant will succeed in calling Israel back to the Lord and will bring salvation to all humankind (vv. 5–6).

Isaiah 50:4–10 shows us that God speaks to and constantly guides his servant (v. 4). The servant is completely obedient to God (v. 5), even though obedience involves personal sufferings

(v. 6). But the sovereign Lord is at work even in the servant's suffering and will completely vindicate him (vv. 7–9). Those who fear God will respond to the servant's word and will trust in the name of the Lord (v. 10).

Isaiah 52:13–53:12 is the last and greatest of these Servant Song sections. God's servant is destined to be exalted (52:13), even though humanity will at first be repulsed by his suffering (v. 14). That suffering is so graphically portrayed in Isaiah 53 that Christ and his cross are unmistakably revealed. God's servant, despised and rejected (vv. 1–3), is pierced for the transgressions of sinners and bears the punishment that brings them peace (vv. 4–5). All of us, like sheep, have gone astray, but the Lord has laid on his servant the iniquity of all (v. 6). The servant died because of and for humanity's transgressions (vv. 7–8) and was laid in a rich man's tomb (v. 9). Yet from eternity God intended to make the servant's life a guilt offering (v. 10). So after death, the servant is restored to life, to see the outcome of his efforts and to be exalted to the heights (vv. 11–12).

These Servant Songs in Isaiah show us not only Jesus but also the character of servanthood. The servant of the Lord, motivated by his or her desire to please God, lives a humble life with others. Responding to God's will, the servant seeks to deliver and to meet the needs of others, even at the price of personal sacrifice.

*In the New Testament.* Two word groups in the New Testament are significant in developing our understanding of servanthood. The word *douleuō* means "serve as a slave." This word emphasizes subjection of one's will to another. In the New Testament, this word is used primarily to picture the believer's relationship with Jesus. Jesus is Lord, and we as his slaves appropriately submit to his will.

The other verb, *diakoneō,* simply means "serve." In the New Testament this word is associated with meeting personal needs of other human beings, particularly the needs of other Christians. *Diakoneō* and its related noun form are linked with many kinds of service in the New Testament, including serving at tables (Luke 10:40), collecting funds for needy brothers (Acts 11:29; 2 Cor. 8:4), and sharing Christ's word (2 Tim. 4:11; 2 Cor. 11:8). Serving also encompasses the use of spiritual gifts and ministry in all church offices (1 Cor. 12:4–6).

While there is a basic and vital difference between *douleuō* ("be a slave") and *diakoneō* ("serve"), the Greeks considered each type of service shameful and demeaning. The Greek ideal was that of *aretē,* "excellence," for they believed that one's first duty was to oneself. To achieve excellence a person must have an unfettered personal will. To surrender any rights or even expend time and effort for the sake of others was considered humiliating. How different from Jesus, who came not to be served but to serve. How out of harmony with the Bible, which teaches that we achieve our full potential not by grasping but by what we give.

This brief survey helps us see the essential difference between the servant and the slave in biblical thought. It also helps us grasp something of the uniqueness of biblical servant-hood. A slave, gladly or sullenly, bends his or her will to work at another's command. In the New Testament, committed Christians chose just such a surrender to God's will and so are launched on a life of discipleship.

Although the servant's role does not call for the surrender of one's will to those whom the servant aids, a servant does surrender his or her interests, giving time and effort freely in order to be of help to others. While the secular world sees servants as having low status, both the Old and the New Testament present a different view. Servants are persons of high status in God's kingdom. Their service is offered to a person who is truly important. And the service offered is seen as vital to the welfare of the one served. But most important, servanthood has been modeled for us by our Lord himself, and we gladly choose to follow in his steps.

## JESUS AS SERVANT

The Servant Songs of Isaiah look forward to the ministry of Christ on earth and powerfully portray the nature of his servanthood. But we see servanthood in even sharper perspective as we observe the life Jesus lived as a human being, as reported in the Gospels.

Perhaps Matthew 20:17–34 best sums up both the teaching of Jesus on servanthood and his modeling of servanthood. The mother of two of the disciples has just approached Jesus, begging for her sons the most powerful positions in his coming kingdom. When the other disciples hear about this request, they are rightly upset. With emotions of all aroused, Jesus calls the Twelve together and teaches them something of the uniqueness of life in his kingdom.

You know that the rulers of the Gentiles lord it over them, and their high officials exercise authority over them. Not so with you. Instead, whoever wants to become great among you must be your servant, and whoever wants to be first must be your slave—just as the Son of Man did not come to be served, but to serve, and to give his life as a ransom for many (vv. 25–28).

Immediately after this instruction, Jesus turned and, trailed by his followers, set out from Jericho on his way to Jerusalem. There the crowds that had gathered for one of Israel's great religious festivals would greet him with palm branches and praise. But there, shortly afterward, Jesus' enemies would seize him. With his disciples scattered, Christ would be tried illegally in Jewish courts and then brought to the Romans, whose garrison soldiers would brutally crucify him. And as Jesus started out from Jericho, he knew what lay ahead.

Yet, as Jesus began that last journey toward the place of his suffering, two blind men cried out. They had heard the crowds and, discovering that it was Jesus who passed by, felt a rising hope. Surely this man, who had healed so many, could restore their sight.

The crowds were unsympathetic, telling the blind men to be quiet. Rabbi Jesus was an important person, he would not have time for two worthless blind men.

But Jesus heard their cry. Despite the inner anguish he must have felt as he started out on that last journey, and disregarding his own great need, Jesus stopped for the blind men. He asked them, "What do you want me to do?" (v. 32).

They answered eagerly, "Lord, we want our sight." The Bible says, "Jesus had compassion on them and touched their eyes. Immediately they received their sight and followed him" (vv. 33–34).

We sense here what servanthood really means. Servanthood is Jesus, stopping there on the dusty road and ignoring his own personal burden to care about the needs of others.

For us also, servanthood is putting aside our interests or our pain, having compassion for others, and paying the price of self-sacrifice as we reach out to aid. Living any human life means that we will be in constant contact with others who have needs. Living a human life in union with God means valuing others so much that we are willing to sacrifice ourselves to serve them.

## GROWTH IN SERVANTHOOD

Servanthood is often misunderstood, even by Christians. Some, like the friend I quoted at the beginning of this chapter, seem to think that servanthood means total surrender of one's needs, interests, and very will to others. To them, *servant* suggests a powerless, menial position, in which the servant must always give in to another.

But in Christian servanthood the believer does not surrender his or her will to the persons served. As disciples of Jesus, our commitment is to him. We are not slaves of other people; we are slaves of Jesus Christ. Servanthood does not mean doing whatever other persons *want;* it means doing whatever we can to help meet other people's *needs.*

The biblical distinction between the servant and the slave and the Christian's call to submit his or her will completely to Jesus provide a great release for those who have felt that Christianity calls for a complete surrender of self to others. "Putting others first" has falsely been taken to means always trying to please them, no matter how selfish or immature their desires. But this view simply is not biblical and is *not* implied in Christ's call to servanthood.

What is implied, is a reorientation of our basic attitude toward other persons. We are to see others, as God does, as individuals of great worth and value.

Paul deals with this issue of our attitude toward others in several epistles. Reminding us of Jesus' example, the great apostle charges us, "Do nothing out of selfish ambition or vain conceit, but in humility consider others better than yourselves. Each of you should look not only to your own interests, but also to the interests of others" (Phil. 2:3–4). Paul asks that our attitude be "the same as that of Christ Jesus" (v. 5).

In a series of exhortations in Romans, Paul adds these instructions: "Be devoted to one another in brotherly love. Honor one another above yourselves. . . . Share with God's people who are in need. Practice hospitality. . . . Do not be proud, but be willing to associate with people of low position. Do not be conceited" (Rom. 12:10–16). As in other passages, the emphasis here on love and humility underlines the need to value others highly. Human beings are important to God. Individuals are so important that God was willing to serve us in Jesus, even at the cost of the life of the Son of God. Other persons are to have a similar value in our eyes. They are to have far more value than the time, effort, or money that we may expend to help them as we give ourselves self-sacrificially.

Moreover, servanthood is not designed to meet our ego needs. While servants are highly valued by God, they are not particularly prized by the world or by the immature in Jesus' church. Servants remain unobtrusive; the mop and pail, not the cheers of the crowd, is most often the servant's lot. In the church, Christian servanthood is not exhibited in the pulpit or in the spotlight surrounded by the strains of electronic tunes. The servant, in quiet person-to-person ways, reaches out to help. He or she listens and cares. The servant's ministry behind the scenes does not satisfy ego needs. But each aspect of servant-hood—its attitude toward others, its willingness to sacrifice, and its dismissal of public acclaim—reflects a true spirituality, the living of a human life in union with our God.

What steps can we take to grow in Christian servanthood? First, we need to reach out to know others. Only as we know others will we be able to sense their needs. Hurts are seldom shared with strangers. The *šārat*, that significant servant of the Old Testament, performed his ministry *in the presence of* the one served.

Second, we can practice listening sensitively for the moods and emotions of others. We can learn to listen not just for words and ideas but for what lies behind them. Is there bitterness in the tone? Is it fear that makes the words tumble too fast from a friend's lips? Does a despondent look indicate unknown needs? The servant whom God equips with a "word that sustains the weary" (Isa. 50:4) will be constantly alert to sense the needs of others, ready to respond in a practical way.

Third, we need to establish and maintain personal priori-ties. What will I put first? Will it be my plans, my desires, or even my needs? If God brings a needy person to me, will I be like Jesus in my willingness to put my own concerns aside and respond to the need?

Like discipleship, which calls for full commitment to Jesus, servanthood also calls for commitment. We must commit ourselves, for Jesus' sake and because others are important to him, to sacrifice ourselves to meet the other's need.

**PROBE**

exercises for personal development
case histories
thought provokers

1. Build your own description of God's servant. Read the passages that the author has identified in this chapter as Isaiah's "servant" passages. Underline key verses. Write down your observations. What does each verse or phrase tell you about the life or ministry of a servant? How can you express the servant's life style? Sum up your findings in a paper entitled, "What Servanthood Means for Me."

2. Check the library or your local Christian bookstore for any books on listening. Read one or more carefully, taking notes on how you can become a more sensitive listener. Look particularly for answers to questions such as: How can I listen for feelings? How can I encourage others to share with me? How can I communicate caring? Look too for suggestions on developing these and other listening skills. Sensitive listening that communicates Christian concern is the servant's most effective way to discover needs and to learn what he or she can do to help.

3. Read through one of the longer Gospels and note incidents in which Jesus displays a servant's heart and actions. Cut out each incident and place on separate sheets of notebook paper. Read each one carefully, and jot down observations. Use the incidents as a basis for meditation and prayer.

    In particular, ask God to help you see more clearly what servanthood involves and how you can be a servant. As you pray, ask the Lord to reveal daily those whom you can serve in some simple but significant way.

# Conclusion

Most studies of Christian spirituality follow a path different from that pursued in this book. Looking back, however, I note that the approach I have taken has many elements in common with traditional writings on spirituality. I summarize here the development of the argument traced above in parts 1 and 2.

## A COMMON UNDERSTANDING OF SPIRITUALITY

Christians have from the beginning recognized the existence of a spiritual realm which parallels and influences the material universe in which we live. The nature human beings were given in Creation—the dust of the earth and the vitalizing breath of God—blends the material and the spiritual. In Christianity, spirituality has been viewed as essentially a personal recovery and experience of the unity of these two realms.

Mystics, including many Christian mystics, have sought reunion in a direct personal experience of God. Through prayer and various disciplines, these men and women have sought to draw close to God, to focus heart and mind on him, to love him, and to know him, not with the hearing of the ear but with the directness of spiritual sight.

At the same time, spiritual writers in every Christian tradition have argued that true spirituality must affect the complete human life. The mystic's yearning is at best only one aspect of that reunion of the spiritual and material for which Christians yearn. As Edward Carter wrote, in a passage quoted above in chapter 1,

> This life which Christ has given us, traditionally termed the supernatural life, is not a type of superstructure erected atop man's normal life. The Christian is not one-half natural and one-half supernatural. He is one graced person. In his entirety he has been raised up, caught up, into a deeper form of life in Christ Jesus. Nothing which is authentically human has been excluded from this new existence. What-

ever is really human in the life of the Christian is meant to
be both an expression and a growth of the Christ-life.

The mystic's approach to spirituality is not so much wrong
as it is inadequate. Unity of the material and spiritual is not
found in devotion alone but is to be found in, and expressed
through, the Christian's total life. The greatest mystics of
Catholicism have recognized this fact. And contemporary
Catholic spiritual writers tend to stress a spirituality that bonds
personal devotion and the expression of holiness in ordinary
life.

Protestants, on the other hand, have traditionally tended to
puzzle over what happens inside believers on their spiritual
journey. What enables us to be spiritual? How can those who
have been lost sinners live in harmony with a holy God? Just
how does the Spirit of God work, and just what can we do to
relate rightly to him?

Protestant traditions differ on their answer to such questions. Yet there is an underlying harmony as expressed in the
various theologies. Each Protestant system attempting to explain spirituality sees the spiritual life as a struggle against the
limitations of our humanity. Each system sees the Holy Spirit as
central to Christian spiritual life and experience. The Spirit's
work enables, sanctifies, and transforms us. Also, in each
Protestant system, the spiritual life is a life of faith, a trust in
God's presence, a reliance on him for power to do what is
pleasing in his sight. In each system too, faith is expressed in
obedience, both to the revealed Word and to the promptings of
the Holy Spirit.

Wesleyan, Calvinist, Pentecostal, and Dispensationalist
views differ in many details of just *how* the Spirit works within
us. Yet an underlying harmony of belief does exist. This
harmony and the fact that every tradition has produced truly
spiritual men and women suggest to me that the theological
explanations are not as important as we tend to view them.
Undoubtedly one of our systems is more nearly correct than the
others. But belief in a system does not make a Christian truly
spiritual.

Furthermore, as we look at teaching on the spiritual life in
those different traditions, we note that the spiritual disciplines
suggested within each tradition tend to overlap. The notions of
how individuals take responsibility for their spiritual growth and
of what they must do to mature are strikingly similar.

These points, made in chapters 1–3, establish several important things about Christian spirituality:

● Christian spirituality involves a quest to unify the spiritual and material worlds.

● Christian spirituality is a matter of the believer's total life and experience.

● Christian spirituality cannot really be understood by reference to our various traditions' theological formulations.

● All our traditions affirm basic truths that underlie the various teachings on spirituality.

## A HUMAN LIFE IN UNION WITH GOD

Our initial look at spiritual writers and spiritual theologies, accompanied by a survey of the vivid images and active verbs associated with spirituality in the Bible, provided no single image capable of summing up and vitally expressing the uniqueness of Christian spirituality. We then turned to look directly at the one person who has lived a truly spiritual life in our world. In the words of Jesus Christ, and in Scripture's statements about him, that essential, dominant image does emerge.

We saw that, by Christ's own testimony, he lived his human life in union with God. Jesus Christ, a real human being, united fully in his actions and in his person the spiritual and material realms. He said:

I . . . do the will of him who sent me (John 6:38).

The one who sent me is with me; . . . for I always do what pleases him (John 8:29).

When [a person] looks at me, he sees the one who sent me (John 12:45).

Don't you believe that I am in the Father, and that the Father is in me? The words I say to you are not just my own. Rather, it is the Father, living in me, who is doing his work. Believe me when I say that I am in the Father and the Father is in me (John 14:10–11).

These statements of Jesus provide the dominant image we need: *True Christian spirituality is living a human life in union with God.*

This reality is emphasized in the Epistles. To those who argued that God, as "spiritual," must isolate himself from the material universe, Paul pointed out that Jesus, the "image of the invisible God" (Col. 1:15), won our salvation by his "physical body through death" (v. 22). Those who viewed spirituality as a retreat from this life or thought that God could be found in an ascetic disconnection from the ordinary were shown to be wrong. Spirituality, in Jesus and in the believer, is to be found in the full context of human life.

True spirituality, then, is found not in the monastery but in human relationships. Spirituality is exhibited not only in prayer but also in "compassion, kindness, humility, gentleness and patience" (Col. 3:12). The spiritual person bears with others, forgives whatever grievances he or she may have against others, and loves as Jesus loved.

When we see this kind of spirituality exhibited in Jesus, we realize that, while there is a spiritual realm, it does not really lie outside this world of time and space. Rather, true spirituality invades it! The spiritual person is involved in the affairs of this life and, in his or her ordinary experience, lives a human life that, like Jesus' life, may be lived in union with God.

We find abundant evidence in Scripture that corroborates this concept. Particularly important evidence lies in what has been called Jesus' High Priestly Prayer, which shows us that, just as there was a real union between Jesus and the Father, a real union now exists between the believer and Jesus that is the basis for his enablement in our human lives.

> I pray also for those who will believe in me through their message, *that all of them may be one,* Father, *just as you are in me and I am in you.* May they also *be in us* so that the world may believe that you have sent me. I have given them the glory that you gave me, *that they may be one as we are one: I in them and you in me.* May they be *brought to complete unity* to let the world know that you sent me and have loved them even as you have loved me (John 17:20–23; italics mine).

Our capacity to live a spiritual life depends first on the existence of our real union with Jesus and then on our experience of that union. Only as we choose, as Jesus did, actually to live in union with God will we become spiritual men and women.

The phrase *in union with God* expresses the first essential aspect of true Christian spirituality. The phrase *live a human life* expresses the second. Spirituality is not found in a rejection of our humanity. Spirituality affirms our humanity and must be expressed in all that living a human life involves.

To see what human life does involve, we returned to Genesis. There we found several necessary elements of human nature and of the human condition. Focusing on these elements, we should be able to search the Scriptures and learn how to live that human life in true union with our God.

From this point, the thrust of this book was determined. Without attempting to cover all the issues of human life, it seemed necessary to look at several critical human issues defined in Genesis and woven as consistent themes throughout the Word of God. These issues, listed in table 2, reprinted here from chapter 5, engage us as individuals and also involve our relationships with other persons.

| Human Issue | Individual Aspect | Corporate Aspect |
|---|---|---|
| Identity | Responsibility | Accountability |
| Intimacy | Prayer | Worship |
| Sinfulness | Confession | Forgiveness |
| Lordship | Choice | Freedom |
| Mortality | Suffering | Compassion |
| Holiness | Morality | Justice |
| Commitment | Discipleship | Servanthood |

One other assumption guided the development of the chapters that explored these aspects of living a human life: while the spiritual power is always God's and a faith which relies totally on Christ and his Spirit are necessary elements in true spirituality, a Christian must accept personal responsibility for his or her spiritual progress. The believer must respond in faith to God's Word and must put Bible truths into practice. Only as we act on God's Word does spiritual growth take place.

And so in the chapters which compose the major section of this book, I was not concerned only with describing true spirituality, or exploring what it means for Christians to live a human life in union with God. I was also concerned with suggesting how we can respond to God's description of the spiritual way and with the disciplines which will help us make spiritual progress.

This book is thus not simply a theology of Christian spirituality but is also a manual for personal spiritual development. Only as we practice the disciplines of the Christian life can we expect to grow spiritually. Only as we respond to what we learn and apply it can we know personal growth or experience the excitement of a life that truly is lived in union with God.

## A MODEL OF CHRISTIAN SPIRITUALITY

In this text I have tried to isolate and explore aspects of human life and to discover from Scripture what it means for a human life to be lived in union with God. I do not pretend to have isolated and discussed every relevant human issue. For instance, human beings are physical beings. Our physical nature makes us dependent on material things to meet our physical needs. When a human life is lived in union with God, physical needs and material possessions are kept in perspective. Jesus spoke often of the necessities of life and of the trust in God as Father which keeps us from anxiety and greed. The Gospels and the Epistles each develop the interpersonal corollary that material possessions are to be used to meet the needs of others. Possessions have no value in themselves. But if they are used to honor God in the service of others, they have a high value indeed.

In writing this book I have not attempted to be exhaustive. Instead I have developed an approach to Christian spirituality which leads us beyond a preoccupation with prayer and meditation and obedience, as important as these are, to broaden our vision of the spiritual life and to point out a practical pathway to balanced spiritual growth.

In everything, I have been guided by the conviction that true spirituality is, in its very essence, living a human life in union with God. As we submit all that we are as human beings to Christ, as we respond to the Scripture's vision of a transformed humanity, and as we practice the disciplines that lead to growth, we will know by personal experience the joys and triumphs of true spirituality.

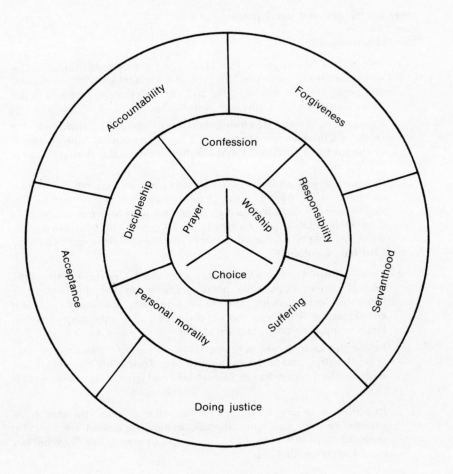

Inner circle: duties to God

Middle circle: duties to oneself

Outer circle: duties to others

**FIGURE 6**

The Duties of Christian Spirituality

**PROBE**

**exercises for personal development**
**case histories**
**thought provokers**

1. The author has suggested at least one other paired human issue which needs to be explored for personal spiritual growth, one rooted in human beings' physical life and their dependence on material possessions for their physical well-being.

   In a group, discuss whether other issues should be included in a study of Christian spirituality. What are their roots in human nature or the human condition? What are their individual and interpersonal expressions?

   In lieu of any exam (if you are using this text in a course), write two chapters on the model of the chapters in part 2. Write them on the implications of our physical nature and on how to live in union with God while relating as a human being to needs and possessions. Or write two chapters on another critical theme of similar significance to Christian spirituality.

2. There is more than one way to organize the topics dealt with in this book. Figure 6, for example, presents Christian spirituality in terms of three concentric circles. The duties represented in each circle are connected in some way with the duties in the adjoining circle(s). Here is another chart, drawn as three concentric circles.

   Revise this chart in any way you chose to express relationships that you see within and between these duties. Review the chapters if you wish, but be prepared to explain and defend your charted representation.

3. Describe in writing any personal spiritual growth you may have experienced by following the disciplines suggested here or by responding in other ways to Christ's call to you to live your human life in union with God.

# Scripture Index